To: _____

From: _____

Why: _____

_____

Only This Morning, You're All Grown Up

An inspiring message from a mother to her daughter

Shared with love by legendary race car driver
Lyn St. James

SOURCEBOOKS, INC.®
NAPERVILLE, ILLINOIS

Published by Sourcebooks, Inc.
P.O. Box 4410, Naperville, Illinois 60567-4410
(630) 961-3900
Fax: (630) 961-2168
www.sourcebooks.com

ISBN-13: 978-1-4022-0722-8
ISBN-10: 1-4022-0722-0

Original internal design by The Design Group, Inc.

A portion of the royalties from the sale of this book will go to the Maxine W. Cornwall Courage Fund in the Lyn St. James Foundation.

Lyn St. James Foundation
PO Box 2246
Indianapolis, IN 44206

www.lynstjames.com

Printed and bound in USA
WP 10 9 8 7 6 5 4 3 2 1

My mother never wrote me any real letters that I recall;

maybe a short note in a card, but that's about it. In fact, I remember mother telling me to always think twice before I put things in writing because you can't take them back.

Mother didn't really have much of a formal education. She wasn't able to attend much school due to her numerous hospitalizations for surgeries and treatments of her polio. She was not confident in her spelling, ability to write well, nor to do math. But she was never at a loss for words, especially when giving out advice, like so many mothers.

She did have a knack for figuring people out. I used to think that God gave her an extra set of antennas to quickly be able to see people as they really were. She also told me many times, "You can never really understand someone until you've walked in their shoes." And I remember going with my mom to get her special shoes made. So, when I saw how difficult it was for her to find shoes that would enable her to walk, it was a graphic lesson for me.

I received this letter from her inside a card. It was so well written, so profound, so global and timeless, so poetic, so extraordinary. I was astounded, and I'm ashamed to say that I recall asking her, "Did you really write this?"

3

Her response was, "Yes, I did. It took me quite a bit of time to put it together, and your Aunt Evy helped me, but I wrote it for you."

When she passed away in 2002, I went through boxes of things and came across the letter inside the card. What a treasure it is. I've shared it with some of my friends, and I shared it with my daughter, Lindsay, on her 21st birthday. The response from everyone was, "You should publish this." So that's why I'm doing this book.

I think we so often pass over or brush off the wisdom of our parents, grandparents, and elders. Yet, what they can offer are frequently pieces of gold. As I get older, I've come to realize that experience and life lessons give us such a different view of the world. We need to listen more, and value the advice of those who see the world differently than we do.

Pearls of wisdom that are given and valued should be shared. I want to share this letter from my mother with you, and I hope you'll share it with your loved ones.

Lyn St. James

To Lyn, from your crazy Mother

Dearest Lyn,

The best things come last.

People will talk for hours saying nothing much,

and then linger at the door

with words that come with a

rush from the heart.

We are all gathered at a doorway today. We linger there

      with our hand on the knob, chattering away like Polonius to Laertes.

Now remember, "Neither a borrower nor a lender be;"—

  and don't forget this above all: **"to thine own self be true."**

But the very best things said often slip out completely unheralded, preceded by, **"Oh, by the way..."**

In real life, when Polonius had finished giving all
   that fatherly advice to his son – who probably wasn't
paying much attention anyway – he must have said,

**"Oh, by the way...if you get into any trouble,
don't forget, you can always call me."**

As we stand in the doorway today,

these are my parting words to my daughter.

There are so many things I want to tell you:

The first thing is **don't be scared.**

You're being flung into a world that's running
about as smoothly as a car with square wheels.
It's okay to be uncertain.

You're now an adult in a time when the leaders of the world
are behaving like children.

**It's a world where the central image
of the day is a terrorist one;
humane concerns inhumanely expressed.**

And the only response to this is impotent fury.
If you weren't a little uncertain, I'd be nervous for you.

Adulthood has come upon you
    and you're not all that sure you're ready for it.

I think that sometimes I'm not ready for adulthood either –

yours or mine.

The day before yesterday, you were a baby.

I was afraid to hold you because you seemed so fragile.

Yesterday, all I could feel was helplessness when you were hurt.

Only this morning, you are grown.

As I get older, **the only thing that speeds up is time.**

But if time is a thief, time also leaves something in exchange;

experience.

I want to squeeze things
great and small
into this lingering good bye.

I want to tell you to **love your work.**

If you always put your heart into everything you do,

you really can't lose.

Whether you wind up making a lot of money or not,

you will have had a wonderful time,

and no one will ever be able to take that away from you.

Keep laughing.

You gurgle when you laugh.

Be sure and laugh three times a day
             for your own well being.

And if you can get other people to join you in your laughter,
you may help keep this shaky boat afloat.

When people are laughing,
they're generally not killing one another.

I have this helpless urge to pass on maxims to you;

things that will see you through. But even the **Golden Rule**

doesn't seem adequate to pass on to a precious daughter.

There should be something added to it.

Here's my Golden Rule for a tarnished age:

Be fair with others, but then keep after them until they're fair with you.

It's a complex world.

I hope you'll learn to make distinctions.

A peach is not its fuzz…a toad is not its warts…
a person is not his or her crankiness.

If we can make distinctions,

we can be tolerant; and we can get to the heart of our problems
instead of wrestling endlessly with their gross exteriors.

Once you make a habit of making distinctions,
  you'll begin challenging your own assumptions.

Your assumptions are your windows on the world.
  Scrub them off every once in a while,
  or the light won't come in.

If you challenge your own assumptions,

   you won't be so quick to accept the unchallenged assumptions of others

      You'll be a lot less likely to be caught up in bias or prejudice,

      or be influenced by people who ask you to hand over

            your brains,

               your soul,

                  or your money

               because they have everything figured out for you.

Be as smart as you can, but remember that

it's always better to be wise than to be smart.

And don't be upset that it takes a long time to find wisdom.

Like a rare virus,

wisdom tends to break out at unexpected times,

and it's mostly

people with compassion and understanding
who are susceptible to it.

The door is inching a little closer toward the latch,

and I still haven't said it.

Let me dig a little deeper.

No matter how loving or loved we are,
it eventually occurs to most of us that deep down inside,

we're all alone.

When the moment comes for you to wrestle with that cold loneliness
which is every person's private monster,

I want you to face the damn thing.

I want you to see it for what it is, **and win.**

Whenever that sense of absurdity hits you,

I want you to be ready.

Life is absurd and meaningless – unless you bring meaning to it,
and unless you make something of it.

It is up to us to create our own existence.

Absurdity will have a hard time getting hold of you
    if you're already in motion.
  You can use the skills of your profession and other skills
      you have learned here:

Dig into the world and push it into better shape.

For one thing, you can try to **clean the air and water.**

You can try to **make the justice system work, too.**

You can **try to find out why**
people of every country and religion have,
     at one time or another,
     found it so easy to make other people suffer.

If you really want to grapple with absurdity,

**try understanding how people can be capable
of both nurture and torture;**

You can try to **stop the next war now,**

before it starts,

And while you're doing all of that,

remember that every right you have as a woman was won for you by women fighting hard.

There are little girls being born right now

who won't even have the same rights you do

unless you act to maintain and extend the range of equality.

The nourishing stew of civilized life doesn't keep bubbling on its own.

Put something back in the pot
for the people in line behind you.

There's plenty to keep you busy **for the rest of your life.**

I can't promise this will ever completely reduce that sense of absurdity,
but it may get it down to a manageable level.
It will allow you once in a while to bask in the feeling that, all in all,
things do seem to be moving forward.

I can see your brow knitting in that way that I love.

That crinkle between your eyebrows that signals your doubt
and your skepticism.

Why – on a day of such excitement and hope –
should I be talking of absurdity and nothingness?

Because **I want you to focus that hope and level of
excitement into coherent rays that will strike
like a laser at the targets of our discontent.**

I want you to be potent; to do good when you can; and

**to hold your wit and your intelligence
like a shield against other people's wantonness.**

And above all, I want you to laugh and enjoy yourself
in a life of your own choosing
and in a world of your own making.

I want you to be strong and aggressive

and tough and resilient and full of feeling.

**I want you to be everything that's you,
deep at the center of your being.**

I want you to have "chutzpah."

Nothing important was every accomplished without chutzpah.

Columbus had chutzpah.
The signers of the Declaration of Independence had it.

Laugh at yourself, but don't ever aim
your doubt at yourself.

Be bold. When you embark for strange places,
don't leave any of yourself safely on shore.

Have the nerve to go into unexplored territory.

Be brave enough to live life creatively.

The creative is the place where no one else has ever been.

You have to leave the city of your comfort
and go into the wilderness of your intuition.

You can't get there by bus, only by hard work and risk,
    and by not quite knowing what you're doing.
What you'll discover will be wonderful.
       What you'll discover will be yourself.

Well, those are my parting words as today's door closes softly between us.
So long, be happy.

Oh, by the way... I love you.

Maxine W. Cornwall

October 14, 1919 — March 18, 2002

Maxine Cornwall was a woman who possessed
great joy and passion for life regardless of limits or
circumstances. She was able to find the center
of your soul with a laser-like beam of compassion
and love. She demonstrated courage and dignity
every day of her life. She loved music; she loved people; she loved to
dance in her mind when her body no longer cooperated; she loved to
play games, and won more often than not. Until the very end, she
remained sassy, loving and appreciative. She was the best mother and
friend a person could have and I consider myself blessed to have been
her daughter. As her only child, she was not particularly happy about
my becoming a professional race car driver, but she supported my
decision. She used to light a candle for me whenever
I was racing. After each race, I would call her, so she
could blow the candle out. I felt like I had an angel riding
on my shoulder. Her spirit and soul touched everyone
she met and we will miss her, but never forget her.

Lyn St. James, one of the first female race car drivers and one of the top 100 Women Athletes of the Century, attributes her vision and spirit to the influence of her mother, Maxine W. Cornwall, who pushed her to educate herself and find her place in the world.

The best things come last.

T H E J U S T P R I N C E

Joseph A. Kechichian and R. Hrair Dekmejian

THE JUST PRINCE
A Manual of Leadership

Including an authoritative English translation of the
Sulwan al-Muta' fi 'Udwan al-Atba'
(Consolation for the Ruler During the Hostility of Subjects)

by
Muhammad ibn Zafar al-Siqilli

SAQI

British Library Cataloguing-in-Publication Data
A catalogue for this book is available from the
British Library

ISBN 0 86356 783 5

copyright © 2003 Joseph A. Kechichian and R. Hrair Dekmejian

This edition first published 2003

*The right of Joseph A. Kechichian and R. Hrair Dekmejian to be identified as the authors of
work has been asserted by them in accordance with the Copyright, Designs and Patents Act of*

Saqi Books
26 Westbourne Grove
London W2 5RH
www.saqibooks.com

For Shaykh Zayed bin Sultan Al Nahyan, a Just Prince

Contents

Acknowledgments

The *Sulwan* offers profound perspectives on leadership that are as applicable today as they would have been in the 12th century or during the age of Machiavelli or even Tacitus. Bringing these perspectives to fruition necessitated a visionary prince who grasped its significance when we first discussed this project with him. We thank Shaykh Sultan bin Zayed Al Nahyan, the Deputy Prime Minister of the United Arab Emirates, for supporting this initiative. Moreover, by agreeing to pen a foreword, Shaykh Sultan clarifies his own vision of a 'just prince' and how his father, Shaykh Zayed bin Sultan, stands as a rare model worthy of emulation. In discussing various interpretations of authority, rulership, and power, Shaykh Sultan projects a vision that augurs well for the future of his country and all those that may wish to conduct business with it. How leaders shape their vision and adapt to changing circumstances can foretell the types of policies they espouse.

Several individuals at the Office of the Deputy Prime Minister in Abu Dhabi, including Khalifah bin Sabha al-Qubaisi, His Highness's assistant office director, and Daham al-Mazrouei, his executive secretary, were gracious with their time and hospitality. To both of them, and many others who have extended legendary Arab hospitality, we owe a special debt of gratitude.

The team at Saqi Books performed in a very professional manner. It was a rare pleasure working with them.

We also thank our respective spouses – Juliette J. Kechichian and Anoush Dekmejian – who allow us to devote attention to scholarly pursuits while they assume additional burdens. Last, but not least, Angelica J. Kechichian deserves special mention for two reasons: first, because she remains a perpetual source of inspiration to her father; and, second, for her impeccable wit.

A Note on Transliteration

A modified version of the Library of Congress transliteration system has been adopted throughout this translation. In rendering Arabic words and names, however, we relied on the style used by the *International Journal of Middle East Studies*. Thus a name that is commonly rendered in English, for example Mohammed, becomes Muhammad, and Mecca becomes Makkah. Whenever known, common English spellings for proper names as well as names of countries were used. For practical purposes, all diacritical marks for long vowels and velarized consonants have been eliminated, although the ' (*ayn*) and ' (*hamza*) were retained. Arabic speakers will appreciate the correct references for the transliterated words throughout the text.

Translating a major work of political philosophy is challenging, to say the least, and this one was no exception. This translation was based on several texts, but we relied primarily on Abu Nahla Ahmad bin 'Abd al-Majid's volume published in Cairo, Egypt by Dar al-Thaqafa in 1978, and another edition by Muhammad Ahmad Damaj, published in Beirut, Lebanon by the Mu'assasat 'Izz al-Din lil-Tiba'a wal-Nashr in 1995. We generally benefited from a first translation by Michele Amari (from Arabic into Italian into English), published in London in 1852. Naturally, we aimed to be meticulous, accurate and readable. We retained much of the original prose, especially the fables that imitate those of the famous *Kalila and Dimna* that were transmitted from India to Persia and the Arab world.

All quotations from the Qur'an are drawn from *The Koran*, translated with notes by N. J. Dawood, London and New York: Penguin Books, 1999.

Maxims from the *Sulwan al-Muta'*

Among the many maxims peppered throughout the Sulwan, *the following stand out for their erudition, depth and longevity. They are gathered here to provide a quick glimpse of Ibn Zafar's philosophical credentials.*

When an issue is uncertain commit yourself into His hands, as He governs destiny.

Who has become rich through pillage shall waste away; who rules by treachery shall be expelled; the army of the unrighteous shall be defeated and the noose of tyranny shall be broken.

Counsel is the mirror of the intellect. If, therefore, you would like to know the capacity of anyone, ask for their advice.

Every sinner will find one to pardon him except the unjust, in whose fall all rejoice with one accord.

Who has waged great injustice shall not flourish. Who is strengthened by malice shall not endure. Who is raised to the throne through violence shall not reign.

Who plants the seeds of knowledge shall reap fame. Self-denial will lead to glory; reflection to wisdom; gravity to reverence, caution to security; pride to hatred; avarice to contempt; ambition to shame; and envy to a crumbling heart.

The king who wallows in pleasure and allows opportunity to escape him shall never attain success in state affairs.

The king who believes that the minds of princes are superior to those of counsellors has fallen into great error. If he acquires the bad habit of contradicting a wise and faithful counsellor — without manifest reason — it is certain that he will never prosper.

One of the most irresistible impulses of the soul is to seek a change of condition. Change is introduced into a being largely due to circumstances, but transforms into corruption through greed. A person who embarks on one change and effortlessly crosses into another must attain the condition most suitable in the intermediate state — between the starting point and the goal — if he is to prosper.

There are three species of creatures, who, if you do not lodge and nourish them as befits their worth, will immediately turn their backs and break with you: these are kings, men of letters and benefactors.

Even as the iron cleaves to the magnet, so does success to patience. Endure, therefore, and you shall conquer.

When you see how a man takes courage and endures, then you may know the quality of his mind.

Greed is the most heinous of all vices. Avarice is the father that begets it; injustice the son to which it gives birth; desire of that which belongs to others its brother; and servility its companion.

If your ears do not enable you to know a man when you are absent, neither will your eyes do so when you see him face to face.

If you would like to know whether good or bad prevails in the mind of a man, ask his counsel. The advice he gives you will reveal his true light.

A lofty spirit will not forget to be grateful whatever wrong he may receive from one to whom he owes a benefit.

If a man has helped you and then turns his back on you or even injures you, do not on that account break with him. Continue to show him gratitude and affection. Such conduct on your part will prove the most powerful intercessor in your behalf.

Sincere advisors do not find favour with the king, unless he is endowed with magnanimity; otherwise they will fail and the flatterers will succeed.

Amongst faithful and far-sighted counsellors, he is most deserving of attention whose prosperity depends on your own and whose safety is tied to yours. He who stands in such a position, exerting himself for your interests, will likewise serve and defend himself while fighting for you.

Dissimulation is a mirage that only deceives short-sighted intellects, but conceals nothing from those who can see through it.

There are two things that deprive a free man of his liberty: rendering homage to virtue and divulging a secret.

If you love at first sight, you may stumble and fall.

Instability is the mark of a vulgar mind, not a lofty spirit.

He who offers princes that which does not please them must not complain if they fail to react.

Stupidity is a veil that prevents understanding from illuminating the right path.

As desire places you in submission to others and enslaves you the more it presses, it is clear that men are slaves of worldly goods, and those who need more have the heaviest weight to bear.

You love the one you have confidence in, who is faithful and deserving of affection.

Honesty and fidelity are praised by everyone and are favoured by all.

Wealth is like water. He who does not open a gate to carry off its overflow drowns in it.

Foreword

by
Sultan bin Zayed bin Sultan Al Nahyan

When Niccolò Machiavelli wrote *The Prince* in 1513, the Italian city-states were in turmoil, subjected to repeated foreign invasions. In the context of the time, his advice to Lorenzo de Medici in Florence came to embody amorality and cynicism, association with corrupt rule and cunning, although Machiavelli was probably both a religious and moral man. Still, what lacked in the Florentine's prose was palpable. 'Machiavellianism' called for a reliance on wicked political steps to accomplish a ruler's objectives to attain and retain power. Such initiatives were considered to be diabolical and, needless to say, Machiavelli's discourses were not always welcome by 'morally inclined' clergymen with equally ambitious political designs on authority. Not surprisingly, while *The Prince* was drafted in 1513 and first circulated around 1516, it was finally published in 1532 – five years after Machiavelli's death in 1527. The book was placed on the Pope's *Index of Prohibited Books* in 1559, where it stayed those few centuries until the Vatican amended its list.

If Machiavelli set out to safeguard his 'master' from large-scale intrigue, instability, invasion, blackmail, fear and violence, he also wished to ingratiate himself with the Medicis to receive political favour. What the advisor hoped for was a lofty post worthy of the advice. In any case, Lorenzo de Medici did not care for Machiavelli's suggestions, and the latter did not receive the hoped-for appointment.

To be sure, Machiavelli's numerous practical recommend- ations stood in stark contrast with what passed as advice at the time. For example, few dared to criticize a dictator who would rely on cruelty to gain and retain power, even if the ultimate objective was the ruler's authority, the nation's security or its welfare. Yet, Machiavelli always disassociated ethics from politics, positing that sacrifices were necessary to preserve and protect any ruler and his community. His complex views assessed the economic, socio-political and military circumstances of an association. Equally important, he evaluated the capacity of a ruler to govern effectively, administer punishment and dispense justice. The Florentine's prince was pragmatic and realistic. He was tolerant but not of dissent. He purported to defend the masses but was intolerant of those who either disobeyed him or threatened the stability of 'his' state. And while he did not neglect fairness, Machiavelli's ideal prince was not primarily motivated by a sense of justice.

Fourteenth-century Italy may well have required a harsh prince but, remarkably, Machiavelli became more popular in the time since. Cromwell, Frederick the Great, Louis XIV, Napoléon, Bismarck, Clemenceau, Wilson, Stalin, Hitler, Roosevelt, De Gaulle, Churchill, Truman and a score of modern rulers referred to the Florentine's book as a source of practical guidance. Dictators and statesmen alike sought to implement his recommendations. Most emulated his suggestions, even if they preferred to couch them in lofty popular rhetoric – perhaps to lessen the impact of devastating blows on their respective societies or hapless colonial subjects.

If necessity propelled certain rulers to adopt harsh tactics to govern, few did so with security, for most eventually confronted the wrath of their populations or colonized subjects one way or another. Upheavals, violence, revolutions and, in certain cases, assassinations, were not prevented. Because Machiavelli's prince lacked justice, he could not rule with legitimacy. Yet, almost 350 years before the Florentine wrote his famous guidebook, a fellow Italian – but of Arab origin – underscored why a ruler could not govern without justice. His advice to *his* prince, analysed and translated in this volume, provides the various missing links between power and virtue.

The *Sulwan al-Muta' fi 'Udwan al-Atba'* (*Consolation for the Ruler During the Hostility of Subjects*), written by Muhammad ibn Zafar al-Siqilli (the Sicilian) in the 12th century, produces, like Machiavelli's *The Prince*, an analysis of power and virtue. Remarkably, the treatise emphasizes justice, which rings true in the 21st century as well.

Ibn Zafar was, first and foremost, a Muslim scholar who was profoundly affected by contemporary developments. What he learned from Arab and Muslim histories determined whatever intellectual capabilities he displayed. Thus, the advice to his prince, even if pragmatic in certain aspects, was justified by pertinent references to the religious dicta of Islamic Law (*Shari'a*). Moreover, like Machiavelli, Ibn Zafar aimed to secure a lofty post with his ruler, certainly to draw financial rewards but also to receive physical and political protection. The main distinction between the two, perhaps due to a different measurement of urgency, time and legal interpretation, hovers around the innate concept of justice. For even if the concept was idealized, it was, nevertheless, something to aspire to.

Yet Ibn Zafar was not just a traditional Muslim who perceived rights or freedoms in terms of law but also in terms of pure politics. It is generally assumed that Muslims, and especially Arabs, perceive the opposite of tyranny as justice (rather than freedom). This is not the case, although some Muslims — especially in the Levant and the festering Ottoman Empire — fell victim to such practices. If certain rulers considered justice as a right to govern and thus assigned the legitimacy of their authority to divine law, others were amply aware of such nuances and shied away from these generalizations. Rather, they ruled through consensus, even when most of the Muslim and Arab worlds lacked the institutions to fulfill the basic requirements of consensus. Muslim legitimacy, certainly in the Arab Gulf region, was — and remains — deeply rooted in tribal customs. And while tribal customs cannot be compared to the democratic institutions that evolved in Western societies, neither can they be dismissed out of hand. Their pertinence to local tradition was and is self-evident to its inhabitants. How they impacted the way of life of millions over the centuries benefited certain rulers who, against some odds, managed to govern well. Ibn Zafar's discourse on justice, therefore, offers a keen awareness of tribal customs that, for better or worse, shape his unique vision of what power and virtue are supposed to accomplish.

Power Within Islamic Principles
Because the world into which Islam was revealed was highly politicized, arguments about God's aims on earth, His

designation of a leader to guide believers and the difficulty of understanding what God's justice ('adl) meant, significantly shaped the debate around power and justice. Moreover, as the Islamic world grew rapidly through the conquest of vast territories, it quickly became apparent that 'raw power' would not be sufficient to provide and ensure stability and prosperity. Capable leaders could and did rule effectively but all worked to create a just public order precisely to embody God's will.

Muslims believe, like all adherents to monotheism, that God is both true and just. Muslims further believe that God's ultimate justice was the main motivation for saving humanity. Because God is truth, there can, therefore, be no doubt about His justice. To cement this principle, God sent us His prophets, the Prophet Muhammad being His last. What often confuses many is that the Prophet Muhammad was not just a religious leader but also a temporal guide. He clearly displayed and excelled in power and, even if he did not choose to separate 'church' from 'state', he nevertheless ruled with a clear notion for justice. In other words, the Prophet's governance in Madina and Makka was the model of rule in which power and justice were balanced. To be sure, much turmoil dominated early Islamic rule, during and after the Prophet Muhammad's life, but his undeniable sense of justice allowed for the development of political jurisprudence (usul al-fiqh al-siyasi) that was fundamentally based on religious doctrine (al-'aqida).

But for the Prophet Muhammad, the harmonious balance between power and justice represented only one aspect of rule. In fact, the Prophet sought to find harmony between justice and virtue as well, cognizant that virtue was an acquired ability. When the Prophet died and the community faced its first major 'political' crisis, many wondered what type of ruler could successfully fulfill God's will in the ideal world. This was when the notion of a 'Just Prince' (*al-Sultan al-'Adil*) first emerged as a topic of discourse. Who could assume power to ensure a just order? Was that candidate qualified, that is, virtuous? These were critical questions because, in Islam, rulers who lacked an ethical foundation could not — and cannot — possibly create a just order. Thus begins the search for a balance between justice and virtue, thereby completing the power loop. In other words, a ruler must exercise power to ensure justice but can only do so if he is virtuous, which, in turn, legitimizes his power. The just Islamic rule necessitates a capacity to govern, fundamental knowledge about one's strengths and weaknesses and an innate sense of justice. These are not easy to fathom or acquire, as the history of the past several centuries amply illustrates.

How Should the Ruler Confront Challenges?
For Ibn Zafar, as for most political philosophers, rulers must try to govern without making fundamental mistakes. To be sure, pitfalls abound, some much more serious than others. Equally important, most statesmen make political mistakes, even if unintended. Understanding one's mistakes and learning from them is among the most difficult propositions confronting statesmen. How a leader addresses such challenges shapes the way he may ensure stability.

First, the alert ruler must ensure that he has full knowledge of events, for knowledge is the key ingredient in all other decisions. What we know and what we do not know inform our responses to a particular event. Lack of knowledge may therefore force a leader to commit the most egregious errors.

Second, a leader must perceive facts for what they are, because what appears to be true may not always be so. Perception also requires that a leader fathom various alternatives as he evaluates how certain decisions may affect his rule, the stability of his realm and the welfare of his subjects. It is an arduous task, necessitating care in assessing various opinions, propositions and options.

Third, a leader must have luck, because circumstances beyond one's control may, at times, force his hand; without a doubt, some are luckier than others. While luck is an intangible element, it can be turned into an asset to serve one's objectives, especially if one reacts in time.

Fourth, a leader must be prepared, and when he determines that his preparation is complete he must prepare some more. One is never prepared for all eventualities; often mistakes are made owing to a lack of preparation. Contingency planning – or lack thereof – may make or break a statesman's resolve to act in a decisive manner.

Fifth, a leader must quickly correct his mistakes and learn not to repeat them. Indeed, common mistakes are repeated time and again because one is loath to acknowledge personal errors. This is where strong and loyal advisors must play their roles, even if rulers are not always willing to listen to their advice. It is the astute statesman who knows how to task his advisors in watching over pitfalls that may result in disaster.

Sixth, a leader must not make the mistake of certainty, because the consequences of his decisions may result in positive or negative results. Given that in the end a policy will either succeed or fail, a leader must learn how to be certain before he reaches a final decision. Once a decision is reached, he must see it through.

Seventh, a leader must not make the mistake of false wisdom, and must be guided by ethical considerations to accomplish his objectives. While innate wisdom is a quality that shapes a leader's character, he must watch for arrogant penchants that will lead him to believe in his capabilities to such an extent that he would forsake sound advice. This is also an area where loyal advisors must play a critical role, if for no other reason than to remind statesmen that all men — including rulers — are mortal, and that one's privileges do not stem from only temporal sources.

Finally, the leader must not make the mistake of believing in his rule *in toto*, but always trust God to guide him. It is remarkable that leaders in Westernized societies frequently call upon the Supreme Being, even if most of them cherish a separation between church and state. For example, American leaders regularly conclude major and minor speeches alike with one of the most elegant phrases ever devised, namely, 'so help me God.' Presumably, they are invoking the Lord's assistance to rule fairly with justice and liberty for all.

Al-Siqilli's Solutions

In the *Sulwan*, Ibn Zafar broaches subjects rarely addressed by our contemporary Muslim writers, including discourses on solutions to issues that can prevent a ruler from governing securely and with legitimacy. For example, the Arab Sicilian addresses the principles of conduct that many leaders ought to practice while serving in government. Towards that end, he distinguishes five philosophical necessities: (1) A strong belief in God as well as a renunciation of injustice; (2) the courage to conquer evil; (3) the patience to always persevere regardless of costs and consequences; (4) contentment and submission to the Will of God against all hardships; and (5) consideration of the burden of rule with cheerfulness. These five points are universal in both nature and substance. While they may seem self-evident to a reader in the 21st century, Ibn Zafar underscored them and illustrated how reneging them would weaken one's resolve and prevent one from following one's principles; his conclusions are astoundingly appropriate even for the 21st century.

Trust in God. Ibn Zafar refers to the Qur'an, the Hadith of the Prophet Muhammad, renowned Muslim jurists, Persian writers, Arab poets, Sassanid historians and various Christian theologians in providing substantial moral and political reflections. He even refers to Saint Luke ('Father Luke') as he weaves political discourse into his numerous narratives, fables and political observations. Naturally, by relying on universal sayings and reflections, the Sicilian ensures that his own assessments do not become obsolete. His entire logic is based on this elegant and pious approach. By 'trusting God' Ibn Zafar correctly concludes that this is the only way and that all others must submit to the eternal truth. Even in modern times, with discussions of the 'end of history' and 'clash of civilizations' so common, man is still profoundly moved by faith, without which most seem to be slaves to materialism. It is a universal yearning, proportionate to each believer, in search of eternal solace.

Fortitude. The pious Ibn Zafar was also a genuine pragmatist, identifying courage as the second necessary principle. His numerous examples emphasize the value of determination in undertaking any task, remaining steadfast against any challenge and responding to any situation. To be sure, this may appear obvious, for determination was an ingredient in most political discourses. Yet, it gained added value and greater depth, especially with respect to the clashes between the Persian and Roman Empires. In modern times, it was certainly applicable to the clashes that pitted the (communist) East against the (capitalist) West. Even if one is weak or facing a superior foe, admonishes Ibn Zafar, one must remain determined to accomplish one's goals. Consequently, fortitude is a requirement that, in the context of political reflections, strengthens one's will to power.

Patience. Patience is the third philosophical necessity: having relied on God and mustered his courage, the prince must prepare himself slowly and surely. According to Ibn Zafar, a ruler should learn when to act and when not to. He should learn the art of patience, as any hasty or ill-conceived move might create unwanted consequences. The concept of time, therefore, takes a new shape in Ibn Zafar's philosophy. A ruler must learn how to manage time, separate the wheat from the chaff, test various theories and seek advice. Time is also valuable to prevent a ruler from acting in haste and with emotion.

Contentment. When Ibn Zafar composed his *Sulwan* — probably for a prince serving in Nur al-Din's court in Damascus, and Abu al-Qasim, the Arab Sicilian Commander — his native Sicily was just about fully integrated by the Normans. The conquests, and what the conquerors stood for, certainly inspired Ibn Zafar to sharpen his prose. Ibn Zafar cautioned his prince to learn the art of contentment and be genuinely satisfied with what he had or had not accomplished, a difficult task under the best of circumstances. Contentment included a practical dimension for the Sicilian, who did not favour hasty adventures. In a sense, Ibn Zafar anticipated that intrigue and the thirst for power — not to mention the desire to dominate — would lead to various calamities. Where one may be and where one may be going at any given time depended on this critical philosophical precept. While ambition certainly has its merits, one must balance it with contentment, especially if one is motivated by faith.

Self-denial. The faithful individual, whose trust in God does not waver and who is courageous, patient and content, must also resist the urges of power and rule with genuine virtue. In some ways, self-denial is the most difficult and complex philosophical ingredient in Ibn Zafar's teachings, because it requires complete intellectual mastery over a situation while remaining totally submissive to God. Yet the ruler who submits to God and rules with justice will accomplish his objectives. He will attain and retain power and learn, through courage, patience, contentment and self-denial, to do so with virtue.

Accountability and Legitimacy

The principles upon which Ibn Zafar's advisory opinions are founded were not applied during the Sicilian's time, nor are they applied today. Few leaders — especially in the West, where separation of church and state is an ingrained political fact — accept the primacy of an absolute and unlimited authority (God) over political life even if regular references to the contrary abound. Machiavelli's *The Prince*, it may be worth recalling, was not motivated by an ethical just order. Earlier, Ibn Zafar attempted to solve the difficulties that beset him by imagining a faultless prince whose government is regulated according to God's will, under strict principles of justice and general concern for the good of those governed. Thus, a Just Prince must combine firmness, strength and patience. All his subjects must be equal. All must accept his power, because it is 'entrusted' into his hands and because he would not be able to wield it if he lacked a clear conscience and was not righteous. A prince should be, in Ibn Zafar's own words, 'more singular than the sphinx, more marvellous than alchemy, and rarer than red gold.' A tall order, indeed.

But at the dawn of the 21st century, is it not possible to imagine how best to instill just rulership in the heart of a prince? Are there impediments that prevent a benevolent ruler from being accountable and legitimate? Is Ibn Zafar's model prince — who could rule through justice and beneficence — impossible to find? In fact, not only is it possible to imagine such a prince, but several, including Shaykh Zayed bin Sultan Al Nahyan (the ruler of Abu Dhabi and President of the United Arab Emirates), rule with precisely such principles. Like many Muslims, Shaykh Zayed's governance approximated the Sicilian's principles because his traditions required him to balance power with virtue and, in doing so, attempt to create an ethically just order. Other rulers throughout the Muslim world, from the Rashidun caliphs to modern times, have sought similar objectives. Few succeeded, but not because their intentions were necessarily negative. Many fell into the traps that power conveniently sets out. Others failed to grasp those principles that may facilitate the fulfilment of divine justice. Still others lacked the ethical notions that ensured respect for the masses. It is often said that one is loath to see one's errors while busy cataloguing those allegedly committed by others. This is the challenge addressed by Ibn Zafar and those who seek to emulate his principles.

BOOK ONE

THE JUST PRINCE

The Significance of Ibn Zafar
al-Siqilli's Work

The central concern of Ibn Zafar al-Siqilli's magnum opus, *Sulwan al-Muta' fi 'Udwan al-Atba'*, is governance — the modalities of rulership to promote a stable and just social order. Written in the literary genre of *furstenspiegel*, or 'Mirror for Princes', the *Sulwan* offers practical advice to the ruler. The book also raises some of the most immutable and persistent philosophical and ethical questions that have confronted thinkers throughout history. Indeed, Ibn Zafar's book does not only contain maxims for a wise ruler to follow, but provides a conceptual framework of religious, moral and humanistic values on which this Sicilian Arab thinker based his advisory precepts to achieve his vision of a just and peaceful society. Moreover, in his conceptualization of power and its role in governance, Ibn Zafar used the historical method, reflecting his conviction that these were transcendent problems affecting the human condition.

Power and Authority: Theoretical Perspectives

The process of governance is as old as the appearance of humankind on earth. As human beings began to congregate together to form distinct societies, the element of power emerged as a central dynamic in defining relations among individuals and groups. Because of innate inequalities in the distribution of power among competing persons and interests, the central issue became the establishment of order in society, i.e. the function of governance by those who were able to accumulate enough power to impose their will. Hence the rise of leaders — the holders of power — as mainstays in the life of societies since early times.

In the sweep of human affairs throughout recorded history, the leadership function has been exercised at different levels of society and in diverse cultural settings by monarchs, princes, tribunes, presidents, prime ministers, tribal chiefs, clerics, ministers and their bureaucratic underlings. As holders of power, leaders are considered by many political thinkers to be key players in the political arena, although their relative importance has produced significant controversy in recent times.[1]

Clearly, among the ancient Egyptians, Babylonians, Chinese, Indians and Persians, the focal power of the ruler was beyond question. In Greek political philosophy, Plato pioneered consideration of the ruler's epicentric role in governing the city state. To Plato, the philosopher-king was the ideal type of ruler, combining theoretical wisdom with practical political experience, a partial embodiment of which was Alexander the Great, pupil of Aristotle, who had in turn been a student of Plato. Plato's concept of the philosopher-

---

1. For a discussion, see R. Hrair Dekmejian, 'Marx, Weber and the Egyptian Revolution,' *The Middle East Journal* 30:2, Spring 1976, pp. 161–162. See also Eva Etzioni-Halevy, *The Elite Connection: Problems and Potential of Western Democracy*, Cambridge, United Kingdom: Polity Press, 1993; Majid Khadduri, *Arab Contemporaries: The Role of Personalities in Politics*, Baltimore and London: The Johns Hopkins University Press, 1973; and, Idem., *Arab Personalities in Politics*, Washington, DC: The Middle East Institute, 1981.

king had a formative impact on both Islamic and Western political thought. In the Muslim context, Abu Nasr al-Farabi synthesized the Platonic and Islamic notions of the ideal ruler as one who is prophet/lawgiver/imam, all combined.[1] This formulation reappeared in different forms in the writings of Ibn Sina, Ibn Bajja and Ibn Rushd.[2] In Western political thought, Plato's model of the ideal ruler was the first formal study of power and leadership, an area of analysis that eventually culminated in the 'Great Man' theory and its modern re-formulations and refutations.

The fundamental question concerns the role of political leadership in the historical process: to what extent do leaders change history? How important are leaders in shaping the political process? Among the ancients, the Platonic notion of the ideal ruler found a practical re-affirmation in Plutarch, whose measure of great men included heroism in war; grace; dignity; and generosity.[3] It was not until the 14th and 15th centuries that the leadership theme re-emerged in Western political discourse, particularly in the writings of Niccolò Machiavelli and, later Thomas Hobbes, who shared a belief in the practical necessity of effective rulership to establish a stable and secure political order.[4] In the aftermath of the

---

1.   Erwin I.J. Rosenthal, *Political Thought in Medieval Islam*, Greenwood Press: Westport, Connecticut, 1985, pp. 128–129.

2.   *Ibid.*, pp. 144, 158, 176, 199–201.

3.   Plutarch, 'Timoleon and Aemilius Paulus', in Barbara Kellerman, (ed.), *Political Leadership*, Pittsburgh, Pennsylvania: University of Pittsburgh Press, 1986, pp. 350–51.

4.   Niccolò Machiavelli, *The Prince*, translated with notes by George Bull, with an introduction by Anthony Grafton, London and New York: Penguin Books, 1999; Idem., *The Discourses*, edited with an introduction by Bernard Crick, using the translation of Leslie J. Walker, S.J., with revisions by Brian Richardson, London and New

(continued...)

French Revolution and the ensuing Napoleonic wars, a renewed focus on heroic leadership was propounded by George Friedrich Hegel and Thomas Carlyle, who saw the march of history as being determined by 'great men'.[1] Carlyle's maximalist position was, in turn, challenged by Herbert Spencer, who posited an evolutionary view of historical change,[2] and by Karl Marx, whose theory of dialectical materialism viewed leaders as pawns of social and economic forces that were the ultimate shapers of the historical process.[3] Indeed, Marx considered as inevitable the overthrow of the capitalist 'ruling class' by a proletarian revolution, which had not materialized by the time of his death in 1883. In an ironic twist, a major error in Marx's theory of revolution was identified by his most famous disciple, V.I. Lenin. In his general antipathy towards ruling classes, Marx was blinded to what Lenin considered imperative: to succeed, revolutions required competent leaders that the proletariat was unable to produce. To address this fundamental missing link in Marxian theory, Lenin organized a leadership 'vanguard' of full-time revolutionaries, who eventually took power in Russia under his personal direction. Noticeably, and in a single sweep, Lenin had resurrected Carlyle's 'Great Man' theory, while combining in himself the

---

(...continued)

York: Penguin Books, 1970. For Hobbes' voluminous contributions, see William Molesworth, (ed.), *The English Works of Thomas Hobbes*, 11 volumes, London, 1839–1845. For a concise introduction, see Michael Oakeshott, (ed.), *Leviathan: Or the Matter, Form, and Power of a Commonwealth Ecclesiastical and Civil*, Oxford: Blackwell, 1946.

1. Thomas Carlyle, 'The Leader as Hero,' in Kellerman, *op. cit.*, pp. 5–9.
2. Herbert Spencer, 'The Great Man Theory Breaks Down,' in Kellerman, *op. cit.*, pp. 10–15.
3. Howard Elcock, *Political Leadership*, Cheltenham, UK: Edward Elgar, 2001, pp. 3–4.

dual functions of revolutionary theorist and practitioner – a modern approximation of Plato's philosopher-king.

Among the greatest critics of Marx were the élite theorists Gaetano Mosca, Vilfredo Pareto and Robert Michels, who emphasized the central role of politics and leaders in shaping social evolution.[1] Attacking Marx's insistence on a violent revolution leading to a classless society, Mosca asserted that after the revolution a new ruling class would replace the old, hence the inescapable permanence of the leadership function in human affairs. It's not surprising that Mosca was the first Western political theorist to recognize Ibn Zafar's importance as a student of power and leadership, and found in him an intellectual soul-mate.[2]

While the great debate raged in 19th-century Europe, a distinguished American political scientist took up the cause of 'great men' as a prelude to his own quest for a leadership role. As a professor at Princeton University and later its president, Woodrow Wilson perceived a 'true leader of men' as the embodiment of the thinker and man of action.[3] This formulation constituted a Wilsonian resurrection of Plato's philosopher-king within a democratic setting. It also was reminiscent of the notion of good leadership as an 'aristocracy of intellect' à la Thomas Jefferson.

Although theorists have persuasively argued that leaders are a necessary and permanent feature in all societies, it should be noted that there cannot be 'a leadership for all

1.   *Ibid.*, pp. 4–5. See also Gaetano Mosca, *The Ruling Class*, edited and revised by Arthur Livingston, New York: McGraw-Hill, 1939, pp. 50–51.

2.   Gaetano Mosca, *Histoire des Doctrines Politiques*, Paris: Payot, 1936, p. 27.

3.   Woodrow Wilson, 'Leaders of Men,' in Kellerman, *op. cit.*, pp. 428–437.

seasons'. As Charles de Montesquieu and Max Weber have postulated, leadership is a dynamic function that varies in nature, scope and importance, depending on the developmental phase of a given society.[1] Consequently, a leader's power and locus of action is determined by his personal attributes and the conditions prevailing in his political environment. Clearly, times of crisis and turmoil require a much greater leadership role than periods of stability and normalcy. Indeed, as Weber theorizes, conditions of social crisis provide an opportunity for the rise of charismatic leaders with a message of salvation to establish a new political order.[2] Herein lies the special salience of Ibn Zafar's *Sulwan*, because its author provides advice to a prince who finds himself in the throes of a revolutionary situation among his subjects. As such, Ibn Zafar goes beyond counselling his prince about the essentials of rulership to providing a stratagem for confronting dire emergencies brought on by insurrectionary situations.

As a political sociologist, Weber was also preoccupied with the problem of legitimacy, the process by which power becomes transformed into authority. Therefore, legitimacy involves the moral right of a ruler to hold power and exercise it in a manner acceptable to the populace.[3] Notably, legitimacy of rulers and legitimation of power were central issues for Ibn Zafar 800 years before Weber's work.

---

1. Charles L. Montesquieu, 'Considérations sur les Causes de la Grandeur des Romains et de leur Décadence,' *Oeuvres Complètes de Montesquieu*, Paris: Gallimard, 1951, p. 70; see also Dekmejian, *op. cit.*, pp. 161–162.
2. Max Weber, *Economy and Society*, translated and edited by Guenther Roth and Claus Wittich, New York: Bedminster Press, 1968, pp. 1111, 1121.
3. *Ibid.*

Ibn Zafar: An Overview

Despite its intrinsic importance, the work of Ibn Zafar al-Siqilli has remained virtually unknown to contemporary Western scholars. A plethora of recent studies on Islamic political thought has been prompted by the rise of Islamist movements in the 20th century.[1] As such, these studies have focused on Ibn Taymiyya and others who serve as the historical anchors of modern Islamist thought, which has detracted scholars from exploring little-known Arab thinkers

1. Among others, see John J. Donohue and John L. Esposito, (eds.), *Islam in Transition: Muslim Perspectives*, New York: Oxford University Press, 1982; Hamid Enayat, *Modern Islamic Political Thought*, Austin: University of Texas Press, 1982; John L. Esposito, (ed.), *Voices of Resurgent Islam*, New York: Oxford University Press, 1983; R. Hrair Dekmejian, *Islam in Revolution*, Syracuse, New York: Syracuse University Press, 1985, 1995; Hichem Djait, *Europe and Islam: Cultures and Modernity*, Berkeley and Los Angeles: University of California Press, 1985; Maxime Rodinson, *Europe and the Mystique of Islam*, translated by Roger Veinus, London: I.B. Tauris, 1987; Barbara Freyet Stowasser, (ed.), *The Islamic Impulse*, Washinhgton, DC: Centre for Contemporary Arab Studies, Georgetown University, 1987; Shabbir Akhtar, *A Faith for All Seasons: Islam and the Challenge of the Modern World*, Chicago: Ivan R. Dee, 1990; Albert Hourani, *Islam in European Thought*, New York: Cambridge University Press, 1991; Ahmad Bin Yousef and Ahmad Abul Jobain, *The Politics of Islamic Resurgence: Through Western Eyes*, North Springfield, Virginia: The United Association for Studies and Research, 1992; John Kelsay, *Islam and War: A Study in Comparative Ethics*, Louisville, Kentucky: Westminster/John Knox Press, 1993; Mohammed Arkoun, *Rethinking Islam*, translated and edited by Robert D. Lee, Boulder, Colorado: Westview Press, 1994; *Islam: Opposing Viewpoints*, n. p., n. c., USA: Greenhaven Press, 1995; John L. Esposito, *Political Islam: The Challenges of Change*, Annandale, Virginia: United Association for Studies and Research, 1995; Fred Halliday, *Islam and the Myth of Confrontation: Religion and Politics in the Middle East*, London: I.B. Tauris, 1995.

whose critical works have lain dormant for centuries. It is safe to suppose that there exist many more unknown jewels of political literature like Ibn Zafar's *Sulwan* on dusty library shelves and in collections of manuscripts. Although a few contemporary editions of the *Sulwan* are available in Arabic, the Sicilian is hardly known even in Arab intellectual circles; nor has his work been accorded the importance that it deserves.[1]

In the West, only a handful of scholars have been familiar with Ibn Zafar's contributions. The pioneer in the discovery of Ibn Zafar was Michele Amari, the distinguished 19th century Sicilian Arabist, who did seminal work on the history of Arab Sicily during his stays in Paris (as a political exile escaping persecution in 1842 and 1849 by the Neapolitan government). Amari discovered eight manuscripts of the *Sulwan al-Muta'* in the Bibliothèque Nationale, which he collated and translated into Italian. He published his Italian manuscript in 1851 with a detailed commentary and notes. An English translation of Amari's work appeared in 1852.[2] Amari was quick to grasp the value of the *Sulwan* as an outstanding political discourse. In his introductory chapter, Amari proudly refers to Ibn Zafar as 'my Arab fellow-countryman of the twelfth century', whose '*Solwan* offers

---

1. For Arabic editions of the *Sulwan al-Muta' fi 'Udwan al-Atba'* (Consolation for the Ruler During the Hostility of Subjects), also known as *Kitab al-Sulwanat fi Musamarat al-Khulafa' wal-Sadat* (Book of Consolations in Conversations with Caliphs and Noblemen), see the following: Abu Nahla Ahmad bin 'Abd al-Majid, Cairo: Dar al-Thaqafa, 1978; and, Muhammad Ahmad Damaj, Beirut: Mu'assasat 'Izz al-Din lil-Tiba'a wal-Nashr, 1995.

2. Michele Amari, *Solwan; or Waters of Comfort by Ibn Zafer*, Volumes I and II, London: Richard Bentley, 1852.

many profound views of policy, which are as applicable now as they would have been in the age of Tacitus or of Machiavel'.[1]

It was a half century later that Amari's Italian rendition of the *Sulwan* came to the attention of Gaetano Mosca, who drew parallels between Ibn Zafar's book and Machiavelli's *The Prince*.[2] As the founder of the modern field of élite studies, Mosca had been instrumental in building upon the intellectual legacy of his great Italian predecessor from Florence. Yet as a Sicilian, Mosca also became keenly interested in exploring the contributions of mediaeval Arab thinkers to the field of political science. In reading the *Sulwan*, Mosca discovered 'a Machiavellism more refined than that of the Florentine Secretary'[3] – a powerful endorsement of Ibn Zafar's work after the passage of eight centuries. Since Mosca, Ibn Zafar has received only brief mention: first in an entry in the *Encyclopaedia of Islam* and second, in a French monograph on Arab miniatures.[4] Ibn Zafar is better known to modern Italian specialists on Muslim Sicily, such as Umberto Rizzitano, who has built upon Amari's pioneering efforts.[5]

Ibn Zafar: A Biographical Sketch

A short, misshapen and ill-favoured man, Abu 'Abdallah Muhammad ibn Abu Muhammad ibn Zafar al-Siqilli al-

1. *Ibid.*, Volume I, p. 2.
2. Mosca, *op. cit.*, p. 27.
3. *Ibid.*
4. Umberto Rizzitano, 'Ibn Zafar 'Abd Allah,' *The Encyclopaedia of Islam*, New Edition, Volume III, Leiden: E. J. Brill, 1971, p. 970; see also Rachel Arié, *Miniatures Hispano–Musulmanes*, Leiden: E. J. Brill, 1969, pp. 1–8. (Hereafter EI.)
5. Umberto Rizzitano, *Storia e Cultura nella Sicilia Saracena*, Palermo: S. F. Flaccovio, 1975, pp. 160, 284–285, 366, 434–435, 450–451.

Makki al-Maliki was born in Sicily in 1104, but lived as a wanderer seeking a livelihood and political haven in mostly inhospitable Arab capitals. He was an unlucky man, whose wisdom and loyalty were seldom appreciated by those in power whom he sought to serve.

The precise chronology of the travels of 'The Sicilian Wanderer' is difficult to establish. Born when Sicily was under Norman rule, Ibn Zafar is thought to have been raised and educated in Makka, the city of his forbears, as denoted by the inclusion of 'al-Makki' in his name. More certain is Ibn Zafar's sojourn to the Maghreb and, after the Norman capture of al-Mahdiyya (1148), his visit to the doctrinally adverse milieu of Fatimid Egypt. Around 1150 Ibn Zafar took refuge in Aleppo, Syria, where he secured a teaching position at Madrasa Ibn Abi 'Asrun. He also enjoyed the patronage of Safi al-Din, a high-ranking official in the court of Nur al-Din Mahmud ibn Zanji (1146–1174). The outbreak of civil war forced Ibn Zafar to leave Syria for Sicily, where he briefly enjoyed the patronage of Amir Abu 'Abdallah ibn Abi al-Qasim ibn 'Ali al-Qurashi, also know as Ibn al-Hajar. Soon thereafter Ibn Zafar left Sicily for Egypt and settled in Hama, Syria, where he died in poverty in 1170 or 1172.[1]

Despite his many misfortunes, Ibn Zafar was highly regarded by his contemporaries as well as later chroniclers, in sharp contrast to the relative oblivion that befell him in the modern Arab/Muslim setting. According to 'Imad al-Din al-Isfahani, who knew Ibn Zafar personally, he is described as 'a

---

1.   On Ibn Zafar's travels, see Yaqut al-Rumi, *Kitab Irshad al-'Arib ila Ma'rifat al-Adib* (Book of Intelligent Guidance and Refined Learning), Volume VII, Cairo: Matba'at al-Hindiyya, 1925, p. 102; and Amari, *op. cit.*, Volume I, pp. 23–28.

mighty genius'.[1] The great geographer Yaqut al-Rumi called Ibn Zafar 'a refined philologist'.[2] The historian Shams al-Din Muhammad al-Dhahabi considered Ibn Zafar 'a brilliant thinker'[3] and Ibn Khallikan, the great chronicler, praised him as 'an accomplished scholar'.[4] Among the epithets of distinction given to Ibn Zafar were *Hujjat al-Din* (Argument of the Faith), *Shams al-Din* (Sun of the Faith), *Jamal al-Din* (Beauty of the Faith), *Burhan al-Din* (Proof for the Faith), *Hujjat al-Islam* (Argument of Islam) and *Jamal al-Islam* (Beauty of Islam).[5] Despite all these accolades and tributes of greatness, Ibn Zafar experienced much poverty and dishonour in his lifetime; after the 1700s, his work was virtually forgotten for 300 years.

Ibn Zafar's Literary Legacy

Ibn Zafar was a prodigious writer with a total literary output of thirty-two books, only a few of which are known to have survived (including the *Sulwan*).[6] An unusually well-rounded individual, Ibn Zafar had a mastery of diverse branches of learning both sacred and secular: theology, civil law, moral philosophy, Islamic law, history, philology and pedagogy.

1. Amari, *op. cit.*, Volume I, p.xx.
2. Yaqut al-Rumi, *op. cit.*, p. 102.
3. Al-Imam Shams al-Din Muhammad ibn Ahmad ibn 'Uthman al-Dhahabi, *Sirat A'lam al-Nubala'* (Biography of Most Learned Nobles), Volume 20, Beirut: Mu'assasat al-Risala, 1985, pp. 522–523.
4. Abu al-'Abbas Shams al-Din Ahmad ibn Muhammad Abu Bakr ibn Khallikan, *Wafayat al-A'yan wa Anba' Abna' al-Zaman* (Obituaries of Eminent Men and Histories of Leading Contemporaries), Volume 4, Cairo: Maktabat al-Nahda al-Misriyya, 1948, p. 29.
5. Amari, *op. cit.*, Volume I, pp. 39–40.
6. *Ibid.*, pp. 39–40; see also Arié, *op. cit.*, pp. 1–4; Rizzitano, *op. cit.*, p. 970.

Moreover, he was well-versed in the history of the Arabs before and since Islam; the traditions of the Prophet; Indian literature; history and literature of the Persians; and the sacred books of the Jews and Christians. He was considered a foremost *mufassir* (exegete), poet, grammarian and man of letters. As a reading of the *Sulwan* illustrates, and although he was a pious Muslim with strong Arab loyalties, Ibn Zafar's intellectual reach extended far beyond the political and cultural confines of *Dar al-Islam*. His advisory opinions carried universal appeal.

2

Counselling the Prince: An Historical Overview

Ibn Zafar's Predecessors

Ibn Zafar's *Sulwan* belongs to that genre of political literature where the writer offers advice to a prince to enable the latter to sustain his leadership role, rule more effectively and secure his realm. This type of writing, commonly known as *furstenspiegel* or 'Mirror for Princes', is best exemplified in the Western political literature by Niccolò Machiavelli's celebrated magnum opus *The Prince*. Under the guise of offering practical advice, many of these authors made significant contributions to the field of political philosophy and the art of governance.

The practice of providing political 'know-how' to those in authority may be traced to ancient times. Among the earliest are the Chinese Confucian writers of the classical age who sought to gain high office in order to reform the government. Mencius visited rulers to dispense advice on good governance. Even more significant were the writers of the Legalist school of Chinese thought, such as Lord Shang and Han Fei, who held high office only to suffer tragic deaths.[1] Another classic of the advisory genre from ancient China is *The Art of War* by

---

1. A. C. Graham, *Disputers of the Tao*, La Salle, Illinois: Open Court Co., 1988.

Sun Tzu, who aimed 'to reach invincibility, victory without battle and unassailable strength through understanding of the physics, politics, and psychology of conflict'.[1] Not surprisingly, this Chinese classic has retained its fame as a sourcebook of guidance in military strategy, politics and even business, almost rivalling Machiavelli's opus.

Although Plato (427–347 BC) did not write a *furstenspiegel* in the narrow sense, he sought to apply a philosopher's scientific knowledge to practical politics as described in his *Statesman, Laws and Republic* and institutionalized in the Academy, the school he founded to provide expertise in framing laws and constitutions for the Greek cities. Preoccupied with finding a remedy for the chaotic state of Greek politics, Plato travelled to Sicily for the express purpose of educating King Dionysius II of Syracuse, in a vain attempt to transform him into a philosopher-king.[2]

A shining example of ancient Hindu political literature is the *Arthasastra*, a detailed manual of statecraft. It is a systematic exposition of rules to acquire and maintain power and modalities for the conduct of foreign policy and military campaigns. This Sanskrit *furstenspiegel* was authored by Kautilya, a Brahmin, and Chief Minister to King Chandragupta (321–296 BC), the founder of the Mauryan Empire.[3]

Providing advice to rulers soon became a universal phenomenon that developed across the centuries throughout

---

1. Sun Tzu, *The Art of War*, translated by Thomas Cleary, Boston & Shaftesbury: Shambhala Publications, Inc., 1988, p. vii.

2. Michael B. Foster, *Masters of Political Thought*, Volume I, Cambridge, Massachusetts: Houghton Mifflin, 1941, p. 24.

3. George Modelski, 'Kautilya: Foreign Policy and International System in the Ancient Hindu World,' *American Political Science Review* 58:3, September 1964, pp. 549–551.

the world. The rise and progressive expansion of Arab power in the decades after the death of the Prophet Muhammad confronted successive Muslim caliphs and sultans with complex problems of governance and administration over an immense realm of countries and peoples stretching from Spain to Central Asia. In the context of the multifaceted challenges of rulership and struggles for power among ruling factions, both official and unofficial advisors emerged in key roles within and on the periphery of the ruling élite. Although some of these advisors were lay functionaries, others belonged to the clerical class (*'ulama'*), who dispensed advice on governance according to Islamic law – a practice that harked back to the beginnings of the Caliphate. A dozen of these luminaries left behind a rich body of literature that represents much of the collective political thought and experience of Muslim thinkers and practitioners of the art and science of governance during the centuries of Islam's ascendance. What follows are brief discussions of their more significant contributions.

Ibn al-Muqaffa' (720–757)

One of the earliest contributors to the genre of 'Mirror for Princes' literature was 'Abdallah Ibn al-Muqaffa', a Persian convert to Islam. This brilliant secretary to the uncle of Caliph al-Mansur was a pioneering figure who effected the emergence of classical Arabic literature through his translations from Persian, such as the Indo-Persian epic *Kalila wa Dimna* as well as his authorship of several *furstenspiegels* on the art of government. Of special significance are Ibn al-Muqaffa''s *al-Adab al-Kabir* (*Great Literature*), *al-Adab al-Saghir* (*Lesser Literature*), and *Risala fil-Sahaba* (*Epistles of the Companions*), which are replete with political advice to the caliph and his courtiers, derived from *khudaynama* chronicles of Persian kings and his own experience and involvement in the affairs of state, which caused his early demise at the hands of his enemies.[1]

Yet Ibn al-Muqaffa''s writings established a powerful precedent to be followed by subsequent authors of tomes to advise rulers, including al-Jahiz, Ibn al-Qutaiba, Tayfur, Ibn Abi al-Rabi', Ibn 'Abd Rabbih, al-Mawardi, Kai Ka'us, Nizam al-Mulk, al-Ghazali, al-Turtushi, Ibn Zafar, Ibn Jama'a, Ibn al-Tiqtaqa and al-Dawani. The most significant precedent Ibn al-Muqaffa' set for this long list of distinguished Muslim writers was to transform the absolutist model of Persian kingship into a more humanistic practice of rulership constrained by Islamic faith with its laws, obligations and equality of all believers before God.[2]

Al-Jahiz (776–868)

A most worthy successor to Ibn al-Muqaffa' was Abu 'Uthman 'Amr al-Jahiz, a famous and prolific writer of *adab* literature, Mu'tazili theology and political discourse. Born and educated in Basra 'in an obscure family of *mawali* from the Banu Kinana and probably of Abyssinian origin, he owes his sobriquet to a malformation of the eyes'.[3] Despite his handicap, he demonstrated 'an invincible desire for learning and a remarkably inquisitive mind urged him towards a life of independence and, much to his family's despair, idleness'.[4]

---

1. F. Gabrieli, 'Ibn al-Mukaffa',' *The Encyclopaedia of Islam*, New Edition, Leiden & London: E. J. Brill and Luzac & Co., 1965, pp. 883–885.
2. Erwin I.J. Rosenthal, *Political Thought in Medieval Islam*, Greenwood Press: Westport, Connecticut, 1985, pp. 68–73.
3. Ch. Pellat, 'Al-Djahiz,' EI, *op. cit.*, p. 385.
4. *Ibid.*

According to a leading historian, al-Jahiz's 'precocious intelligence won him admittance to Muʻtazili circles and bourgeois salons', where he helped define thorny 'problems confronting the Muslim conscience at that time' ranging from how best to harmonize faith and reason, the delicate question of the Caliphate and the even more difficult and defining issue of various 'conflicts between Islamic sects and the claims of the non-Arabs'.[1] In time, al-Jahiz won recognition for his voluminous writings, which provided comprehensive advice to the caliphs al-Maʼmun and al-Mutawakkil on how to govern; the qualities of the ideal Muslim ruler; the behaviour of courtiers; the practices of effective governance as expressed in his *Kitab al-Taj* (*Book of the Crown*); and other contributions.[2] Although his physical appearance may have affected his career in the Abbasid court, al-Jahiz's role as an *eminence grise* accorded him regular access to members of the ruling élite.[3] Al-Jahiz occupies a key place in Muslim political thought. His ability to manipulate rhetoric and humor, his gift of providing useful advice without offending and his capacity to overcome natural handicaps were instrumental in making his talents useful to the Abbasid cause.[4]

Ibn Qutaiba (828–889), Tayfur (819–893) and Ibn Abi al-Rabiʻ (d. 894)
After al-Jahiz, the most notable exponent of *adab* writing was Abu Muhammad ʻAbdallah Ibn Qutaiba al-Daynuri. Born in Kufa, Iraq, this Hanbali theologian of Iranian descent and leading *qadi*, was instrumental in Caliph al-Mutawakkil's

---

1. *Ibid.*
2. *Ibid.*, p. 386; see also Rosenthal, *op. cit.*, pp. 75–77.
3. Pellat, *ibid.*, p. 385.
4. *Ibid.*, p. 387.

campaign to replace Mu'tazili ideology with Sunni traditionalism.[1] Despite his espousal of orthodoxy, as an official ideologue of the new order, Ibn Qutaiba was an eclectic intellectual who also wrote on secular subjects. He studied philology and was the first representative of the eclectic school of Baghdad philologists that succeeded the Kufa and Basra schools of rationalist thinking (*ahl al-ra'i*), while jurisprudence (*fiqh*) was under development.

Although engaged in theological polemic, Ibn Qutaiba's chief works were directed to the training of an ideal clerk who would loyally serve his ruler. Four of his studies that may be said to form a series were geared towards that objective: 1) the *Adab al-Katib* (*Training of the Clerk*) provides detailed instruction on writing and is a useful compendium of Arabic style; 2) the *Kitab al-Ma'arif* (*Book of Knowledge*) describes how an advisor should gather knowledge to better serve his leader; 3) the *Kitab al-Shi'r wal-Shu'ara'* (*Book of Poetry and Poets*) highlights the critical importance of poetry as a form of communication. (Given the value of this medium for Arab societies then and now, Ibn Qutaiba's foresight further illustrates an appreciation for how best an advisor may serve his ruler); 4) the most important study of the set, the *'Uyun al-Akhbar* (*Sources of Information*), deals in ten chapters with lordship; war; nobility; character; science and eloquence; asceticism; friendship; requests; food; and women. This is a heavily illustrated volume with examples from history, poetry and both Arabic and Persian proverbs.[2] Ibn Qutaiba was

---

1. G. Lecomte, 'Ibn Kutayba,' EI, *op. cit.*, pp. 844–847.
2. For additional details, see Abu Muhammad 'Abdallah ibn Qutaiba, *Adab al-Katib* (Training of the Clerk), edited by Max Grunert, Leiden: E. J. Brill, 1900; Idem., *Kitab al-Ma'arif* (The Book of Knowledge), edited by F. Wtistenfeld, Gottingen, 1850; Idem, *Kitab al-Shi'r wal-*
(continued...)

greatly influenced by Ibn al-Muqaffa' and al-Jahiz and their Indo-Iranian antecedents, although his Arabic prose is superior for its simplicity, facility and modernity.[1]

A contemporary of Ibn Qutaiba, Ahmad Abu Tahir Tayfur was an historian and *littérateur* of Baghdad. Tayfur's literary career brought him into contact with high officials. Of particular relevance is a letter Tayfur wrote to his son, who had become a provincial governor during the caliphate of al-Ma'mun, which offers detailed advice about the ruler's duties and the maxims of good governance.[2]

Another jurist of this period was Shihab al-Din Ahmad ibn Abi al-Rabi'. An advisor to the Caliph Abbas VIII al-Mu'tasim, the son of Harun al-Rashid, Ibn Abi al-Rabi' authored *Suluk al-Malik fi Tadbir al-Mamalik (A King's Behaviour to Govern Kingdoms)*.[3] Ibn Abi al-Rabi' relied on Greek philosophy – which asserted that man possessed civic attributes – but placed his discourse within an Islamic context. Man, posited Ibn Abi al-Rabi', was capable, but more so when he relied on God. Likewise, he asserted that rulers were capable of governing, but did so more effectively and justly when they applied God's laws.[4]

(...continued)

      Shu'ara' (Book of Poetry and Poets), edited by M. J. de Goeje, Leiden: E. J. Brill, 1904, and Idem, *'Uyun al-Akhbar* (Sources of Information), edited by C. Brockelmann, Leiden: E. J. Brill, 1900.

1.   *Ibid.*, pp. 846–847.

2.   F. Rosenthal, 'Ibn Abi Tahir Tayfur', EI, *op. cit.*, pp. 692–693; see also Rosenthal, *op. cit.*, pp. 76–77.

3.   'Adil Fathi Thabit 'Abd al-Hafiz, *Shar'iyyat al-Sulta fil-Islam* (Legitimation of Authority in Islam), Alexandria, Egypt: Dar al-Jami'at al-Jadida lil-Nashr, 1996, pp. 166–171.

4.   *Ibid.*, pp. 167.

Ibn 'Abd Rabbih (860–940)

Among the few Andalusian writers of works on princely
conduct was Abu 'Umar Ahmad ibn 'Abd Rabbih of Córdoba,
Spain, who followed the *adab* tradition of al-Jahiz and Ibn
Qutaiba. He lived during the apogee of Arab rule in Spain
under the Marwanid dynasty. For three decades he was an
official panegyrist of the Marwanid rulers and served as
laureate of Caliph 'Abd al-Rahman III (912–961). His *al-'Iqd
al-Farid* (*The Unique Necklace*) is an encyclopaedic compilation
of knowledge that includes chapters on government, good
conduct, war and rulership.[1]

Al-Mawardi (974–1058)

Abu al-Hasan 'Ali al-Mawardi was a Shafi'i jurisprudent
(*faqih*) of Basra, an eminent *qadi* of great learning and author
of seminal books on Islamic law and government including *Al-
Ahkam al-Sultaniyya* (*Princely Rules*), *Qawanin al-Wizara wa Siyasat
al-Mulk* (*Ministerial Laws and the Politics of Authority*) and *Nasihat
al-Muluk* (*The Advice of Rulers*).[2] These writings discuss various
principles of political science, with special reference to the
functions and duties of caliphs, their chief ministers and
other viziers. They highlight the dynamic relationships
between various social groups and government officials, as
well as the myriad measures required in different situations to
strengthen the ruler's power and ensure victory.[3]

Al-Mawardi's proficiency in jurisprudence, ethics, political
science and literature proved useful in securing respectable
posts throughout his long life. As a trusted advisor in the
Abbasid court in Baghdad and in his writings, al-Mawardi

1. C. Brockelmann, 'Ibn 'Abd Rabbih', EI, *op. cit.*, pp. 676–677.
2. C. Brockelmann, 'Al-Mawardi', EI, *op. cit.*, p. 869.
3. 'Abd al-Hafiz, *op. cit.*, pp. 171–178.

sought to strengthen Sunnism and the power of the caliphs
against the sultans and provincial governors. He was entrusted
with important diplomatic missions by the caliphs al-Qadir
(991–1031) and al-Qa'im (1031–74) to negotiate with
emerging rivals such as the Shi'ite Buwayhid rulers of Iraq.[1]
A man of upright reputation and modesty, al-Mawardi
effectively assumed the combined functions of political
theorist, jurist, diplomat and court counsellor. He is
considered the author of the 'Doctrine of Necessity' in
Muslim political theory because he believed that unlimited
powers delegated to regional governors tended to create chaos
– hence his support for a strong caliphate. Yet, he also
favoured clear principles for the election of a caliph, and
identified key qualities for 'voters' including the necessity of
a certain degree of intellect and the demonstration of sound
character.

Kai Ka'us (b. 1020) *and Nizam al-Mulk* (1018–1092)

Despite al-Mawardi's best efforts, the Abbasid Caliphate
continued to decline in the 11th century, and lost power to
the Seljuk sultans. The period of Seljuk ascendance produced
two major advisory tomes by non-Arab writers – the
Qabusnama of 'Unsur al-Ma'ali Kai Ka'us and the *Siyasatnama*
of Abu 'Ali al-Hasan al-Tusi Nizam al-Mulk.[2] Kai Ka'us was
the penultimate ruler of the Ziyarid dynasty that ruled the
southern littoral of the Caspian Sea under the Seljuks.
Written in the Persian *andarz* style (giving counsel to rulers),
the *Qabusnama* was intended to provide practical guidance to

---

1.   C. Brockelmann, 'Al-Mawardi', EI, *op. cit.*, p. 869.
2.   Rosenthal, *op. cit.*, pp. 78–83.

his son and successor, Gilan Shah.[1] The book's introduction and forty-four chapters cover a wide range of topics, including kingship, leadership in battle and administration. Since its appearance in 1083 the *Qabusnama*, a work readily accessible on account of its direct style, numerous aphorisms and historical anecdotes, remained popular particularly in Persia and the Ottoman Empire.

Another 'Mirror' of great renown is the *Siyasatnama* or *Siyar al-Muluk* (*The History of Kings*), written by Abu 'Ali al-Hasan al-Tusi Nizam al-Mulk, the famous minister of the Seljuk sultans Alp Arslan and Malikshah. After Alp Arslan's assassination in 1072, a ruthless Nizam al-Mulk dominated Malikshah and in effect became the actual ruler of the Seljuk Empire. Written in 1091–92, just prior to Nizam al-Mulk's own assassination, the *Siyasatnama* details in fifty chapters advice to the sultan and the shortcomings and failures of Seljuk rule, which he had vainly sought to correct.[2] The addition of eleven chapters a year after the *Siyasatnama* was first published in 1092 highlights Nizam al-Mulk's sense of failure in providing a sound system of governance, as dangers threatened the empire, from the Isma'ilis in particular. Still, Nizam al-Mulk, like Cardinal Richelieu in France several centuries later, was a patron of the arts, generously supporting poets and writers. Remarkably, he also founded several colleges whose ethos and teachings were based on the Ash'ari *Kalam* (dialectical theology) and the Shafi'i school of law, to which he adhered. These madrasas, including the famous al-

1. C.E. Bosworth, 'Kay Ka'us,' EI, *op. cit.*, p. 815.
2. H. Bowen and C.E. Bosworth, 'Nizam al-Mulk,' EI, *op. cit.*, pp. 69–73.

Nizamiyya of Baghdad, contributed greatly to the Sunni revival in the central and eastern lands of Islam.[1]

Al-Ghazali (1058–1111)

One of the foremost theologians of Islam, Abu Hamid Muhammad al-Ghazali was a mystic and reformer of the Muslim faith. In 1091, al-Ghazali was sent by Nizam al-Mulk to teach at the al-Nizamiyya madrasa in Baghdad. Although popular within both religious and political circles, al-Ghazali sought to distance himself from the vicissitudes of government affairs. He left teaching after experiencing an intense spiritual struggle and took up the mystical life of the Sufi for twelve years. Al-Ghazali returned to teaching and produced several major studies, including his most important work, *Ihya' 'Ulum al-Din* (*The Revival of the Religious Sciences*).[2] A semi-autobiographical work, *al-Munqidh min al-Dhalal* (*Deliverance from Error*) was also composed, although his *Nasihat al-Muluk* (*Advice to Kings*) sets standards for kingly behaviour and provides guidance on dealing with ministers and subjects.[3] Despite his high stature, al-Ghazali remained uninvolved in government work and political affairs because of his true calling as a religious reformer, mystic and thinker who successfully reconciled Sufism with Islamic orthodoxy.[4]

Al-Turtushi (1059–1126)

A traditional Arab *faqih* born in Spain, Abu Bakr Muhammad al-Turtushi settled in Alexandria, Egypt, where he educated

---

1. *Ibid.*
2. W. Montgomery Watt, 'Al-Ghazali,' Encyclopaedia of Islam II, *op. cit.*, pp. 1038–1041.
3. Frank Ronald Charles Bagley, *Ghazali's Book of Counsel for Kings*, London: Oxford University Press, 1964, pp. 45, 63, 80, 106.
4. W. Montgomery Watt, 'Al-Ghazali,' EI, *op. cit.*, pp. 1038–1041.

many disciples including such famous figures as Ibn al-'Arabi and Ibn Tumart (d. 1130), the future Mahdi of the Muwahhidun movement in North Africa.[1] Al-Turtushi wrote *Siraj al-Muluk* (*Lamp for Rulers*), a large compilation (64 chapters) of moral maxims, anecdotes and advice on rulership dedicated to his patron, the counsellor al-Ma'mun ibn al-Bata'ihi.[2] The encyclopaedic dimensions of Turtushi's book provided considerable material for Muslim political thinkers of subsequent generations. Although Ibn Khaldun criticized al-Turtushi in *The Muqaddima* for being a compiler without originality, he himself benefited from the wealth of historical information and political insights contained in the *Siraj al-Muluk*.[3]

Ibn Zafar's Successors

Ibn Zafar al-Siqilli was al-Turtushi's immediate chronological successor. As such, he provides the intellectual link between the long line of *furstenspiegel* authors going back to Ibn al-Muqaffa' and subsequent writers of the 'Mirror' or related genres such as Ibn Jama'a, Ibn al-Tiqtaqa, Ibn Taymiyya and al-Dawani.

Ibn Jama'a (1241–1333)
A direct intellectual descendant of al-Mawardi and al-Ghazali, Badr al-Din Ibn Jama'a was a Shafi'i jurist, theologian and

---

1. A. Ben Abdesselem, 'Al-Turtushi,' EI, *op. cit.*, pp. 739–740.
2. *Ibid.*
3. 'Abd al-Hafiz, *op. cit.*, pp. 150–159; see also Ibn Khaldun, *The Muqaddima* (Introduction to the Science of History), translated by F. Rosenthal, abridged and edited by N.J. Dawood, New Jersey: Princeton University Press, 1967, pp. 41–42.

teacher. His book on constitutional law, *Tahrir al-Ahkam fi Tadbir Ahl al-Islam* (*The Formulation of Orders to Guide Muslims*), outlines the ruler's obligations towards his subjects as well as his need to seek advice from the *'ulama'* in legal matters.[1] Although a conservative theologian, Ibn Jama'a was also a pragmatist, offering rulers worldly counsel in the genre of the 'Mirror for Princes.'[2]

Ibn al-Tiqtaqa (1262–?)

Born of noble lineage, Safi al-Din Muhammad ibn 'Ali ibn Tabataba, known as Ibn al-Tiqtaqa, was the Shi'ite representative (*naqib*) of al-Hilla in Iraq. During his visit to Mosul he wrote *Al-Fakhri* (*On the Systems of Government and Muslim Dynasties*), for Fakhr al-Din 'Isa ibn Ibrahim, the ruler of the city. It included a *furstenspiegel* and a history of caliphs and wazirs, with detailed biographies.[3]

Despite his allegiance to Shi'ism, Ibn al-Tiqtaqa provides a realistic assessment of the factors responsible for the success or failure of rulers in Islamic history. In order to ensure the ruler's success, Ibn al-Tiqtaqa lists ten qualities based not only on moral standards but also on mastery of the art of rulership. Ibn al-Tiqtaqa was concerned with the practical politics needed to sustain the ruler and his state, and had considerable influence on the work of Ibn Khaldun.[4]

---

1. Rosenthal, *op. cit.*, pp. 43–51.
2. Kamal S. Salibi, 'Ibn Djama'a,' EI, *op. cit.*, pp. 748–749.
3. Ibn al-Tiqtaqa, Muhammad ibn 'Ali, *Al-Fakhri* (*On the Systems of Government and Muslim Dynasties*), translated by C. E. J. Whitting, London: Luzac, 1947. See also F. Rosenthal, 'Ibn al-Tiktaka,' EI, *op. cit.*, p. 956.
4. Rosenthal, *op. cit.*, pp. 62–67.

Ibn Taymiyya (1263–1328)

Taqi al-Din Ahmad ibn Taymiyya, the pre-eminent but highly controversial Hanbali theologian and jurisconsult, played a significant role in influencing successive rulers and affairs of state in both Syria and Egypt.[1]

Although Ibn Taymiyya did not write strictly in the 'Mirror' genre, his voluminous publications, religious edicts (*fatwas*) and personal involvement in political affairs, doctrinal polemics and military campaigns made him a controversial figure who faced frequent persecution and imprisonment.[2] As an activist advocate of Hanbali puritanism, Ibn Taymiyya emphasized that rulers should always be guided by Islam's teachings, which would require them to seek advice from the *'ulama'* as the guardians of the faith.[3] Ibn Taymiyya's doctrinal and political legacies have had a formative impact on Islamic political thought and society, particularly in the development of contemporary revivalist ideologies and movements.

---

1. Ibn Taymiyya's writings were largely forgotten after his death. The Salafi movement revived them during the rise of the so-called 'Wahhabi awakening' in Saudi Arabia especially after the 1930s. See, for example, George Makdisi, 'Ibn Taimiya: A Sufi of the Qadiriya Order,' *American Journal of Arabic Studies* I (1974), pp. 118–129; see also Salah al-Din al-Munajjid, ed., *Shaykh al-Islam Ibn Taymiyya: Siratuhu wa Akhbaruhu 'inda al-Mu'arrikhin* (*Shaykh Ibn Taymiyya: Biography and Views According to Historians*), Beirut: Dar al-Kitab al-'Arabi, 1976. For a Saudi perspective on the role of Ibn Taymiyya, see Muhammad Jalal Keshk, *Al-Sa'udiyyun wal-hal al-Islami* (The Saudis and the Islamic Solution), Washington, DC: n.p. 1982, especially pp. 85–108.

2. R. Hrair Dekmejian, *Islam in Revolution*, Syracuse, New York: Syracuse University Press, 1995, pp. 37–40.

3. H. Laoust, 'Ibn Taimiya,' EI, *op. cit.*, pp. 951–955.

Al-Dawani (1427–1503)
A teacher, philosopher and *qadi* of Fars, Muhammad ibn As'ad Jalal al-Din al-Dawani wrote *Akhlaq-i Jalili* (*Practical Philosophy*) – a popular version of Nasir al-Din Tusi's *Akhlaq-i Nasiri* – for Uzun Hassan, the Aq Qoyunlu ruler. To al-Dawani, a righteous ruler is necessary to maintain 'the equipoise of the world'.[1] He courageously argued that, in addition to righteousness, the ruler – clearly, Uzun Hasan – must learn certain practical rules of governance in order to enjoy his power under God's *Shari'a*.[2] Moreover, he argued that a ruler needed supreme law as well as monetary power to rule effectively; he must also have and display unique qualities, including those that would allow him to lead 'men to perfection'. Importantly, al-Dawani did not simply identify force as a tool for rulership but, like Ibn Zafar, defined good government as one that is based on God's justice. He boldly called on the just ruler to become 'the shadow of God upon earth, His representative (*khalifat Allah*), and the deputy (*na'ib*) of the Prophet Muhammad'.[3] Al-Dawani's work is important, as he summarizes much of the literary heritage of Islam including political philosophy, law and practical wisdom on rulership. As such, his work represents the culmination of intellectual currents until the 14th century, when Muslim power had passed on to the Ottoman Turks and Persian Shahs.

1. Muhammad ibn As'ad Jalal al-Din al-Dawani, *Akhlaq-i Jalili* (*Practical Philosophy of the Muhammadan People*), translated by W. T. Thompson, London: Luzac, 1839. See also Ann K. S. Lambton, 'Al-Dawani,' EI, *op. cit.*, p. 174.
2. Rosenthal, *op. cit.*, pp. 221–222.
3. Lambton, *op. cit.*, p. 174.

The Western Tradition

To place the *Sulwan al-Muta'* within the larger context of its literary genre, it is important to present a brief overview of the rich tradition of *furstenspiegel* writing in Western countries. Although Machiavelli's *The Prince* would become the most popular work of this type, many such books were produced earlier, as well as during and after his lifetime.

As a distinctive form, the appearance of advisory books can be traced back to the emerging Italian city-states of the 13th century. The earliest example of this genre is *Oculus Pastoralis* (1242), by an anonymous author; its tenets were later expanded in books by Giovanni da Viterbo and Brunetto Latini.[1] With the spread of factional conflicts in the Italian city-states, princely government acquired greater acceptance. One result was works by such writers as Petrarch, Dante and others, seeking to justify centralized authority to insure social peace, while emphasizing the need to govern with justice and clemency.[2]

The 14th and 15th centuries saw a proliferation of panegyrics and books dedicated to various dukes, princes and popes by functionaries like Ferreto de Ferreti (b. 1296), Pier Paolo Vergerio (b. 1370), Uberto Decembrio (b. 1350), Francesco Patrizi (b. 1412), Bartolomeo Sacchi (b. 1421), Diomede Carafa (b. 1407) and Giovanni Pontano (b. 1426). A similar flowering of the advisory genre occurred in northern European countries, where kingly power was already ascendant.

---

1. Quentin Skinner, 'Political Philosophy' in *The Cambridge History of Renaissance Philosophy*, ed. by Charles B. Schmitt, et al., Cambridge: Cambridge University Press, 1988, pp. 389–390.
2. *Ibid.*, pp. 409–423.

In England, Sir Thomas Elyot (c. 1490) wrote of the virtues that princes needed to cultivate, while the great political theorist Thomas More produced a comprehensive critique of the social order that included a cynical view of advisors, a role he soon assumed only to face execution.[1] Among the French humanists writing advisory books were Josse Clichtove (b. 1472) and Guillaume Budé (b. 1467), who presented his book *The Education of the Prince* to King Francis I,[2] By mid-16th century the 'mirror' tradition had spread to the Iberian countries, with books authored by Jeronimo Osorio, Felipe de la Torre, Pedro Ribadeneyra and Juan de Mariana. One of the most comprehensive and popular such works was Antonio Guevara's *The Dial for Princes*, which included behavioural advice to rulers as well as nobles, courtiers and other officials.[3] Meanwhile, there was an upsurge in the publication of educational manuals in Germany, two of the most notable authored by the German humanists Jacob Wimpfeling (b. 1450) and Johann Strum (b. 1507).[4]

The two most significant *furstenspiegel* books with a lasting impact were *The Prince* (1513) and Desiderius Erasmus' *The Education of a Christian Prince* (1516). Written within three years of one another, the Florentine and the Dutchman provided sharply contrasting solutions to the political instability that pervaded their respective milieux. Unlike the crafty Florentine diplomat, Erasmus was a priest whose fundamental frame of reference was the Christian faith and its

---

1. Quentin Skinner, *The Foundations of Modern Political Thought, Vol. I*, Cambridge: Cambridge University Press, 1978, p. 218.
2. *Ibid.*, p. 214.
3. *Ibid.*, pp. 214–215.
4. *Ibid.*, p. 214.

practice in the process of governance. Machiavelli wrote to instruct a ruler who had just taken power, focusing on how to keep and perpetuate it through a mix of coercive and manipulative stratagems to be used outside the existing Christian moral order. On the other hand, Erasmus sought to reinforce the existing order of hereditary monarchies because he considered discord and civil strife too dangerous, costly and illegitimate except against tyranny.[1] The problem for Erasmus was how to prevent tyrannical rule through the proper education of those who would inherit power. Implied in his political philosophy is a contract between ruler and subjects: the people's consent to submit to a prince, according to Erasmus, is conditional on the expectation that his rule will be based on justice, benevolence and the general good. Hence the imperative to educate the prince from childhood to serve the people through modesty, magnanimity and good laws while avoiding flatterers, heavy taxation and war.[2] Ultimately, the virtuous conduct of a ruler would validate his legitimacy — a concept that would have an abiding influence in shaping the development of democratic theory.

In keeping with the practice of his contemporaries, Erasmus dedicated his book to Prince Charles of Aragon and later to Henry VIII, in a thankless search for a permanent advisory position which was not fully realized. In retrospect, Machiavelli's work endured precisely because he challenged the conception of princely virtue that was held by his contemporaries. One highly placed practitioner of the Machiavellian ideal was Cardinal Richelieu. Ironically, despite

---

1. Erasmus, *The Education of a Christian Prince*, edited by Lisa Jardine, Cambridge: Cambridge University Press, 1997, p. vii.
2. *Ibid.*, pp. 1–110. See also Skinner, *The Foundations of Modern Political Thought*, pp. 222–223.

his priestly rank, Richelieu's advocacy and practice of harsh royal absolutism was a far cry from the ideals of Erasmus, a Catholic priest of an earlier generation.

Cardinal Richelieu (1585–1642)

Cardinal Richelieu was the pre-eminent architect of the French state under a powerful monarchy. As Secretary of State for Foreign Affairs (1616) and later as Prime Minister of France, Richelieu imposed upon the unruly French his vision of power and greatness based on the doctrine of the divine right of the king to establish peace and order in society. After earning the confidence of the young King Louis XIII, the cardinal proceeded to unite the country by disciplining the clergy, the nobility and the Huguenot opposition in order to make the monarch the unchallenged master of France; the country then emerged as a major power in Europe. Although a devout Catholic, Richelieu held the French state above the Church and used religion as an instrument to promote the King's authority and policies. An advocate of harsh rule and a potent manipulator of power, Richelieu's indispensable advisory role is reflected in his writings, particularly in the *Testament Politique*, where he discusses the king's weak decision-making style in a chapter titled 'Le Conseil du Prince':

> The sad state of your affairs seemed to force you to hasty decisions, without permitting a choice of time or of means; and yet it was necessary to make a choice of both, in order to profit by the change which necessity demanded from your prudence ... Notwithstanding these difficulties which I represented to your Majesty, knowing how much kings may do when they make good use of their power, I

ventured to promise you, with confidence, that you would soon get control of your state, and that in a short time your prudence, your courage, and the benediction of God would give a new aspect to the realm.

I promised your Majesty to employ all my industry and all the authority which it should please you to give me to ruin the Huguenot party, to abase the pride of the nobles, to bring back all your subjects to their duty, and to elevate your name among foreign nations to the point where it belongs.[1]

Not one to leave opportunities slip by, on his deathbed Richelieu designated Cardinal Mazarin his successor, thus ensuring that the unity of France under strong rule would be maintained.

Karl Phillip Gottfried von Clausewitz (1780–1831)

Clausewitz was a Prussian soldier and intellectual who rose from a middle-class social background. His military service was extensive: he saw combat against the armies of the French Revolution and Napoléon and served as a prominent military educator and staff officer with political/military responsibilities at the very centre of the Prussian state.

Clausewitz's fame is due to the importance and influence of his magnum opus *On War*, one of the best known studies

---

1.   Cardinal Richelieu, *Political Testament*, in J.H. Robinson, ed., *Readings in European History*, 2 volumes, Boston: Ginn, 1906, pp. 2:269–270. See also Hantaux, ed., *Maximes d'état et fragments politiques du cardinal de Richelieu*, Paris, 1880; Avernel, ed., *Lettres, instructions diplomatiques et papiers d'état du cardinal de Richelieu*, 8 volumes, Paris, 1853–1877; and Horric de Beaucaire, ed., *Mémoires du cardinal de Richelieu*, Paris, 1908.

on the theory of warfare and strategy.[1] His ability to dissect various issues earned him a strong reputation both on the battlefield – resurrecting Prussia after its near-destruction by Napoléon in 1806 and participating in the latter's defeat at Waterloo – and in political circles. His advice was sought by Prussian statesmen because he did not spell out a program or prescribed solutions. Rather, because he understood that his readers would face unpredictability, he addressed the all-too-human nature of strategic problems. He attempted to develop human capital, to help his masters as well as his readers develop their own strategic judgment to deal with ever-changing environments.

Like most 'advisors', Clausewitz was both admired and misunderstood. His famous line, that 'war is merely the continuation of policy by other means' was vilified for its lack of morality. In fact, Clausewitz would have agreed that war should not be seen as just another routine tool for politicians. He approached strategic theory through realism, which described the uncertainties of world events, taking into account both human weakness and the complexity of the environment. He maintained that statesmen need to assess their rapidly changing environments as they devise approaches and adopt various policy options.[2]

Richard Elliot Neustadt (1919–)

A distinguished political scientist and pioneer in the study of the American presidency, Richard Neustadt served in key

---

1. Karl von Clausewitz, *On War*, translated by O. J. Matthijs Jolles, Washington DC: Infantry Journal Press, 1950.
2. On Clausewitz's strategic thought, see John M. Colins, *Grand Strategy*, Annapolis, MD: Naval Institute Press, 1973, pp. xx-xxv, 17, 21, 221, 224.

positions in the federal government as well as the top ranks of the professorate at Cornell, Columbia and Harvard universities. For three decades he held staff and advisory positions at the Bureau of the Budget; Senate subcommittees; the State Department; the Democratic Platform Committee; and the presidency under John F. Kennedy and Lyndon Johnson. In 1960 Neustadt published his magnum opus *Presidential Power*, which comes closest to being a *furstenspiegel* that shaped the Kennedy presidency, in view of the author's close association as special consultant with the then-president-elect.[1] Although Neustadt authored other important books,[2] *Presidential Power* has become a classic for students of the presidency and practitioners of political leadership. His main argument is that election to the presidency does not guarantee the incumbent success as an effective leader, unless he knows how to maximize his power in a competitive political arena. Thus presidential power depends on a president's capacity to persuade others to support his program; succeed in establishing a reputation as a professional politician; and display an ability to shape popular perceptions to uphold his public prestige.[3] Neustadt uses four criteria to gauge a president's efficacy: First, he asks whether the leader has met the goals of his agenda; second, has he a 'feel' for power; third, how does he react to crises, and is he able to operate effectively under duress; and fourth, is he aware of his legacy — in other words, does he assess the

1. *Who's Who in America*, Volume 2, 53rd ed., 1999, p. 3257.
2. *Alliance Politics* (1970); *The Swine Flu Affair* (1978, 1983); *Thinking in Time* (1986); *The Skybolt Crisis in Perspective* (1999).
3. Richard E. Neustadt, *Presidential Power*, New York: John Wiley & Sons, 1960, pp. 33–107.

consequences of his decisions?[1] A respected teacher and compassionate individual, Neustadt retired from Harvard's John F. Kennedy School of Government in 1989.[2] His memoranda were recently published and are widely consulted.[3]

1.   Richard E. Neustadt, *Presidential Power and Modern Presidents: The Politics of Leadership from Roosevelt to Reagan*, New York: The Free Press, 1990, p. xx.

2.   As experienced by R. Hrair Dekmejian, who had the good fortune to have been Neustadt's student at Columbia University in 1962.

3.   Charles O. Jones, ed., *Preparing to be President: The Memos of Richard E. Neustadt*, Washington DC: The American Enterprise Institute Press, 2000.

3

The *Sulwan al-Muta'*: Analysis of a Magnum Opus

Existing manuscripts of Ibn Zafar's masterpiece bear one or both of two titles: *Sulwan al-Muta' fi 'Udwan al-Atba'* (*Consolation for the Ruler During the Hostility of Subjects*) or *Kitab al-Sulwanat fi Musamarat al-Khulafa' wal-Sadat* (*Book of Consolations in Conversations with Caliphs and Noblemen*). The *Sulwan*, more than any of his other works, brought Ibn Zafar considerable fame and posthumous recognition, and was translated into Persian and Ottoman Turkish.[1] In retrospect, it would appear that the popularity of the *Sulwan* was a consequence of its political content, focusing on the practical counsel it offered Persian and Ottoman rulers after the decline of Arab power.

Ibn Zafar's Historical Milieu

Ibn Zafar's work needs to be analysed against the backdrop of the political developments of his time, as well as the strategic position of Sicily in the conflict between the Muslim World and Christian Europe. The 12th century saw a decline of Arab-Muslim influence that, undoubtedly, marked Ibn Zafar. The Aghlabid conquest of Sicily in 827 was followed by the

---

1. Victor Chauvin, *Bibliographie des Ouvrages Arabes*, Liège: Imprimerie H. Vaillant-Carmanne, 1892, pp. 175–177.

rule of the Fatimids and their Kalbite partisans who, in turn, lost power in 1052 amid internecine conflicts between competing factions. African Arabs fought Spanish Arabs, Sunnis clashed with Shi'is and Arabs struggled with Berbers.[1] A period of anarchy ensued, where rival *qa'ids* (lordlings) ruled over the island, opening the way for the Norman invasion that began in earnest in 1061 and was completed by 1097.[2] Roger I presided over a Christian kingdom where Muslims occupied key positions in the Norman court as well as in the military, in a unique milieu of Christian-Muslim symbiosis and coexistence.[3]

As the centre of a flourishing culture, Sicily became a bridge for cultural transmission between the Muslim World and Christian Europe. Under Roger II, Sicily's Arabophile culture reached a zenith, though after his death in 1154 a period of Muslim restlessness ensued, particularly during the reign of William II (1166–1189).[4] Notably, as Ibn Zafar was born under Norman rule, his worldview and aspirations were shaped as a Muslim facing the consequences of Islamic decline at home and abroad. It was this environment of political upheaval and personal uncertainty that gave birth to the *Sulwan al-Muta'*.

---

1. For a detailed account, see Leonard C. Chiarelli, *Sicily During the Fatimid Age*, Doctoral Dissertation, Department of History, University of Utah, June 1986, pp. 119–123.

2. Francesco Gabrieli, *The Arabs: A Compact History*, translated by Salvator Attanasio, Westport, Connecticut: Greenwood Press, 1981, p. 136.

3. *Ibid.*, p. 136.

4. Abu al-Husayn Muhammad ibn Ahmad ibn Jubayr, *Rihla* (Travels), Leiden: E. J. Brill, 1907, pp. 341–342.

Two Princely Patrons

Ibn Zafar upheld the ruler's role as the essential feature of a stable political order and the maintenance of the general good. However, as a realist, he recognized that all too often failure was the common destiny of rulers, that good rulers were a rarity and effective governance required learning based on practical maxims and ethical values that he was prepared to provide. But who was this worthy leader Ibn Zafar wanted to help succeed in governance?

Al-Siqilli dedicated editions of his book to two different patrons. The first edition of the *Sulwan* was dedicated to an unknown ruler facing a revolutionary situation in Syria; he may have been the ruler of Damascus, who later was expelled by Nur al-Din.[1] In his preface, Ibn Zafar states that the book was written at the request of 'a noble king', for his personal use in facing an incipient political crisis.[2]

More consequential from an historical perspective is the book's second edition, which Ibn Zafar dedicated in 1159 to Abu 'Abdallah Muhammad ibn Abu al-Qasim ibn 'Ali 'Alawi al-Qurashi. A leader of the Muslims of Sicily, Abu al-Qasim had shown munificence towards Ibn Zafar. In an effusive dedication to '*qa'id al-muslimin*', Ibn Zafar offers Abu al-Qasim 'the choicest and most excellent present that might find favour in his eyes, and be valuable and worthy of his status'.[3]

---

1. Michele Amari, *Solwan; or Waters of Comfort by Ibn Zafer*, Volume I, London: Richard Bentley, 1852, p. 109.

2. *Ibid.*, pp. 31–32. See also Muhammad ibn Zafar al-Siqilli, *Sulwan al-Muta' fi 'Udwan al-Atba'* (Consolation for the Ruler During the Hostility of Subjects), translated by Joseph A. Kechichian and R. Hrair Dekmejian, appended text, p. 128. (Hereafter — *Sulwan*, appended text).

3. *Sulwan* — appended text, p. 141. In addition to the *Sulwan*, Ibn Zafar presented Abu al-Qasim with three other books: *Asalib al-Ghaya*; *al-*
(continued...)

Scion of a large Sicilian Arab family whose members had traditionally been military commanders, Abu al-Qasim had returned to Sicily in the 1150s to assume a military position in the Norman government.[1] Soon, the Arab nobleman was confronted with challenges to his position from within the Muslim community as well as from King William II (1166–1189), whose weak government could not secure the well-being and loyalties of an increasingly restless Muslim population.[2] Thus, for a leader in Abu al-Qasim's tenuous position, Ibn Zafar's book may have been intended as a welcome source of political guidance, helping to 'meet every vicissitude of fortune'.[3]

Method of Analysis: Historicism

A distinguishing characteristic of Ibn Zafar's book is the use of historical methodology in the derivation of his maxims on rulership. This approach sets him apart from earlier Islamic theorists as well as from many of those who followed him. Unlike such Muslim philosophers as al-Kindi (d. 873), al-Farabi (d. 950) and Ibn Rushd (d. 1198), who were influenced by Greek thought, Ibn Zafar belongs to a category of thinkers whose ideas developed within a more authentic Islamic mould. These included Ibn Abi al-Rabi' (d. 894), al-

---

(...continued)
> *Muthanna*; and the *Durar al-Ghurar*.

1. On Abu al-Qasim's leadership role, see the first-hand account by Ibn Jubayr, Rihla, *op. cit.*, p. 341; also Michele Amari, *Biblioteca Arabo-Sicula*, Volume I, Torino-Roma: Ermanno Loescher, 1880, pp. 101–102.
2. Ahmad T. Madani, *al-Muslimun fi Siqilliya wa Janub Italiya* (The Muslims in Sicily and South Italy), Cairo: n. p., 1948, pp. 50–112.
3. *Sulwan* – appended text, p. 140.

Juwayni (d. 1283), al-Mawardi (d. 1058) Ibn Taymiyya (d. 1328).[1] In sharp contrast to these *fuqaha'* (legists), whose political thought and rules of governance typically were deduced (*istinbat*) from the Qur'an and Sunna, Ibn Zafar was a thoroughgoing historicist and rationalist. To be sure, he does not defy the authority of the religious texts, but seeks empirical grounding for his maxims in past events and the experience of Arab caliphs, Persian kings and Byzantine rulers. These are supplemented with Arabic poetry and sayings as well as Indian fables and tales. In fact, Ibn Zafar is careful to note that the contents of his book — facts, fables and deductions — do not conflict with the *Shari'a*.[2] He proceeds analytically by first quoting the Qur'an and the Sunna, and then goes outside the scriptural framework to support his arguments by real or supposed historical examples, reinforcing them with his own observations. Such resort to historical and experiential analysis constitutes a notable departure from the norm for a writer of the 12th century.

Still, the *Sulwan* synthesizes much of the wisdom found in 'The Mirror for Princes' literature that preceded Ibn Zafar. He complements these with his own unique insight and analysis based on a rich historical legacy. Indeed, the *Sulwan* reflects the convergence of six civilizational currents: ancient India, Sassanid Persia, Hellenism, Jewish history, Christianity and the Muslim/Arab civilization. Aside from his own Muslim/Arab heritage, Ibn Zafar's work is powerfully influenced by the history of Persia, which provided him with numerous models of kingship and a source of historical romances, tales and maxims. Of course, Persia had by then

---

1. 'Adil Fathi Thabit 'Abd al-Hafiz, *Shar'iyyat al-Sulta fil-Islam* (Legitimation of Authority in Islam), Alexandria, Egypt: Dar al-Jami'at al-Jadida lil-Nashr, 1996, pp. 150–191.
2. *Sulwan* — appended text, pp. 133–134, and 141.

become a key point for literary transmission from India to the Islamic world, as exemplified by Ibn al-Muqaffa's translations – particularly of Bidpai's well-known *Kalila wa Dimna*, a source of imitation for Ibn Zafar and his predecessors writing in the 'Mirrors' genre. More surprising was Ibn Zafar's knowledge of Christianity and Judaism as reflected in several of his books, including the *Sulwan* and *Khayr al-Bashar*.[1] The integration of these diverse historical, cultural and religious currents informed Ibn Zafar's peculiar *weltanschauung* – a generally dark outlook on the human condition, which required not only divine intervention, but immediate action by a strong, capable and just ruler.

Five Maxims

Ibn Zafar sets very high standards for his ideal ruler, who is perceived as a supremely unique individual, 'more singular than the sphinx, more marvelous than alchemy, and rarer than red gold.'[2] The underlying reason for Ibn Zafar's quest for a ruler of extraordinary qualities is the heavy political burden that is placed upon his shoulders. In fact, this ideal prince is expected to establish not only an orderly polity, but one based on justice. Therefore, Ibn Zafar's prince should not only be powerful and capable, but also righteous.

To help the ruler in this difficult task, Ibn Zafar sets his maxims within a five-fold conceptual framework that offers general remedial guidelines (*sulwanat*) from which he later derives specific rules and strategies of governance. The five maxims are:

---

1. Amari, *op. cit.*, Volume I, pp. 52–53;
2. *Sulwan* – appended text, p. 325.

- Trust in God (*Tawfid*). Trust in God and advance resolutely if the cause is just, or abandon it if it is unjust.

- Fortitude (*Ta'assi*). Hold to your course of action with fortitude and bravery until the crisis is over.

- Patience (*Sabr*). Persevere with patience.

- Contentment (*Rida*). Submit to God's will, should the issue prove unfortunate.

- Self-denial (*Zuhd*). Give up the vanity of earthly power should it prove to be too heavy a burden.[1]

The foregoing formulation represents a cyclical dynamic of action for a ruler to follow throughout his career from beginning to end, dealing as well with specific challenges that confront him in the routine of governance. This 'rulership cycle' constitutes the analytical structure of the *Sulwan*, where Ibn Zafar devotes individual chapters to each of its five conceptual components. Taken individually and collectively, they reflect Ibn Zafar's own value system which defines the counsel he proffers to his prince.

Trust in God
From its onset to culmination, Ibn Zafar's 'rulership cycle' is grounded in his unshakable faith in an omnipotent God. Indeed, to Ibn Zafar, the total spectrum of human existence and behaviour is ordered by the Divine Being, who is all-powerful, compassionate and merciful. Though he was born in Norman-ruled Sicily, Ibn Zafar thought and worked within

---

1.   Amari, *op. cit.*, Volume I, pp. 124, 144.

the Muslim *umma*'s frame of reference. He wrote as a Muslim for two Muslim princes, the first ruling the Syrian part of the *umma* and the second, Abu al-Qasim, a Muslim vassal prince to Sicily's Christian potentates. Consequently, Ibn Zafar modelled his ruler after the theocratic pattern set by the early caliphs, where the rulership function proceeded from the Islamic essence of the state.

For Ibn Zafar, it is not enough for the ruler to be Muslim; he must be a true believer as well, for several interrelated reasons. As a faithful ruler, he would first enjoy God's blessing against his foes; he would be guided by the precepts of the faith to rule with justice; and his authority would be reinforced by the legitimacy derived from Islam, as well as his observance of its precepts. Thus, Godliness becomes a prerequisite for virtuous rulership.

With trust in God, the ruler is advised to advance resolutely, but only if the cause is just. The determination of whether a cause is just or unjust is left to the prince, who, Ibn Zafar hopes, will be guided by Islamic criteria of justice. Indeed, to Ibn Zafar, justice constitutes the single most important basis of legitimacy, as opposed to the use of violence that automatically de-legitimizes its user. Towards that end, he states:

> He who has waged great injustice shall not flourish.
> He who is strengthened by malice shall not endure.
> He who is raised to the throne through violence shall not reign.[1]

---

1. *Sulwan* – appended text, p. 181.

Fortitude

Once a cause is found to be just, the prince should proceed with fortitude and bravery until the challenge is overcome. For Ibn Zafar, the Prophet Muhammad best exemplifies fortitude, as he endured the sufferings inflicted by his enemies with courage and later defeated them.[1] The Sicilian considers fortitude 'the virtue of noble men'[2] and reminds the prince that he should not despair when calamities befall him, but rather thank God that He has spared him from suffering an even worse fate.[3] Inculcated with such feeling, the ruler will manifest not only fortitude but also endurance. Yet, to endure, the prince must also possess a prime asset: patience.

Patience

Basing himself on the Prophet's example and sayings, Ibn Zafar considers patience a key attribute of successful rulership. Patience that combines firmness, moderation and perseverance is seen as the master virtue that rules over all other virtues.[4] In adversity, patience is like a coat of arms that promotes endurance and success: 'Endure ... and you shall conquer.'[5] Ibn Zafar defines the patience of kings as consisting of three clusters of elements: forbearance, which gives birth to clemency; watchfulness and foresight, which lead to prosperity of kingdoms; and courage, which leads to the ruler's firmness and readiness to defend the state.[6] Finally, patience is the ladder to reach contentment – Ibn Zafar's fourth maxim.

---

1. *Sulwan* – appended text, pp. 192–193.
2. *Ibid.*, p. 193.
3. *Ibid.*, p. 193.
4. *Ibid.*, pp. 230–232.
5. *Ibid.*, p. 230.
6. *Ibid.*, p. 232.

Contentment

In accordance with the second and third maxims, fortitude and patience, Ibn Zafar counsels the prince to do his utmost to prevail against enemies in securing power. Although Ibn Zafar enjoins the ruler to do everything humanly possible to shape his destiny, he also wants to prepare his master for the possibility of failure. If a ruler does his best to follow the prescribed maxims but still fails, he must accept his fate with contentment because it is God's will. Consequently, Ibn Zafar advises: 'It is better to govern with contentment than be governed by it. Incline yourself to contentment before you are compelled to it by necessity.'[1]

Self-denial

At the conclusion of the 'rulership cycle' is abdication – to give up the vanity of earthly power should it prove to be too heavy a burden. As a faithful Muslim, Ibn Zafar depicts the world as 'a temporary shelter' where the possession of power and wealth is transitory. He posits: 'Let him who longs to obtain power know how to abdicate.'[2] It is noteworthy that Ibn Zafar bases this discourse on the precedent established by the Prophet himself: When God gave Muhammad a choice to be 'a prophet-king or a prophet-servant of God', he chose the latter.[3] To emphasize the Prophet's disdain for worldly power, Ibn Zafar quotes the tradition of 'Abdallah ibn Mas'ud[4] – an interpretation that seems at variance with the prevailing view of contemporary Islamist ideologues who

---

1. *Ibid.*, p. 269.
2. *Ibid.*, p. 334.
3. *Ibid.*, p. 304.
4. *Ibid.*, p. 305.

advocate the establishment of God's sovereignty on earth.[1] The Sicilian's fundamental point is that beyond the possession of power and wealth, there is something transcendental for the believer to pursue: the commitment to Godliness. This devotion can be observed in the actions of several exemplary rulers: Mu'awiya ibn Yazid's abdication of the Caliphate to embrace Islamic piety; the Greek king's turn from worldliness to God; the Ossetian king's conversion to Christianity and retreat into monastic life; and Babak ibn Ardashir's refusal to accede to his father's absolutist ways in ruling Persia.[2] Thus ends Ibn Zafar's cycle of rulership, which begins with trust in God in the quest for power, and ends with the abandonment of power in exchange for Godly piety, whereby inheriting the rewards of the afterlife.

Idealism versus Realism: Mosca's Paradox

Grounded at both ends in religious idealism, Ibn Zafar's fivefold dynamic of maxims may well be dismissed by atheists, cynics or realist strategists as being too idealistic and moralistic for success in the brutal arena of politics, where only the fittest are expected to survive. However, a closer reading of the *Sulwan* reveals that the wise Sicilian Arab was deeply aware of the practical requirements of governance. Indeed, within the macro framework of five general rules, Ibn Zafar offers a multitude of micro maxims to guide the ruler in his struggle to prevail in troubled times. These include tactics and stratagems that challenge the moral parameters of Ibn Zafar's larger conceptual scheme, pointing to a

---

1. R.Hrair Dekmejian, *Islam in Revolution*, Syracuse, New York: Syracuse University Press, 1995, pp. 41–44, 75–96.
2. *Sulwan* – appended text, pp. 322–335.

contradiction of significant proportions. It was none other than Gaetano Mosca who discerned this paradox in the *Sulwan* when he stated: 'Parmi les maximes contenues dans ce travail on en peut citer deux, l'une qui présente un charactère antimachiavelique, et l'autre d'une machiavelisme plus raffinée que celui du secrétaire florentin.'[1] ('Among the maxims contained in this work we may discern two types: the one displaying an anti-Machiavellian quality, the other a Machiavellism more refined than that of the Florentine secretary himself.')

To be sure, Mosca's observation is correct. In his quest to achieve *praxis* – to derive operational rules of princely conduct from his macro framework based on religion – Ibn Zafar had to sacrifice some of his own beliefs and principles. Among these rules, the most important may be summarized by the formula: *Tadbir* + *Hila* + *Quwwa* = Victory. When faced with a powerful antagonist, the ruler should use a combination of planning (*tadbir*), artifice (*hila*) and force (*quwwa*). Therefore, in choosing alternative plans of action, the leader would have to engage in a phased process of decision-making as follows:

Tadbir. The first step to be taken by the prince is to begin planning and strategizing by assessing the nature of the challenge facing him. Such assessment requires first-hand information, because:

> ... If a man embarks on any undertaking according to hearsay, he will build upon possibilities; but if he regulates

---

1. G. Mosca, *Histoire des Doctrines Politiques*, Paris: Payot, 1936, pp. 26–27.

it according to what he sees with his own eyes, he will build upon certainties.[1]

Thus, reliable intelligence is needed about the strengths and weaknesses of the foe, the strategy, experience and psychological disposition of the enemy camp.[2] In weighing such intelligence, one must differentiate between reality and disinformation fed by spies,[3] as well as assess the capacity of an informant to report information with accuracy.[4]

But before formulating his response, the leader's strategizing process requires two additional functions: wise counsel and sound deliberation. Ibn Zafar warns that 'the counsel devised at first sight is worthless' and 'the best counsel is that which has been proven by reflection, and adopted after mature deliberation'.[5] Elsewhere, he states with poetic eloquence:

Counsel is the sword of wisdom. If a sword is the keenest and has been sharpened with the best care, and its blade most diligently polished, then surely the counsel which has been the most frequently deliberated and the longest weighed will be better than all others.[6]

Clearly, Ibn Zafar saw the investigatory, consultative, and deliberative functions as essential prerequisites to the employment of artifice (*hila*) and, ultimately, force (*quwwa*).

---

1. *Sulwan* — appended text, p. 162.
2. *Ibid.*, pp. 159–160, and 249.
3. *Ibid.*, pp. 237–240.
4. *Ibid.*, pp. 237 and 240.
5. *Ibid.*, p. 162.
6. *Ibid.*, pp. 162–163.

If artifice proves sufficient to overcome a foe, then why use force against him?[1]

Hila. The employment of *hila* (ruse or artifice), or a stratagem based on guile and trickery (*makida*), is proposed by Ibn Zafar as a possible alternative to the use of force. The instruments of *hila* could include spies, propagandists and *agents provocateurs* to spread disinformation and dissension in the enemy camp. Without a doubt, for Ibn Zafar — who so often preached truth and morality — the use of artifice is a contradiction. He resolves it by stating that the end justifies the means. In other words, the use of falsehood is permitted, but only for a *raison d'état*:

> Falsehood is like poison. It may cause death if used alone but, when mixed in medicine by an apothecary, may be of service. A king may not permit falsehood except when used for the good of the state, for example, to deceive an enemy or conciliate the disaffected.[2]

Nevertheless, Ibn Zafar is quick to warn his master about the need for secrecy and selectivity in employing artifice, fearing that such secrets may be compromised by disloyal counsellors:

> Likewise, kings must only allow such poisons to be kept in the hands of sound men, who would know how to withhold them from those with evil hands.[3]

---

1. *Ibid.*, p. 161.
2. *Ibid.*, p. 295. See also Amari, *op cit.*, Volume II, p. 151.
3. *Ibid.*, p. 295.

Al-Quwwa al-Mutlaqa. When all else fails, the prince should resort to force, and to the fullest extent possible. Even when employing raw force, the prince is urged to use artifice tactically to mislead his enemy and catch him by surprise. However, Ibn Zafar places preconditions which the prince needs to consider in deciding upon the use of force. One essential factor is the psychological predisposition of the prince with respect to his foe. In order to have a chance of success, the user of force should not proceed from a self-imposed position of psychological inferiority towards an enemy, however powerful.[1]

In considering the use of force, Ibn Zafar advises the prince not to challenge the enemy unless he knows him to be weaker than himself;[2] nor should the prince treat his enemy with compassion (*ihsan*) or become distracted by his words and lose the chance to destroy him.[3] Indeed, Ibn Zafar does not believe that 'the base nature of man' can be changed, and no amount of conciliation will turn an enemy into a friend, which necessitates total destruction of the foe.[4]

Theories of Revolution

Interspersed throughout the *Sulwan* are theories of revolution, its causes, manifestations and suggested modalities to confront it. As a general rule, Ibn Zafar writes that revolutions develop against sovereigns ruling by hereditary right, who have become lethargic and corrupted by the pleasures of the palace, convinced that they can continue to

---

1.   *Sulwan* – appended text, p. 182.
2.   *Ibid.*, p. 161.
3.   *Ibid.*, pp. 257–259.
4.   *Ibid.*, pp. 211 and 279.

rule on the basis of the legitimacy of their illustrious ancestors without special effort on their part.[1] The government of such a monarchy is imperiled by certain 'maladies' – the pride, ire and rapacity of the king that lead to abuse of power and the use of violence, triggering rebellion among his subjects.[2]

Specifically, Ibn Zafar places the onset of revolutions to 'heart-burnings' among the masses, meaning a combination of deprivation and suffering, accompanied by newly acquired 'audacity of the masses' to challenge those in authority.[3] Hence the dialectical relationship between the dominant classes – characterized by the 'insolence of the great', 'timidity of the rich' and the 'carelessness of those with plenty' – and the masses in ferment, manifesting a 'readiness to express the imaginings of the mind'; the 'confidence of the poor'; and the 'wakefulness of those who suffer'.[4]

Within the context of the foregoing macro-level causal factors, Ibn Zafar identifies two micro-level triggers of revolution concerning the ruler's treatment of subjects: partiality that awakens hatred and mildness that encourages audacity among the populace.[5] Here, Ibn Zafar displays a unique appreciation of the role of social classes and class struggle as casual factors of political unrest that would require different modalities of treatment in order to sustain the ruler's authority. He identifies three classes. At the top are the notables, who need to be shown impartiality, courtesy and benevolence. Next are the middling castes of merchants,

---

1. *Ibid.*, p. 242.
2. *Ibid.*, pp. 246–247.
3. *Ibid.*, p. 264. See also Amari, *op. cit.*, Volume II, pp. 98–99.
4. *Sulwan.*, appended text, p. 265.
5. *Ibid.*, pp. 264–265.

artisans and servants, who should be treated with a mix of gentleness and severity as appropriate. At the bottom of the social ladder is the populace 'that always supports those who advocate causes without questioning either their words or their actions'.[1] As such, they must be ruled by fear without harshness and by punishment without excess.[2] Ibn Zafar is acutely aware of inter-class conflict as a cause of revolution. Therefore, he urges the ruler to keep his subjects within their castes.[3]

In this context, he is particularly concerned about the role of the middle classes — merchants, artisans and servants — who will leave their castes if the ruler uses force against them, and proceed to join 'the military order' and precipitate a mass uprising.[4] In recognizing the revolutionary potential of the middle classes, Ibn Zafar is a true precursor of later theorists who saw the pivotal role of these social categories in leading challenges to royal authority.[5]

Equally significant to Ibn Zafar is the role of 'the blind fanatic' (*al-ta'assub al-a'ma*), who uses religion to rally the populace against the ruler and, once in power, rules with an authority more absolute than that of the sovereign.[6] Basing himself on examples from Islamic and pre-Islamic history, Ibn Zafar correctly diagnoses the rise of commoners to supreme power in times of upheaval, backed by the urban underclasses

1. *Ibid.*, p. 259.
2. *Ibid.*, p. 259.
3. *Ibid.*, pp. 243–244.
4. *Ibid.*, pp. 243–245.
5. Thomas H. Greene, *Comparative Revolutionary Movements*, 3rd ed., Englewood Cliffs, New Jersey: Prentice Hall, 1990, pp. 43–45, 67–68.
6. *Sulwan* – appended text, pp. 246–247. See also Amari, *op. cit.*, Volume II, p. 67.

– a phenomenon so pervasive in recent European history – which is seen by political theorists as the onset of totalitarian dictatorship.[1] In warning the ruler about 'the blind fanatic' who uses religion as an instrument of mass mobilization, Ibn Zafar undoubtedly had in mind such charismatic revolutionaries as Hamdan Qarmat, the Iraqi peasant whose Batini message brought together peasants, artisans and emigrants to terrorize the 'Abbasid Caliphate in the ninth and tenth centuries.[2]

Beyond revolutions brought on by tyranny and governmental misconduct, Ibn Zafar further identifies the causes of rebellion against non-tyrannical rulers. In such times of normalcy, people become disconnected because of their 'ignorance of the immutable principles of truth and justice, and from the arrogance engendered by a long period of prosperity'.[3] Here, Ibn Zafar is pointing to what modern political sociologists call an 'end of ideology' situation in a developed polity where a society's belief system, which legitimizes the ruling order, has eroded and the populace become arrogant and spoiled in an environment of material abundance.[4] Should the ruler treat such people with gentleness and appeasement, they will become more violent and impetuous, because of their affliction with four of the most ignoble passions: anger, sensual pleasures, greed and

---

1.   Carl J. Friedrich and Zbigniew K. Brzezinski, *Totalitarian Dictatorship and Autocracy*, New York: Fredrick A. Prager, 1963, pp. 17–26.

2.   On the Carmathians or Qaramita, see Philip K. Hitti, *History of the Arabs*, 10th ed., London: Macmillan, 1970, p. 444.

3.   *Sulwan* – appended text, p. 243.

4.   Daniel Bell, *The End of Ideology*, New York: Free Press, 1962.

idleness. Such people, posits the Sicilian, can only be cured by fire and steel.[1]

Elsewhere, Ibn Zafar advises a ruler facing an external threat to refrain from mobilizing the masses – that is, putting swords in their hands – because instead of fighting the enemy they will turn against the king, unlike soldiers who are willing to sacrifice their lives for his glory.[2] However, Ibn Zafar warns, 'the lower classes ... abhor the military, at whose hands they are frequently subjected to outrage and oppression.'[3] On the other hand, should the military be treated with gentleness, 'the whole nation finds fault with the sovereign'.[4] To illustrate his analysis, Ibn Zafar seeks to clarify the ruler's perception of the true sentiments of his subjects towards him:

> The masses do not look upon the king as a member of the human family, but consider only his peculiar characteristics: his isolation, dignity, and the elevation of his office; therefore, they turn against him and unite with those who are on par with themselves.[5]

Without a doubt Ibn Zafar is more profoundly distrustful of the masses – because of their greater propensity to be carried away by passions – than the upper classes, who are seen as more capable of rational behaviour. In this respect, he stands out as a forerunner of later analysts of élite behaviour.

---

1. *Sulwan* – appended text, p. 243.
2. *Ibid.*, p. 244.
3. *Ibid.*, p. 245.
4. *Ibid.*, p. 245.
5. *Ibid.*, p. 246.

The Virtuous Prince

As stated above, Ibn Zafar's concept of the virtuous prince combines the attributes of competence and justice. Thus, the virtuous prince should possess the necessary skills to rule effectively as well as the ethical compass to rule with justice. This combination of ability and morality is a peculiar aspect of Ibn Zafar's model of leadership, where the ruler's moral character shapes his governance. But what is the utility of making moral character one of two elements of virtuous rulership?

First, an ethical prince who rules with justice will please God. Second, a prince ruling justly and capably is bound to increase his legitimacy among his people, thereby maximizing his authority and the country's stability. For Ibn Zafar, the mix of effective and ethical rule is good policy for the prince, both to secure his realm on earth and salvation in the afterlife. This dynamic interdependence between effective rule and ethical governance is the *leitmotif* that guides Ibn Zafar's various formulations in defining the specific attributes of the virtuous prince. In one of the most eloquent passages in the *Sulwan*, Ibn Zafar speaks through Babak addressing his father Ardashir, the founder of the Sassanian dynasty, about his ideal king:

> It is he who fills the eyes of his people with glory, their ears with the sound of his praise, who inspires their understandings with reverence, and their hearts with affection. The monarch, whose clemency embraces all things, whose justice never errs, whose government is upright, and the vigour of his arm so strong that the heart of the guilty tremble as their swords fall to the ground. It is he who preserves the just from injustice, the monarch

whose valour enables men, and whose moderation and generosity captivate their affections.[1]

Babak's recitation about the model king includes eleven useful attributes that may, in turn, be divided into three functional categories considered essential for good governance:

1. the evocative/inspirational function, or the ability to communicate with the populace to inculcate in them a sense of identification with the symbols of the ruler's glory and authority;

2. the ethical policy function, or the willingness to base his behaviour, policies and decisions upon a set of moral precepts, i.e. valour; uprightness; clemency; justice; moderation; and generosity;

3. the coercive function, or the possession of coercive capability and the willingness to use force vigorously when necessary. The first two functions promote the ruler's legitimacy, rhetorically through inspirational messages and reinforced by socially beneficial policies. As the ruler's legitimacy is heightened, his need to employ coercive means is minimized. In the opposite case, a badly ruled polity will rely on maximal force to compensate for low legitimacy. This inverse relationship, based on a reformulation of Max Weber's theories on power, legitimacy and authority, may be expressed in graphic form:

$$\text{Control} = \text{Legitimacy} + \text{Force}^2$$

1. *Ibid.*, p. 323.
2. R.Hrair Dekmejian, *Egypt Under Nasir*, London: University of London Press, 1972, pp. 9–12.

Bad Government: Control Based on Increasing Force

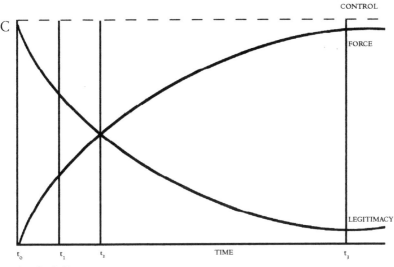

At t_0, C = L, F = 0.
Realistically '0' can never be reached.

Good Government: Control Based on Increasing Legitimacy

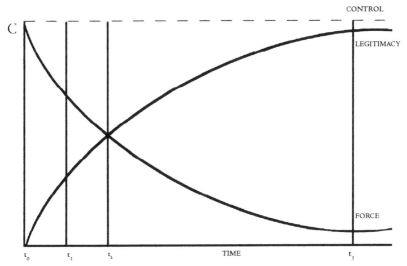

At t_0, C = F, L = 0.
Realistically '0' can never be reached.

The Ruler as Servant

Among Ibn Zafar's novel ideas is his view of rulership as a form of slavery to serve the masses. To Ibn Zafar, the act of governance is a two-way street. The prince's duty is to serve his subjects, and in return they will grant him their obedience, i.e. the legitimacy he needs to govern securely and effectively. Indeed, the ruler and the ruled are bound together in a reciprocal relationship, reminiscent of Mu'awiya's famous maxim about his hair binding him to the people: 'when they pull, I loosen, and if they loosen, I pull.'[1] The ruler-cum-servant dynamic is succinctly expressed in the *Sulwan* through the mouth of the 'wild elephant', as follows:

> ... The most enslaved is the king, because he is bound to serve his subjects both with body and mind. This is because the ruler must govern them; instruct them; defend them; provide for their prosperity; restrain the disobedient; assist the oppressed; ensure free movement; strengthen frontiers; devise and apply laws; collect excessive wealth and expend it for the public good; prevent revolution; eliminate civil discord and sedition. Besides all this, the king stands in need of his subjects; endures various difficulties; must protect himself; carry on the duties of state; seek out those who are able to give him good and honest counsel; and be prepared to repulse enemies.[2]

---

1. Philip K. Hitti, *History of the Arabs*, 10th ed., London: Macmillan, 1970, p. 197.
2. *Sulwan* — appended text, pp. 327–328.

According to Ibn Zafar's 'wild elephant', therefore, the virtuous prince is a public servant striving for the general good. Yet such service is clearly a heavy burden requiring not only selflessness and a sense of moral duty, but also great stamina and a capacity to perform multifaceted tasks on many fronts. To be sure, Ibn Zafar's virtuous ruler is an exceptional individual — the embodiment of a charismatic steward of the people.

The Graceful Prince

The concept of a person endowed by God with exceptional qualities, described as 'gifts of grace', harks back to the Greeks and to biblical literature. The possessor of these divine gifts (*charis*) is said to be 'charismatic', a term traditionally associated with prophets, religious teachers and, in recent times, with revolutionary leaders and military heroes.[1] Writing in the 12th century, Ibn Zafar's conception of the virtuous prince adheres to the religious meaning of charisma, where the ultimate source of these 'gifts' is the Almighty. In other words, it is God who has graced a particular prince with extraordinary qualities in order to serve His purpose. Once again, Ibn Zafar cites Babak, who vainly struggles to instruct his father Ardashir, in the ways of righteousness:

... It is not every monarch upon whom such grace is bestowed, but only on those who, irrespective of their

1. R. Hrair Dekmejian, 'Charismatic Leadership in Messianic and Revolutionary Movements,' in *Religious Resurgence*, edited by Richard T. Antoun and Mary Elaine Hegland, Syracuse, New York: Syracuse University Press, 1987, pp. 82–93.

personal interests, place themselves on a level with the poorest of their subjects and so illustrate their selflessness. It is those who devote their power and all the time required to the affairs of state, thus escaping the charge of indolence. It is those who deny every breath of passion, when it behooves them to take with one hand and give with the other, to raise one person to a post of confidence and dismiss another, to grant or refuse, and to punish or pardon. It is by these means that they avoid every shadow of injustice. Therefore, to possess these qualities is more singular than the sphinx, more marvellous than alchemy, and rarer than red gold.[1]

It is significant that Ibn Zafar's prince is endowed by God with His grace *because* he is selfless, administers justice impartially, is not indolent in governing and upholds the interests of the poor. In short, Ibn Zafar's virtuous prince is a supremely Godly personage, who governs energetically and dispenses justice selflessly, but also humbles himself to 'the level of the very poor'. In modern parlance, he is a steward of the downtrodden, and even a 'class traitor' in the eyes of those upholding the narrow self-interest of the dominant élites.

The Pragmatic Prince

Can so virtuous a prince survive in the world of power politics? Ibn Zafar's answer is in the affirmative, unless God wills it otherwise. To be sure, Ibn Zafar is not an utopian idealist, but a realist who personally witnessed a half dozen

---

1. *Sulwan* — appended text, pp. 324–325.

wars, rebellions and civil disorders while living in Syria, Sicily, Egypt and the Maghreb. He remains consistent throughout the *Sulwan* in proposing a 'political formula' of personality traits and actions needed to maximize the ruler's chances of success against adversaries.

It is towards that end that Ibn Zafar offers a political formula of five main virtues in which the prince ought to surpass all others: first, paternal mercy for all subjects; second, vigilance over the populace; third, courage to defend the people; fourth, sagacity to delude foes; and fifth, prudence to take advantage of every opportunity.[1] When facing adversity, he advises the ruler to have patience; fight depression; execute strict justice; secure the roads; protect people seeking refuge; conciliate alienated subjects; and show generosity as well as clemency.[2] Elsewhere, Ibn Zafar points to the example of Caliph Musa al-Hadi who had strength of mind, a quick eye, sagacity, courage and vigour.[3] Because of the vicissitudes of power, says Ibn Zafar, the most prudent ruler is the one who prepares for every contingency by keeping a faithful counsellor; a sharp sword; a speedy stallion to escape if further resistance is impossible; a beautiful woman whose love will preserve him; and an impregnable fortress for refuge.[4]

He warns against such vices as kingly pride, ire, vanity, rashness, sloth, greed, rapacity and preoccupation with sensual pleasures that distract the ruler from his duties and tasks of rulership.[5] To be sure, the passions of a 'man of reason are

1.   *Ibid.*, pp. 202–203.
2.   *Ibid.*, p. 259.
3.   *Ibid.*, p. 234.
4.   *Ibid.*, p. 255.
5.   *Ibid.*, pp. 243–247.

subordinate to his judgment,' because he regulates them 'according to the dictates of reason.'[1] Yet, as a good Muslim, Ibn Zafar tells the ruler that 'worldly materialism' breeds opposition, and that the good prince should practice abstinence, 'a virtue followed only by the chosen.'[2]

The Sicilian Arab does not limit himself to the enumeration of the general attributes of a virtuous ruler, but applies them to specific problems of governance. Consequently, a wise prince should be aware of 'the five signs' that bring about the demise of rulers: first, a belief in gossip and those who cannot foresee the consequences of actions; second, turning against those whom he ought to love; third, lacking sufficient revenue; fourth, favouring one and dismissing another based upon caprice, not reflection; and fifth, despising the counsel of men of wisdom and experience.[3]

In the end, Ibn Zafar's conception of the pragmatic ruler is one who is watchful and proactive, identifying problems as they arise and dealing with them before they cause discord and sedition.[4] A ruler should seek information on the popular mood and needs to address the specific complaints of his subjects — because 'subjects first shake their tongues and then their fists'.[5] Indeed, the ruler must not ignore rebellious words, but confront opponents and critics before limited dissatisfaction leads to bigger problems. In order to control his subjects' rebellious tongues and stay in power, a ruler will have to win his subordinates' hearts by administering justice

---

1. *Ibid.*, p. 279. Here the Platonic influence is obvious.
2. *Ibid.*, p. 306.
3. *Ibid.*, p. 183.
4. *Ibid.*, pp. 264–265.
5. *Ibid.*, p. 258.

impartially, lightening taxes and exempting them from tariffs.[1] Ibn Zafar goes as far as to advocate a redistribution of wealth, to 'collect excessive wealth and expend it for the public good.'[2] He asserts that 'all men have a right to share in the goods of this world and to enjoy them in turn'.[3]

Finally, in confronting opponents, Ibn Zafar counsels the ruler not to use violence (*'unf*) prematurely, because his subjects (*al-ra'iyya*) will be pushed to a mass uprising against their will.[4] Instead, the ruler first needs to use patience and compromise. However, at some point, the ruler may have to use toughness, because, says Ibn Zafar, unlimited softness (*lin*) and compromise, will bring harm to the ruler, as in the case of the Caliph 'Uthman, whose leniency resulted in his death at the hands of enemies.[5]

A Good Counsellor

One of the most persistent themes in the *Sulwan* is the imperative necessity of having a good counsellor, as well as the elaboration of the qualities required of such a person. Ibn Zafar prefaces his maxims by warning the ruler against advisors who seduce others with 'flattering words'. To underline his own integrity and utility as an advisor, the Sicilian Arab asserts that princes rarely are able 'to secure an honest and able minister, a learned and faithful counsellor,

---

1.   *Ibid.*, p. 258.
2.   *Ibid.*, p. 328.
3.   *Ibid.*, p. 194.
4.   *Ibid.*, pp. 264–265.
5.   *Ibid.*, pp. 263–264.

one who should act with firmness and self denial and to fulfill God's will'.[1]

To Ibn Zafar, the best advisor (*wazir*) is one who combines philosophical wisdom with political experience – a concept that harks back to Plato's model of the philosopher-king. Thus the wise prince should remember: 'Counsel is the mirror of the intellect. If, therefore, you would like to know the capacity of anyone, ask him for advice.'[2] Moreover, the good counsellor should be faithful to the prince, and able to view things from his master's perspective to better protect the latter's interests by planning for every contingency.[3]

The failure of *wazirs* to provide the ruler with useful advice is another recurrent theme in the *Sulwan*, with its examples of advisory deficiency owing to incompetence, dishonesty, timidity or the desire to be 'a chameleon living in the trunk of some tree ... until these calamities end'.[4] After empirically demonstrating the danger to the ruler of being bound by the counsel of his official circle, Ibn Zafar stresses the necessity of seeking advice from outside this entourage. This age-old problem of executive decision-making is analysed by Ibn Zafar through historical examples where rulers reach out to an 'old man' to seek honest advice in times of crisis.[5] Could it be that the 'old man' is Ibn Zafar himself? A poor, unfortunate man seeking recognition and employment, the Sicilian Arab was at pains to tell the prince that his maxims were only known to professional counsellors, who kept their secrets from others.

---

1. *Ibid.* p. 126.
2. *Ibid.*, p. 162.
3. *Ibid.*, pp. 203–205.
4. *Ibid.*, p. 156.
5. *Ibid.*, pp. 153 and 172–174.

In a number of separate passages, Ibn Zafar summarizes the qualities that princes should seek in choosing their ministers and advisory staff. One such exemplary passage focuses on Jalis, the Arab teacher of Bahram, son of the Persian King Yezdejird:

Bahram held Jalis in great esteem because of his dignity, refined manners, literacy, political and historical knowledge and analytical clarity.[1]

In this case Ibn Zafar emphasizes the character, wisdom and intellectual qualities of Jalis, which a capable advisor should possess to properly instruct and guide his prince. These qualities, however, are necessary but not sufficient for a model counsellor to be effective; he also needs practical experience in different fields, astuteness, firmness and operational ability in war. These characteristics are succinctly ascribed by Ibn Zafar to the *wazir* of the Persian King Sapor:

He was a man of mature years, astute, firm, clear-sighted, experienced in business, a theologian, and well-versed in languages, literature, science and the stratagems of war.[2]

As if these qualities were not sufficient, Ibn Zafar adds that the good counsellor should combine fidelity to the ruler with the courage to provide truthful advice even when it might not please his master.[3] Nevertheless, Ibn Zafar recognizes that in the final analysis, the element that binds the counsellor to the prince is the commonality of their

---

1. *Ibid.*, p. 271.
2. *Ibid.*, p. 197.
3. *Ibid.*, p. 273.

interests and, ultimately, their shared destiny. He forewarns the prince:

> Amongst the faithful and far-sighted counsellors, he is most deserving of attention whose prosperity depends on your own, and whose safety is tied to yours. He who stands in such a position, exerting himself for your interests, will likewise serve and defend himself while fighting for you.[1]

When taken together, Ibn Zafar's various depictions of the good counsellor actually represent his view of himself in terms of wisdom, experience, fidelity and truthfulness — qualities that he wished to bring to the service of the two successive princes to whom he dedicated the *Sulwan*. It was unfortunate that his sincere exertions in writing the *Sulwan* were not crowned with long-term success. At best, Ibn Zafar al-Siqilli held brief periods of advisory work for Abu al-Qasim, the Sicilian commander and, possibly, for the unknown ruler in Syria.

---

1.   *Ibid.*, p. 273.

4

Ibn Zafar and Machiavelli: A Comparative Analysis

Here are two thinkers separated by 350 years, writing insightfully and passionately about the fundamentals of political authority and rules of governance for their respective patrons and reaching remarkable conclusions that continue to reverberate in the 21st century.

In comparing and contrasting Ibn Zafar's *Sulwan* with Machiavelli's *The Prince*, one is struck by important similarities as well as significant differences that deserve careful analysis. The similarities between the two thinkers pertain to the commonality of their objectives, methods and worldviews, as well as certain maxims on governance and parallels in the two thinkers' respective historical environments. Differences spring from their distinct personalities, particular belief systems and contrasting visions of man's ultimate destiny.[1]

---

1. For a preliminary analysis, see R. Hrair Dekmejian and 'Adil Fathi Thabet 'Abd al-Hafiz, 'Machiavelli's Arab Precursor: Ibn Zafar al Siqilli', *British Journal of Middle Eastern Studies* 27:2, 2000, pp. 135–137. This comparison excludes *The Discourses*.

Crisis Environments

Both the Sicilian Arab and the Florentine Secretary were theorists of crisis, which defined their environments and shaped their writings and behaviour. Caught in their respective environments of crisis, both Machiavelli and Ibn Zafar shared an overwhelming aspiration to help establish a stable political order that would also provide them with rewarding careers.

The Florentine Republic had fallen in September 1512; in August 1513 Lorenzo de Medici, the Pope's nephew, assumed power. Machiavelli, who had been in government service for fourteen years as a bureaucrat and diplomat, was dismissed and imprisoned by the new regime. After suffering torture by *strappado*,[1] he was released from jail and retreated to his farm to write, vainly seeking return to full-time government service.[2] Similar misfortunes visited Ibn Zafar in his desperate quest for a secure livelihood for himself and his family. The 12th century had witnessed the decline of Muslim power, amid internecine conflicts and wars with Christian lords, which drove Ibn Zafar to a life of itinerancy and poverty.

Two Princes, Two Authors

As related earlier, both the *Sulwan* and *The Prince* are pre-eminent examples of *furstenspiegel* literature, aiming to provide

---

1. A method of torture whereby a prisoner is lifted by a rope tied to the wrists and dropped without touching the ground. See Niccolò Machiavelli, *Selected Political Writings*, Edited and translated by David Wootton, Indianapolis, Indiana: Hackett Publishing Co., 1994, p. xi. (Hereafter Machiavelli/Wootton).
2. *Ibid.*, p. xxvii.

powerful patrons with advice in statecraft in return for a position within the ruler's official circle. In the case of the *Sulwan*, it was written at the request of an unknown Syrian ruler who appears to have ended up a failure; a second edition was dedicated to the Sicilian Arab commander Muhammad ibn Abu al-Qasim ibn 'Ali al-Qurashi, who subsequently lost his position in the Norman Court. In a similar vein, Machiavelli first intended to dedicate *The Prince* to Giuliano de Medici (1479–1516), brother of Pope Leo X. Eventually, *The Prince* was dedicated to Giuliano's nephew, Lorenzo de Medici (1492–1519), who became ruler of Florence in 1513.[1]

As one would expect, Machiavelli's dedicatory letter to Lorenzo and Ibn Zafar's prefatory notes to his two princes are full of effusive praise, expressions of humility, and readiness

---

1. In fact, Machiavelli's dedication takes the form of a 'letter' to Lorenzo de Medici that in and of itself is a rare *tour de force*. See Niccolò Machiavelli, *The Prince*, translated with notes by George Bull, with an introduction by Anthony Grafton, London: Penguin Books, 1999, pp. 1–2. Machiavelli illustrated his disappointment in failing to secure a political appointment with Lorenzo by dedicating – actually presenting as a gift – his *Discourses* to Zanobi Buondelmonti and Cosimo Rucellai to 'depart from the usual practice of authors, which has always been to dedicate their works to some prince, and, blinded by ambition and avarice, to praise him for all his virtuous qualities when they ought to have blamed him for all manner of shameful deeds.' The Florentine underscores the point that princes must be held in esteem 'not because they have the power to be generous,' but simply because they are generous. His indictment is sharper when he continues: 'In like manner, (one) should admire those who know how to govern a kingdom, not those who, without knowing how, actually govern one.' See Niccolò Machiavelli, *The Discourses*, Edited with an introduction by Bernard Crick, using the translation of Leslie J. Walker, S. J., with revisions by Brian Richardson, London: Penguin Books, 1998, pp. 93–94.

to further the interests of their sovereigns. Yet both men entertained hopes that transcended their immediate personal and political concerns. They both advocated political unity — Machiavelli calling for a united Italy and Ibn Zafar hoping for a resurgent and united Islamic Arab realm. Their parallel pursuit of these noble goals was prompted by their shared idealism, with which they also hoped to advance their individual fortunes by winning appointments to government positions. In this sense, the Sicilian and the Florentine were both hoping to convince their respective princes of their personal loyalty and functional usefulness to the pursuit of a stable political order. Moreover, both writers were urging the rulers to adopt their respective programs and policies, which would secure princely power as well as benefit their subjects and the larger interests of the Italians and Arabs, respectively. Thus, while selfishly pursuing their individual careers, the two men sincerely believed that their advocacy of a strong and secure ruler was a moral end that would provide stability and some benefit for their peoples.

Methods of Analysis

The similarity in their objectives also extends to the methodologies employed by both writers in formulating their maxims. Both Machiavelli and Ibn Zafar use a largely historical method, based on examples of the successes and mistakes of rulers past, combined with their own personal experience in the political life of Italy and the Arab world, respectively. Both men possessed great historical knowledge, a shrewd understanding of the forces shaping their environments, and pride in their own abilities as experts on the affairs of state.

In contrast to Machiavelli's more direct approach in stating his maxims, Ibn Zafar often prefers to use fables to place words in the mouths of animals and real or imagined individuals, as a means to distance himself politically from expressing a point of view that might be used against him by his enemies or taken as an insult by the prince. In addition, Ibn Zafar – working within an Islamic context – opts to rely on scriptural quotations repeatedly, implyng that his writings, in content and form, were religiously lawful and legitimate.[1] No such constraints encumbered Machiavelli's writings, although he was careful to use phraseology designed to minimize the chances of alienating Lorenzo de Medici and other influential individuals.

In addition to their use of historical examples and personal experience to develop their maxims, the two thinkers were thoroughgoing rationalists who counselled against 'passions' and sentimentality in political analysis as well as in the conduct of affairs of state. Equally significant is their shared realization of the gap between theory and practice, as well as what modern comparative theorists call the problem of establishing equivalence between past events, decisions and situations and their applicability to new conditions.[2] To be sure, Machiavelli advocates imitating his Roman ancestors, while Ibn Zafar seeks to selectively emulate examples from Arab, Persian and Byzantine history. Yet both thinkers are mindful that old strategies of action need to be adapted to

---

1. Muhammad ibn Zafar al-Siqilli, *Sulwan al-Muta' fi 'Udwan al-Atba'* (Consolation for the Ruler During the Hostility of Subjects), translated by Joseph A. Kechichian and R. Hrair Dekmejian, appended text, pp. 128–138.

2. Adam Przeworski and Henry Teune, *The Logic of Comparative Social Inquiry*, New York, New York: John Wiley, 1970, pp. 113–131.

changed circumstances.[1] Of course, such adaptation requires considerable learning by a prospective ruler, and, both wonder what could happen if the ruler were incapable of learning how to transform the maxims into effective policies. Ibn Zafar and Machiavelli would heartily agree that the ruler's only salvation is to find a trusted, intelligent and capable counsellor and listen to his advice.

Selecting Good Advisors

The advisory function, or staffing, constitutes an essential element in the rulership process. However powerful and competent, rulers cannot by themselves govern successfully without the help of functionaries who possess specialized knowledge and skills in various aspects of governance. Thus, the quest for a good staff of advisory personnel has been a persistent problem in the annals of leadership since time immemorial. Advisors have the capacity to harm or sustain rulers regardless of their formal titles or type of political system; history is full of poor or bad advisors who were the bane of the existence of numerous kings, caliphs, princes, presidents, prime ministers and others in authority. It is not surprising, therefore, that both Ibn Zafar and Machiavelli were acutely concerned with the role of counsellors in their substantive writings. As perceptive students of history and astute observers of the dynamics of power and authority in their own time, these men could not do otherwise. Yet, in a more immediate sense, by highlighting the role of advisors, *they were writing about themselves and their own aspirations* to gain advisory employment in the retinue of their prospective

---

1.   *Sulwan*, appended text, pp. 155–160. See also Machiavelli/Wootton, *op. cit.*, p. xxxv.

patrons. This was the fundamental purpose of authorship of their respective *magnum opera*. It may consequently be safe to conclude that their vision of good counsellorship was one shaped by their own self-view and sense of utility to those in power.

Reading Ibn Zafar and Machiavelli makes it painfully obvious that little has changed in the persistent dysfunctionality of the staffing process throughout the centuries. Both writers point to unsavoury characters who tend to populate the ranks of counsellors: sycophants, flatterers, opportunists, egotists, incompetents and men of doubtful loyalties. To address this problem, Ibn Zafar states that a king's first duty is to find 'a faithful counsellor, from whose advice he may seek assistance in good as well as in adverse fortune',[1] while Machiavelli considers the choice of good advisors to be 'of foremost importance'.[2] Still, how shall the ruler select his advisors, and what should the criteria be for selection? Both writers share the view that a leader's choice of advisors mirrors his own self in terms of personality, character and ability. For Ibn Zafar, the choice of good advisors is a reflection of a ruler's wisdom and recognition of the necessity to solicit sound advice.[3] In selecting an advisor, Ibn Zafar states:

> Counsel is the mirror of the intellect, if therefore, you would like to know the capacity of anyone, ask for advice.[4]

He further posits:

---

1. *Ibid.*, p. 255.
2. Machiavelli/Wootton, *op. cit.*, p. 70.
3. *Sulwan*, appended text, p. 272.
4. *Ibid.*, p. 162.

If you would like to know whether good or bad prevails in the mind of a man, ask for his counsel.[1]

Similarly, Machiavelli is frank in telling Lorenzo de Medici:

Rulers get the advisors they deserve, for good rulers choose good ones, bad rulers choose bad ones. The easiest way of assessing a ruler's ability is to look at those who are members of his inner circle.[2]

Among the qualities that define Ibn Zafar's good counsellor are loyalty; wisdom; experience; shrewdness; frankness; vigilance; dignity; knowledge of literature, politics and history; and analytical skills.[3] Although Machiavelli would not take exception to these attributes, he provides 'one infallible way for a ruler to judge his advisor':

When you see your advisor give more thought to his own interests than yours ... then you can be sure such a person will never be a good advisor. You will never be able to trust him, for he who runs a government should never suggest anything to his ruler that is not in the ruler's interests.[4]

Machiavelli's supreme criteria for selecting a good advisor — upholding the ruler's interests above one's own — finds repeated affirmation in the *Sulwan*,[5] written, it may be worth recalling, some 350 years earlier. Ibn Zafar goes further,

1. *Ibid.*, p. 250.
2. Machiavelli/Wootton, *op. cit.*, p. 70.
3. *Sulwan*, appended text, pp. 183, 248–249 and 276.
4. Machiavelli/Wootton, *op. cit.*, p. 71.
5. *Sulwan*, appended text, pp. 205, 249–251, 273 and 292.

pointing out the solidifying effect of the interacting dynamic of interests between ruler and counsellor:

> Amongst faithful and far-sighted counsellors, he is most deserving of attention whose prosperity depends on your own, and whose safety is tied to yours. He who stands in such a position, exerting himself for your interests, will likewise serve and defend himself while fighting for you.[1]

This dynamic of mutuality of interests is expressed somewhat differently by Machiavelli, who emphasizes the need to provide material and honorific rewards to keep the advisor satisfied, effective and loyal to his prince:

> ... The ruler, in order to get the best out of his advisor, should consider his advisor's interests, heaping honours on him, enriching him, placing him in his debt, ensuring he receives public recognition, so that he sees that he cannot do better without him, that he has so many honours he desires no more, so much wealth he desires no more, so much status he fears the consequences of political upheaval.[2]

Having established their criteria for selecting good advisors, Ibn Zafar and Machiavelli are at pains to urge the ruler to solicit truthful advice actively and wisely, while stressing that the final determination of policy should be the ruler's prerogative.[3] Both warn that the ruler's failure to seek

---

1. *Sulwan*, appended text, p. 273.
2. Machiavelli/Wootton, *op. cit.*, p. 71.
3. Machiavelli/Wootton, *op. cit.*, pp. 72–73.

and follow sound advice will have serious repercussions for his ability to govern.[1]

Yet, despite their best efforts, these two aspirants for counsellorship had limited success in gaining secure positions in government. Ibn Zafar appears to have worked for Safi al-Din, a notable in Nur al-Din's court and, later, served Abu al-Qasim in Sicily for a brief period prior to his second trip to Syria, where he died a broken man in 1170 or 1172. Machiavelli was never allowed to return to government service except near his life's end, when he briefly served as official historian of Florence. Here were two great minds and competent advisors whose counsel went unheard, and their aspirations remained mostly unfulfilled during their lifetimes. Fame, honour and recognition would only come after their death and, ironically, mostly by non-countrymen.

The Religious Prince versus the Secular Prince

The significant similarities between Ibn Zafar and Machiavelli should not obscure the differences between them, both in degree and kind. These variances were the product of the specific historical environments in which Ibn Zafar and Machiavelli lived and worked as well as their contrasting views and religious beliefs.

Machiavelli, a product of the Italian Renaissance, had rebelled against the ideological constraints of the Roman Catholic Church, which he saw as a main impediment to Italian unity. Therefore, his maxims on power are divorced from religious, moral and social concerns. In essence he was a secularist who believed that Christianity tended to make

---

1.   *Ibid.*, p. 71; see also *Sulwan*, appended text, pp. 183 and 249–250.

people servile, although he urged rulers to use religious ceremonies and practices as tools to legitimize their power and unite the populace.[1] To Machiavelli, power is the supreme virtue; religion, economics, and morality are important only when they have a bearing on politics.[2] For Ibn Zafar, himself a *faqih*, the situation is almost completely reversed. In sharp contrast to Machiavelli's pioneering quest for secularism, Ibn Zafar functioned largely within the confines of the Muslim *umma* and its religious-political legality and morality, which imposed certain constraints on his political thought and advice to the prince. Consequently, Ibn Zafar advises the ruler to place his trust in God and exercise patience, righteousness and magnanimity towards his subjects, not only because such policies will maximize his chances of securing power, but also because they would satisfy the requirements of virtuous rulership as defined by Islamic religious standards.

Remarkably, and even when he uses the theological and philosophical language of the ancient Indians, Persians and Christians, Ibn Zafar remains within the religious and moral framework of Islam. As a man of faith, Ibn Zafar – writing in the 12th century – could not be expected to have any understanding of Machiavelli's modernizing secularism. On the contrary, Ibn Zafar, operating within Islam's theocratic universe, depicted his virtuous ruler as a believer whose religious faith would and should shape his governance. To the Florentine, religion was but an instrument to be manipulated by the prince who did not have to share the religious beliefs of his subjects, although he should 'appear' to be pious and religious. It must be emphasized that, while Ibn Zafar was

---

1. Machiavelli/Wootton, *op. cit.*, pp. 116–121.
2. Geoge H. Sabine, *A History of Political Thought*, 3rd edn, New York, New York: Holt, Rinehart and Winston, Inc., 1961, p. 351.

well aware of the misuse of religion by impious Muslim rulers, he was equally and abundantly certain about his vision of the righteous prince in both theory and practice. Therefore, to the Sicilian Arab, the quest for worldly power is a priority for any prince, but is only second to God's blessings and heavenly salvation.

Worldviews and Human Nature

Ibn Zafar and Machiavelli lived in political environments of perpetual conflict and, consequently, shared a deeply negative view of the human condition. As he looked at the Arab/Muslim scene of the 12th century, the Sicilian Arab saw a fractionalized realm, brought on by the institutional decline of the Caliphate politically and spiritually. Protracted infighting within the Islamic orbit between Sunnis and Shi'is, and Arabs and Persians, had created a power vacuum inviting conquest by Mongol, Norman and Turkic warlords. Similar gloom and doom pervaded Machiavelli's Italy, where the Church was beset with institutional decay and corruption. The papacy was too weak to unify Italy, but retained enough power to prevent unity under any other ruler.[1] The result was continuous warfare among Italy's five principalities and intervention by outside powers, amid rampant cruelty, murder and debauchery.[2]

As products of their respective chaotic environments, it was not at all surprising that the Sicilian and the Florentine developed negative perceptions of human nature. To Ibn Zafar, evil is generally inherent in human beings, which

---

1. *Ibid.*, p. 337.
2. *Ibid.*, pp. 337–38.

cannot be changed.[1] Yet, this view of human nature places Ibn Zafar in a quandary, because of the religious framework from which he proceeds. As a Muslim, he is inclined to acknowledge the possibility of moderating human passions through education and religious belief.[2] Machiavelli's judgment is more categorical; he views human nature as selfish, aggressive and acquisitive,[3] which places men in a condition of constant conflict and competition that would result in anarchy unless restrained by laws backed by a powerful ruler. Consequently, the ruler's power to restrain bad behaviour should be accompanied by encouraging vigorous religious observance among the people as a means to reduce corruption as well as promoting obedience and the legitimacy of the ruling order.[4] In this sense, religion becomes an instrument of the state, unlike in Islam where, theoretically, the function of the state is to promote religion.

Qualities of the Prince

Although faith plays an important role for a prince who seeks to govern with a certain degree of legitimacy, Ibn Zafar and Machiavelli are in substantial disagreement in identifying the qualities that a virtuous prince should possess. For Machiavelli, the virtuous prince is one who has the will as well as the ability to achieve power and establish a stable political order. Indeed, the Italian word *virtù*, used repeatedly by the

---

1. *Sulwan*, appended text, pp. 186–187 and 211.
2. *Ibid.*, p. 293. Note that Ibn Zafar appears to hold contradictory views of human nature.
3. Machiavelli/Wootton, *op. cit.*, pp. 54, 82, 159 and 161.
4. Michael B. Foster, *Masters of Political Thought*, Volume I, Cambridge, Missouri: Houghton Mifflin Co., 1941, pp. 274–75.

Florentine, means something different than 'virtue' or 'valour' as the measure of a good person.[1] The bearer of *virtù* is a *virtuoso* in the art of governance.[2] Consequently, power becomes the supreme virtue, as 'Machiavellian' has come to mean.

Despite his acute concern with the efficacy of rulership, and though he wrote three and a half centuries before the Florentine, Ibn Zafar could not have accepted Machiavelli's advocacy of power as the ultimate virtue. The Sicilian Arab's virtuous prince was expected to bear a greater burden than the Florentine's worldly one. To be sure, virtuosity to Ibn Zafar meant the acquisition of power to establish a just society under Divine Law, which would ultimately produce both worldly and heavenly rewards. Accordingly, he lists a long chain of moral and instrumental qualities ranging from trust in God, fortitude, patience, contentment and self-denial to paternal affection, vigilance, courage, sagacity, foresight, generosity, firmness, impartiality and righteousness. Although Machiavelli would approve of some of these instrumental maxims directly affecting the quest for power, he would have no sympathy with Ibn Zafar's religious and moral maxims — a fact that points to a more fundamental difference between the two thinkers, one involving the ruler's actual versus perceived possession of qualities. To Machiavelli, the ruler need not have positive qualities, but must appear to have them. The prince must be perceived as sympathetic, religious, trustworthy, honest, and compassionate; but he must be prepared to break these maxims if necessary, to hold on to power by becoming cruel, dishonest, inhuman and, even,

---

1. *Ibid.*, p. 277.
2. Machiavelli/Wootton, *op. cit.*, p. xxix.

irreligious.[1] Clearly, a ruler with such attributes would not be generally acceptable to the Sicilian Arab moralist. Yet, as Mosca discovered in reading the *Sulwan*, Ibn Zafar would recommend using artifice (*hila*), ruse (*makida*) and falsehood (*kazb*) for the 'good of the state'.[2] However, Ibn Zafar expects his prince to *be* good, Godly, and humane. He rejects the notion that a prince can only *appear* to have these positive qualities as Machiavelli posits. Moreover, it is not enough for the ruler to have good qualities; he must act accordingly in his efforts to create a just society, except in situations of extreme crisis when the use of deception and falsehood are permitted as an absolute necessity.

This significant difference between the Sicilian and the Florentine underscores the sharp contrast between the Muslim religious moralist and his amoral, irreligious counterpart, even if both aim to achieve similar objectives for their respective princes. Ends do justify means, but at least in the case of Ibn Zafar, that end is a justly governed polity within a divinely sanctioned framework.

Rules of Governance

Distinctions notwithstanding, in the practical aspects and policies of governance Ibn Zafar and Machiavelli share common ground to a considerable extent in their focus on power, the art of ruling and mechanics of statecraft, because of their shared goal to safeguard the ruler's power. These commonalties may be summarized as follows:

- Refrain from oppressing the people;

---

1. Machiavelli/Wootton, *op. cit.*, p. 55.
2. *Sulwan*, appended text, p. 295.

- Avoid being hated or despised by acting rapaciously towards the masses;
- Ensure that your subjects have an interest in keeping you in power;
- Do not show excessive leniency;
- Avoid excessive self-confidence, timidity and carelessness;
- Be vigilant and ready for all eventualities with enough resources, sufficient reserves, troops, funds and fortifications;
- Learn from the lessons of history and the actions of great men;
- Be ready to take advantage of opportunities in times of war or peace;
- Display strength of character, courage and nobility.

Both theorists recognize the utility of the combined effect of legitimacy and force to maximize the ruler's control over his realm. In fact, both underscore the importance of engendering love (legitimacy) among the citizenry towards the prince, as well as fear of his power (force). These commonalties notwithstanding, Ibn Zafar and Machiavelli would differ on the balance between the two elements of rulership. The *faqih* would tend to stress the legitimacy/love component in contrast to the Secretary's emphasis on force/fear. In Machiavelli's own words:

> ... One ought to be both loved and feared; but since it is difficult to accomplish both at the same time, I maintain it is much safer to be feared than loved, if you have to do without one of the two. Still a ruler should make himself

feared in such a way that if he does not inspire love, at least he does not provoke hatred.[1]

There is another important similarity between the two writers' views concerning the tactics used to secure princely power. For both men the employment of tactical flexibility is a cardinal virtue. Machiavelli's advice to the prince to combine the attributes of the lion and the fox, i.e. force and trickery,[2] has an exact parallel in Ibn Zafar's prescription to use force (*quwwa*) and artifice (*hila*). Neither writer recommends the use of force alone, or to rely on it indiscriminately. Rather, both emphasize a reliance on persuasion, propaganda and trickery and, when necessary, they call on the ruler to act decisively in the affairs of state. It is under such circumstances that both thinkers agree on the use of even ruthless force against internal or external foes, that requires a strong military force of loyal soldiers. In the end, both men believed in the absolute necessity of having a powerful prince to prevent anarchy. However, unlike Machiavelli, Ibn Zafar would object to acquisition of power by force or use of unethical means.

Fate versus Will

In matters of statecraft, what are the limits of human action as distinct from fate and fortune? Both Machiavelli and Ibn Zafar place a strong emphasis on the determining role of human capability. To Machiavelli, half of the world's affairs

---

1. Machiavelli/Wootton, *op. cit.*, pp. 51–52.
2. Machiavelli/Wootton, *op. cit.*, pp. 54–63.

are governed by fortune and half by man.[1] Ibn Zafar refrains from citing such percentages, although his repeated exhortations to the prince to persevere places him squarely on Machiavelli's side. In both cases, the prince will not succeed if he lacks the 'will to power' — the combination of skill, strength and ambition to succeed, which Machiavelli calls *virtù* (virtuosity) and Ibn Zafar, *ta'assi* (fortitude). Such determined princes will do their utmost to shape their destiny. Yet, should everything fail, Ibn Zafar's ruler is enjoined to submit to God's will and with contentment accept his fate in the hope of gaining reward in heaven. No such optimistic future awaits Machiavelli's prince, for whom failure constitutes the ultimate end.

In the final analysis, here are two authors whose political discourses would readily fit the realist school of modern political science, of which Machiavelli is considered the founder. Yet Ibn Zafar is a realist with a conscience, governed by the dictates of his faith-based morality. In the chaotic circumstances that beset the Italian peninsula in Machiavelli's time, clearly, there was a loosening of ethnical standards as the Church became party to protracted political struggles among the princes, leading to the erosion of its role as guardian of Christian morality. These factors propelled the Florentine to break out of the Church's institutional and moral parameters, to embrace a secular pragmatism that later fuelled a full-blown Renaissance with undeniable benefits both to rulers and masses. In contrast, Ibn Zafar was no rebel, only a critic, and a religious and political reformer who remained obedient to the laws and ideological crucible of Islam.

---

1.   Machiavelli/Wootton, *op. cit.*, pp. 161–165, 187–189

Ibn Zafar: A Retrospective Assessment

In offering the *Sulwan* to readers at the onset of the 21st century, it is worthwhile to look back at its humble author and the fruits of his creative mind to search for wisdom and insights that may be relevant to people living in today's troubled times marked by violence, inequity and the perils of globalization. Reflecting on the *Sulwan* and the analysis presented in the foregoing chapters, it becomes manifest that the lessons gleaned from Ibn Zafar's life and thought are significantly useful and applicable to the contemporary common man, as much as to those who are entrusted with the exercise of authority regardless of their religious, national or cultural identity.

Universality and Modernity

Although Ibn Zafar wrote for the benefit of his patrons in power, most of his maxims have universal validity because they transcend the narrow confines of his time and place. For this reason Ibn Zafar and the *Sulwan* enjoyed considerable posthumous recognition among intellectual circles and rulers of the Muslim world until the 1700s. Clearly, the recent revival of interest in his work also testifies to its innate intellectual and historical value that have rendered it a 'classic' of the Arab *furstenspiegel* genre as well as of mediaeval Arab political literature. In retrospect, this poor but brilliant *'alim* constitutes an important transmission link between the accumulated wisdom of the past and intellectuals who succeeded him until the present time. A man of extraordinary broad learning and general knowledge, Ibn Zafar drew upon a 'data sheet' that was virtually universal for his time — Hindu, Zoroastrian, Jewish, Christian and Muslim. These he summarized in twenty-five folk tales, historical narratives and romances, interspersed with his own precepts, maxims, poetry and analysis, to produce the *Sulwan*. Beyond the book's immediate advisory function is the author's message to later generations of readers. If this was his hidden intention, he certainly succeeded with the *Sulwan*, although most of his other books are lost without much hope of retrieval.

Apostle of a Moral Order

Despite its manifestly political content and objectives, the *Sulwan* stands first and foremost as a profoundly moral treatise. Even as he explicates such amoral subjects as the dynamics of power, theories of revolution and maxims of effective governance, Ibn Zafar never deviates from placing these mundane concerns within a moral framework. Indeed, the whole corpus of his political wisdom is imbued with the norms of moral conduct for the virtuous prince as well as the broad sweep of humanity, because Ibn Zafar's penultimate quest is not power but justice: a society at peace with itself and with its Divine Creator.

Indeed, moral imperatives propounded by the Sicilian sage are interspersed throughout the *Sulwan* that, undoubtedly, have concrete relevance to all societies. A compendium of these norms of good behaviour reveals the broad dimensions of Ibn Zafar's moral compass and its relevance to the human condition today.

Positive Guidance

Among Ibn Zafar's very broad compendium of positive norms are: tolerance; thoughtfulness; learning; uprightness; forgiveness; fortitude; abnegation; charity; mercy; patience; modesty; steadfastness; humility; faithfulness; selflessness; abstinence; austereness; impartiality; benevolence; contentment; truthfulness; honesty; clemency; courage; righteousness; graciousness; rationality; generosity; foresight; compassion; endurance; hope; gentleness; kindness; piety; understanding; and optimism.

Negative Guidance

Ibn Zafar cautions the just ruler to avoid the following vices: covetousness; lying; vanity; rashness; arrogance; sensuality; idleness; hatred; anger; ignorance; passions; obstinacy; greed; corruption; avarice; insolence; injustice; pride; egotism; indolence; and rapacity.

As discussed above, the quest for just rule led Ibn Zafar to devise and recommend the adoption of a broad set of what might be termed in modern terminology as 'principles of tolerance.' At times, he admonishes the prince to display magnanimity, stay above the fray and, while acting in a firm manner, practice tolerance. Although steeped in the religious sciences, ethics and traditions, Ibn Zafar was a modern man for his time, as reflected in his open-minded pursuit of knowledge in diverse fields, peoples, faiths and cultures. Despite the calamities that befell him and his family, he remained an idealist and optimist, in his belief in human progress and the perfectibility of man through education and religious guidance.

Tolerance and Moderation

In his tumultuous lifetime, Ibn Zafar experienced jealousy and intolerance as a writer, teacher and counsellor. In the prefatory dedication to his first patron, he seeks to protect himself with scriptural quotations because, he states, '... under such sanction, no one can find fault with the work I have undertaken'.[1] He proceeds to express an unwavering faith in the 'intellect of man' who 'makes himself master of various forms of eloquence ...' and concludes: 'Nor is there anything that is beyond his power to achieve.'[2] These words appear to be clearly directed at his critics, possibly to some conservative personages with parochial views or even religious extremists. Similarly, in the dedicatory note to the Sicilian Amir, Abu al-Qasim, Ibn Zafar defiantly addresses his opponents:

> I propose to treat my subjects in such a manner that is not prohibited by the *Shari'a* or offensive to anyone's ears.[3]

Thus Ibn Zafar's efforts to combat intolerance towards his own work as well as his political and moral maxims manifest a persistent and pervasive commitment to moderation both in religion and governance. He expressly warns the prince about the role of 'the blind fanatic' who uses religion as an instrument to mobilize the masses and overthrow the ruling order; once in power, such a person would rule as an absolute

---

1. *Sulwan* — appended text, p. 133.
2. *Ibid.*, p.138.
3. *Ibid.*, p. 142.

tyrant under the guise of religious purity.[1] In view of his own painful experience and historical knowledge of intolerance and fanaticism, Ibn Zafar preached moderation, devoid of anger, inflexibility and extremism. As an apostle of religious and political temperance, the Sicilian's message is supremely relevant to the Muslim *umma* of the 21st century as a remedy for its conflicts. Moreover, Ibn Zafar's example as a precursor of Islamic moderation would also benefit non-Muslims in seeing a brighter vision of Islam than that preached by its extremist fringe and detractors in the West.

Virtuous Leadership and Social Justice

The pervasive tone of realism embedded in the pages of the *Sulwan* constitutes a reflection of Ibn Zafar's tortured soul and turbulent political environment, which prompted this perpetual itinerant to seek a powerful ruler capable of establishing a peaceful society. However, in his readiness to advocate the urgent necessity for a powerful prince, Ibn Zafar is not prepared to bestow absolute power and legitimacy upon such a ruler. He repeatedly warns the prince through tales and historical examples about the perils of royal absolutism and the disasters that befall kings and populace as a consequence of tyrannical rule. He is painfully aware that unrestrained power is dangerous, and he would heartily agree with a well-known adage used in contemporary Western political discourse: 'Power corrupts, and absolute power corrupts absolutely.' This is the fundamental reason why Ibn Zafar places legal and moral constraints on the ruler's behaviour.

---

1. *Ibid.*, p. 246.

Therefore, the ruler must be a man of faith and behave under its norms both in his personal as well as political life. Not only is the ruler expected to operate within the parameters of the Islamic code of conduct, but he needs to translate the moral maxims of that code into policies to fashion a society based on justice. Only then will the ruler be accorded legitimacy — the moral right to hold power and exercise authority. Herein lies the contemporary significance of Ibn Zafar's masterwork to leaders everywhere, regardless of political, social or religious system. In these troubled times, reading the wisdom of a 12th-century Arab sage provides leaders with spiritual consolation, sound advice on governance and an admonition that is especially relevant in today's global community: *that good society can only be established over the pillars of a moral order, and that a ruler becomes virtuous only when he proceeds to build a polity based on social justice.*

BOOK TWO

Sulwan al-Muta' fi 'Udwan al-Atba'
(Consolation for the Ruler During the Hostility of Subjects)

by

Muhammad ibn Zafar al-Siqilli

Preface to the First Edition

In the name of God, the Merciful, the Compassionate, Muhammad ibn Abi Muhammad ibn Zafar, the poor and lowly servant of the Lord, content to abide His holy will, whose sins may God forgive, thus writes:

Gratitude to God is the noblest garment which man can wear; and praise of Him the surest means to obtain the blessings of this life, and of that which is to come. Glory to God, who gives us endurance as a pledge for success, and friendship as a refuge in misfortune. Glory be to Him, who spreads an impenetrable veil over the mysteries of fate, and restrains the loftiest intellects behind the wall of uncertainty; to Him, who leads the submissive on smooth and pleasant paths, but drives forward the reluctant, until, stumbling and murmuring, they obey his decrees.

He, whose name is praised, has said:

It may well be that you dislike a thing which God has meant for your own abundant good. (4:19)

Blessed be our Lord Muhammad, whom He has sent to bear witness, and to proclaim good tidings; to admonish men and call them to faith, and to be, by the will of God, a shining light unto their eyes. May the blessings of the Most High be showered upon him!

And praise be to God, who created the children of Adam in so noble an image, and caused the plants of the earth to spring up by means of the waters of heaven for their use; supplied them with such abundant means of subsistence; instructed them by the ministry of the prophets, who taught them to distinguish right from wrong in their actions; placed both the mighty and the lowly under the governance of princes, commanding all mankind to follow their wise precepts and those of holy men and enjoining them to afford the former all the assistance in their power in the right way, even as to princes he committed the execution of the most noble and arduous tasks.

For the burdens of rulers are heavy, and their office is full of labour. Their duty is to guard their subjects from those who would seduce them with flattering words; to secure them from all danger in their houses and in the highways; to defend them from their enemies not only from war and violence, but by artifice and subtlety; to restrain the strong from oppressing the weak, and the wicked from injuring the upright; to instruct the ignorant; to cut off, in times of sedition, the diseased members of the social body; to levy upon the goods of their subjects dues prescribed by the law of God, and employ the revenue thence accruing for the public benefit.

For all these reasons, the work performed in a single day by a just prince is more meritorious than 60 years of fighting in the Holy Wars. For this cause, likewise, he shall obtain an honourable place in the presence of God, at the end of the world, as we read in the *Sahih,* on the faith of 'Abdallah ibn 'Umar, according to whom God's apostle said: 'Just princes

are seated on thrones of light at the right hand of the Most
Merciful God; and there also are those who have observed
justice in their judgment towards their kindred.'

One of the most genuine and authentic traditions of Ibn
Shihab is the following, which he obtained from Humayd ibn
'Abd al-Rahman, who had it from Miswar ibn Mukhrama
himself; namely, that he, having been once sent to Mu'awiya
(the founder of the Umayyad dynasty), afterwards related the
following discourse:

'Having', said he, 'entered the presence of Mu'awiya, and
saluted him, he questioned me thus:

"Whence is it, O Miswar, that you make such complaints
against the Caliphs?"

"Permit me to expound them," I replied, "and listen with
indulgence to that which I shall say in their justification."

"In the name of God," replied Mu'awiya, "reveal the
offspring of your soul without fear."

'Then I did not hesitate to repeat all that I had ever said
against him and, Mu'awiya having heard me, answered, "O
Miswar, I am assuredly not free from faults; but, tell me, have
you never committed any which make you fear eternal
damnation, unless you obtain the pardon of God?"

"Yes, God knows I have," I replied. And the Caliph
resumed:

"What reason have you, then, for supposing that you are
more worthy of His forgiveness than I, who have in my favour
the merit of having so often concluded peace between men,
caused the divine laws to be observed, fought in the Holy
Wars, and accomplished so many great works that neither you
nor I should be able to number them? I am indeed so heavily
laden with the burden of my duties that I do not doubt God
will graciously accept my good works, and pardon my evil

ones. Moreover, as often as I have had to choose between God and the world, I have always chosen God."'

'In reflecting upon this discourse', said Miswar, 'I held myself for vanquished.' And he never afterwards uttered Mu'awiya's name without saying, 'May God prosper him!'

The author says: This likewise is the opinion of the wisest jurists concerning those princes who have not yet fully attained high standards of justice. But this cannot be said of princes in our own times, to whom it rarely happens to secure an honest and able minister, a learned and faithful counsellor, one who should act with firmness and self-denial, and to fulfill God's will!

It is moreover related that 'Umar ibn 'Abd al-'Aziz sought to restrain the arrogance of the Bani Marwan and the rest of the Umayyads – to cause justice at their and their retainers' expense. The Bani Marwan had committed misdeeds with impunity. They assembled and hastened in great indignation to the palace, where they found 'Umar's son, 'Abd al-Malik, and addressed him in these words:

'Tell the Commander of the Faithful that we will not submit quietly to the regulation by which he loots us of that which was granted to us from the public treasury by the princes, his predecessors, and wrests from our hands the possessions which we held, to bestow them upon others, under pretext that they were usurped by us. Why should he pretend to inquire into a matter which has been decided after mature examination by another monarch?'

'Abd al-Malik went instantly to report this to his father, whom he found with 'Amr ibn Muhajir, a man the Caliph relied upon in public matters. 'Umar, having heard him, fixed his eyes on the ground, and remained for some time silent and absorbed in profound meditation. Then raising his head, and turning to 'Abd al-Malik, 'What do you say to this, my son?' he asked.

And 'Abd al-Malik replied, 'O, Commander of the Faithful, go forward in the path which God has prescribed to you, even if you knew that the stroke of death was impending over both of us!'

'And what do you think of it?' inquired the Caliph of Ibn Muhajir, who replied:

'God said to the prophet: "And now we have set you on the right path. Follow it, and do not yield to the desires of ignorant men; for they can in no way protect you from the wrath of God. The wrongdoers are patrons to each other; but the righteous have God Himself for their patron."' (45:17–18)

Upon which 'Umar exclaimed: 'Praise be to God who has given me you two and who confirms me in my purpose.' Thus 'Umar ibn 'Abd al-'Aziz considered it good fortune to be assisted by two counsellors at such a juncture. Alas! Why is it that after so many generations men have become ungodly?

We find, moreover, that the same 'Umar ibn 'Abd al-'Aziz, having once written to Salim ibn 'Abdallah to inquire on the conduct of Caliph 'Umar ibn al-Khattab – whose conduct he proposed to imitate, receiving this answer:

'You do not live in 'Umar's days, nor in the midst of a generation like to that over which 'Umar ruled. Nevertheless,' continued Salim's letter, 'keep a strict watch over your officials, and make frequent examinations into their conduct, so that they may fear you. Confirm in their office those with whom you are satisfied, and remove those who displease you. If you bestow or take away office not from respect of persons, but for the service of God, you may hope that he will furnish you with assistants capable of seconding you.'

And this is very true, as is proven by the saying of the Apostle of God: 'To him who is imbued with the fear of the Lord shall be made,' to the end of this tradition.

A noble king, in both deed and purpose, whose justice is acknowledged by all, who is known for the habit of reflection, is gifted with high intellectual powers, filled with love for science – that satisfies his heart and mind, who is addicted to the speculations of moral philosophy, who is assailed by a rebel aspiring to wrest the kingdom from him by force. In the midst of such a great crisis, the king has asked that I write a book.

This request to write a book of philosophy and erudition was made to comfort him. Once I accepted the task, and did not despair in being able to relieve him from his sorrows, it occurred to him that my work would not have the power to dissipate his sadness, nor to afford relief to the afflictions of his soul, unless it were written in the style of *Kalila wa Dimna*.

This prince had granted me his cordial friendship, his generous support and a degree of intimacy that he displayed as openly in public as in private. My soul recoiled from the idea of refusing him consolation in his agony. Therefore, I proceeded to select from amongst the best and rarest Arab writings on moral philosophy, narratives concerning Commanders of the Faithful, and ancient monarchs. I polished up the rough edges of these narratives, using my utmost diligence to make their meaning plain. I inserted, as in a nest, philosophical maxims, and tied them to certain famous personalities into whom I have breathed the breath of lofty spirits, donned them in the mantle of regal bearings, filled their minds with lofty thoughts, and suspended from their shoulders the sword of Arabian or foreign dominions. I have opened every chapter with a few verses from the Qur'an, and some traditions from the Prophet Muhammad, may whom God bless with praise and worship. Lastly, I have placed my stories in gardens, for the delight of the heart as well as the ears, and to combat faults of habit or character.

I have titled this book *Sulwan al-Muta' fi 'Udwan al-Atba'* (*Consolation for the Ruler During the Hostility of Subjects*). The term *sulwan* is the plural of *sulwana*: a shell Arabs believe can gather water. If a person in love drinks from it he will immediately recover. The *Rajiz* has said: 'Not even were I to drink the *sulwan*, should I find peace. Not even were I rolling in wealth, could I live without you.'

The wealth of which I speak is five-fold: first, trust in God; second, fortitude; third, patience; fourth, contentment, and fifth, self-denial.

Therefore, here are various parables that I have succeeded in collecting, all from original narratives translated into Arabic; which parables I have sought to enliven with some eloquence, as I have introduced various philosophical sayings through the mouths of animals. But first I must premise one consideration to shield myself from men of shortsightedness.

And this consideration is the same that is recorded upon good authority by the imam and jurist Abu Bakr Muhammad ibn Husayn 'Ajawi. The latter relates that the Commander of the Faithful, 'Umar ibn 'Abd al-'Aziz, attending funeral services for a member of the House of Umayyad, asked those present to remain still, while he — uttering a cry — went forward into the tombs.

His attendants waited for him a long time, and when he returned, with red eyes and the veins of his neck all swollen, they said to him: 'You have lingered a long time, O Commander of the Faithful! What has detained you?'

And 'Umar replied: 'I have been amongst the sepulchres of those most dear to me. I saluted them; but no one returned my salutations; and when I turned my back to leave, the earth cried unto me: "'Umar, why do you not ask what is become of the arms?"

"What is become of them?" I asked.

'And the earth replied: "The hands have been separated from the wrists, the wrists from the forearms, the forearms from the elbows, the elbows from the joints of the shoulders, the joints from the shoulder-blades."

'And as I turned to leave, the earth called to me once more: "Why, 'Umar, do you not ask me what is become of the trunks?"

"What?" I replied, and the earth resumed:

"The shoulders have been parted from the ribs, and afterwards, in succession, the ribs, and the backbone, the hip-bones, the two thigh-bones, and in the lower extremities, the knees, the legs, and the feet, have been severed from one another."

'I then sought to withdraw, and the voice cried to me for the third time: "Attend to me, 'Umar; do you have no shrouds that will not wear out?"

"And what shrouds will not wear out?" I asked.

'And the earth answered: "The fear of God, and obedience to His will."' And so on to the end of the tradition.

O reader, may God be gracious to you, attend to these words that 'Umar attributed to the earth, to which, as inanimate matter, it appears absurd to ascribe flowery and elegant language. 'Umar, nevertheless, represented the earth as repeatedly calling upon another person, questioning, relating and admonishing which, assuredly, had never really come to pass. But he used this language metaphorically, because having called to mind these philosophical admonitions, he was minded to cast them in the form of a narrative, dividing them into questions and answers, attributing them to others and placing them in the tongue of the inanimate earth. He did so because he perceived that the bearers would be more forcibly driven to reflection, and more urgently moved to relate the matter to others. For if he had said, 'Reflecting upon the state of those who are buried, I perceive that they must be reduced by the earth to such and such a condition,' his warning would not have been expressed with nearly the same vigour that it derived from the original form.

Likewise 'Umar ibn Abu Bishr relates that 'Ali, the Commander of the Faithful, upon whom be the peace of God, one day haranguing the people and being interrupted by their clamours, descended from the tribune and said: 'These people, 'Uthman and myself, are in the same situation as the three bulls, one white, the other red, and the third black, which lived in a jungle together with a lion. Whenever the lion attacked one of these three bulls, they, by uniting their forces, repulsed him so that he was unable to devour them.

But one day the lion said to the black and red bulls: "The colour of this white bull will some day cause us to be discovered in the jungle in which we dwell. If you would suffer me to do so, I would eat him up, and thus we should remain securely concealed, for no one would be able to discover us, seeing that your colour harmonizes with mine and mine with yours." The two bulls, therefore, closed their eyes to what was going on; and the lion, having devoured the white bull, remained with them, and when he sought to attack them, they united together against him.

Then, turning to the red bull, the lion said: "This black fellow will bring disaster upon us, for his colour attracts the eye. Contrive, therefore, to leave him alone, and I will eat him up, and then you and I shall remain here in safety, for the colour of my hide resembles yours, and yours and mine are the same." Accordingly, the black bull was forsaken by the red one and slain by the lion, who lived for a short time in peace with the survivor, until one day he called out to him: "Oh! Red bull, I am coming to devour you."

"You, to devour me?" replied the bull. And the lion replied, "I, myself."

"Since there is no help for it, then," exclaimed the unfortunate animal, "at least wait until I have cried out three times." The lion thereupon drew back, and the bull cried: "Not today, not today, you do not slay me; he slew me when he devoured the white bull; he slew me when he devoured the black bull; he slew me when he devoured the red bull.'"

'Thus', continued 'Ali, 'I was lost on the day of 'Uthman's slaughter.' And this he repeated three times.

The example here gives abundant evidence to the lawfulness of the species of fiction that I have undertaken to relate. To the same effect, it is well to recall that which is related of Nu'man ibn Bishr, the companion of the Prophet. At the time that he governed the city of Kufa [Iraq] for the Caliph Mu'awiya, the latter ordered him to give ten dinars as additional pay to every individual whose name was inscribed on the rolls of the *Diwan*. Nu'man, believing this measure to be inexpedient, did not carry it into effect; hence, one Friday, when he was haranguing the people from the tribune, they cried out to him: 'In the name of God, O Ruler, give us the additional stipend.'

'Do you not perceive', he replied, 'that the dispute between us exactly resembles that which came to pass between the hyena, the fox, and the crocodile? The hyena and the fox, going to the den of the other beast, called to him: "O Abu Husail!"

"I am at your orders," he replied, and they continued: "We came so that you may act as a judge between us."

"The judge must be sought in his own house," replied the crocodile.

'And the hyena resumed, "My eyes hurt me."

'Crocodile: "It is the effect of the heat."

'Hyena: "I gathered some fruit."

'Crocodile: "A good thing."

'Hyena: "And the fox ate it up."

'Crocodile: "Well, he took care of himself."

'Hyena: "But I gave him a blow with my paw."

'Crocodile: "So much the worse for him."

'Hyena: "The fox gave me another in return."

'Crocodile: "A noble animal will avenge itself."

'Hyena: "Now decide between us."

'Crocodile: "Tell a woman one story, and then a second, and though she makes a face over it, tell her ten."'

All these sayings are common adages, and are to be found in all collections. Although the retailers of proverbs, while recording Nuʿmanʾs sayings, have in some degree altered some words. But I have chosen here to revive Nuʿmanʾs memory, and relate that which a companion of the Prophet held it lawful to say, when haranguing the people from the tribune in the assemblage of Friday because, under such sanction, no one can find fault with the work I have undertaken.

All Muslims, moreover, agree in admitting that the marvellous narratives devised by gifted persons are a lawful imitation of the specimen contained in the Qur'an, in the parable of the 'Ant and the Gnat.' For all beings endowed with vital and intellectual faculties superior to those of the above-named insects enjoy them as a special gift of God, differing alike from animal instinct and prophetic inspiration. Thus God, whose name is praised, has said:

God created you, and He will then reclaim you. Some shall have their lives prolonged to abject old age, when all that they once knew they shall know no more. All-knowing is God and mighty. (16:70)

He said, moreover:

We have cast veils over their hearts lest they understand it, and made them hard of hearing. (17:46)

Which saying conveys the idea that God has bestowed knowledge of himself and of his unity upon all created beings. According to some, indeed, this celebration of the praises of God consists only in the marvels of the creation, and the goodness of the Creator, which, being contemplated by a man of enlightened intellect, give him occasion to admire the unity, power, and wisdom of God.

But this opinion only holds good with regard to reflections that the mind of man may make concerning inanimate things, and can by no means be applied to such as are endowed with life. Accordingly, it is related in the tradition of Abu al-Dirda', that the Apostle of God once said, 'No bird nor fish was ever captured except for having neglected to celebrate the praises of God.' Maymun ibn Mahran likewise relates that the truthful Abu Bakr, may God be well pleased with him, once saw a crow expanding its broad wings, and said: 'No game is ever taken, nor does any tree perish, except for having neglected to celebrate the praises of God.' And so on to the end of this tradition.

Lastly, God himself has informed us how He enabled the ant to give wise counsel to her companions, and to warn them to beware of the destruction which was impending upon them, and how He granted her the privilege of knowing Solomon, upon whom be peace, and his armies; as may be seen by the language held by this insect to the other ants, saying:

When they came to the Valley of the Ants, an ant said: Go into your dwellings, ants, lest Solomon and his warriors should unwittingly crush you. (27:18)

God, moreover, enabled her to discern the justice and clemency of Solomon, and made her understand, that had he perceived the ants, there would have been no cause to fear that he should exterminate them, which may be perceived from the expression: 'And perceive it not.' Here, as some believe, the personal pronoun *Hum*, which governs the verb 'to perceive', relates to the ants, which would imply that they did not perceive their companion who was giving them this good advice. But the former interpretation is the better one, for, properly speaking, the pronoun *Hum* relates to beings endowed with reason.

Elsewhere God himself informs us that He inspired the lapwing with the knowledge that Solomon himself was ignorant of the things which He had revealed to her, as may be seen by the words of the lapwing:

The bird, who was not long in coming, said: I have just seen things unknown to you. (27:21)

Moreover, God gave her to know the different races of men, and the ability to distinguish Arabs from barbarians and truthful men from liars, as we read in the same verse:

With truthful news I came to you from Sheba, where I found a woman reigning over the people. (27:23)

Whereas the inhabitants of that country were indeed descended from Sheba, the son of Himyar, He gave her to know, moreover, the appearance and the condition of men, so that she could distinguish men from women, and kings from vassals; for in the following verse the lapwing continues: 'I found a woman reigning over the people,' namely, over Sheba.

He gave her to understand how kings accumulate many different kinds of possessions and are desirous of heaping up treasure, as is shown in the rest of the verse: 'She is possessed of every virtue,' namely, everything which it is customary to offer to princes. God likewise gave her knowledge of the several kinds of rubies and pearls, and that these gems are of great price, and increase the value of that which is adorned with them, for at the end of the verse we find: 'And has a splendid throne,' splendid, that is, after the manner of men.

He gave her to recognize the form of prayer, which is accompanied with prostration, to understand that this was an act of atonement and devotion, and to perceive that the people of Sheba worshipped not God but the sun as we learn from the words:

I found that she and her subjects worship the sun instead of God. (27:24)

He gave her to know the existence of Satan and his tendency to work that which is evil; and that there is in all the world but one path which leads to God, and that is the religion which is acceptable to Him; that Satan turns men aside from this path; and that whoever forsakes it goes astray, as we read in the continuation of the verse:

Satan has seduced them and debarred them from the right path, so that they might not be guided to the worship of God, who brings to light all that is hidden in the heavens and the earth and knows what you conceal and what you reveal. (27:25)

He gave her to know that worship is due to God, and that He alone is the divine Essence. And again:

There is no god but Him. (27:26)

He gave her to know that God orders one hidden substance in Heaven – water – and another on earth – the germ of plants – and that He alone draws forth both the one and the other, which is alluded to in the words of the lapwing, who incidentally brings forward this idea to arouse men to admiration of the Godhead and to show that God has a right to the adoration of all His creatures, being their Creator and He who provides them with subsistence. He gave her also to understand that the hidden things are as well known to God as those that are visible, as we find in the words:

Who brings to light all that is hidden in the heavens and the earth and knows what you conceal and what you reveal. (27:25)

Lastly, God gave her to know that He is seated upon a throne, beside which all the glories of all the thrones of earth vanish, as may be learned from the expression: 'the Lord of the Glorious Throne' (27:26) in which the definite article points out the inferiority and worthlessness of the throne of Balkis, Queen of Sheba, which is designated as 'a splendid throne' (27:24). God therefore granted to the lapwing to understand all these doctrines, which dazzle and confound the minds of men.

To return to my subject, I declare that when the knowledge of facts and the deductions to be drawn from them are unfolded before the intellect of Man, he makes himself master of various forms of eloquence, and from the sense of hearing to which language is addressed, proceeds to communicate by imagery with that of sight. Nor is there anything that is beyond his power to achieve. I therefore commence my task by praying to God that He would aid me to attain my objective, and direct my words to so high a purpose that they may serve as a preparation for a future state. For He alone does what He wills. He is the Mighty and Valiant. Power and goodness dwell in Him alone.

Preface to the Second Edition

In the name of God, the Merciful, the Compassionate, Muhammad ibn Abi Muhammad ibn Zafar, the poor and lowly servant of the Lord, content to abide His holy will, whose sins may God forgive, thus writes:

Gratitude to God is the noblest garment a man can wear, and praise of Him the surest means to obtain the blessings of this life, and of that which is to come. Glory is to God, who gives us endurance as a pledge for success and friendship as a refuge in misfortune. Glory be to Him, who spreads an impenetrable veil over the mysteries of fate, and restrains the loftiest intellects behind the wall of uncertainty; to Him, who leads the submissive on smooth and pleasant paths, but drives forward the reluctant, until, stumbling and murmuring, they obey His decrees.

He, whose name is praised, has said:

It may well be that you dislike a thing which God has meant for your own abundant good. (4:19)

Blessed be our Lord Muhammad, whom He has sent to bear witness, and to proclaim good tidings; to admonish men and call them to piety; and to be, by the will of God, a shining light unto their eyes. May the blessings of the Most High be showered upon him!

I say, further, that amidst the chances of a stormy and wandering life, in which manifold tribulations have succeeded each other, the Most High, whose name be praised, has led me to separate the brotherhood of those who pardon the errors of the high-minded and draw sighs from the bosoms of the envious, the Lord of Lords and Leader of Leaders, Abu 'Abdallah Muhammad ibn Abi al-Qasim 'Ali ibn 'Alawi al-Qurashi, may God bless him, crown his enterprises with success, and to be his patron and his guarantee evermore. When he came into the world he was called to sit in high places, but was likewise warned of the snares which therein abound. Hence his labours are directed towards that which is eternal, not towards that which passes away. He gathers together that he may scatter abroad, not that he may lay up for himself; he dispenses his bounty for the love of God, not to obtain the praise of men; and he shows kindness as a brother to advance justice and piety, not to court affection by flattery. He adorns his chieftain-ship with a spirit to meet every vicissitude of fortune. He does not listen to slanderers, neither is he stingy with his wealth. Such is his disposition that, beside it wrath cannot raise its head; such the firmness of his sway that the people under his guidance need fear no calamity. Therefore I renew my thanks to God, who has given me in this brotherly kindness a strong defence, a sure refuge, abundant wealth, and fountains of living water.

Verses

Under His protection we have all that we can wish for, love, choices and desire.

He guards us from all that may be displeasing to us; and if anything appears desirable unto us, He hastens to let us judge of it by proof.

We lean upon Him for support, as upon a father.

We have tested Him both in good days and bad ones, and in both we have experienced His generous protection.

Furthermore, I swear that if gratitude were not both a sacred tie and obligatory duty, I would, in order to please him, have destroyed that which I unfolded when the Almighty spared me the sorrow of his death, and of continuing to live when deprived of him; I would have concealed when I then set forth to show how ready is the gratitude for his benefits, how lasting his praise in the mouth of his faithful adherents. So, may providence not stay its hand from succouring him; may it restrain calamity's footsteps from overtaking him; glorify evermore through him the high places of power; and frustrate the cunning devices of his enemies. Amen. Amen.

When, by the abundant seed of gifts the harvest of affection was brought forth, and gratitude raised to the highest pitch, I sought to offer him the choicest and most excellent present that might find favour in his eyes and be valuable and worthy of his status; nor could I find any more than learning, which he so ardently loves, wisdom, which he has ever fondly cherished, and literature, which he diligently pursues both by nature and by learning, giving it a place in his mind as well as in his heart.

I therefore presented him with the *Asalib al-Ghaya fi Ahkam al-Aya (Paths Leading to the Goal of the True Interpretation),* in which book I discussed eleven interpretations that lead to the understanding of both the explicit and deductive meanings of the divine saying:

> Believers, when you rise to pray wash your faces and your hands as far as the elbow, and wipe your heads and your feet to the ankle. (5:6)

I added to my gift *al-Muthanna* (*Guide to Perfect Apprehension*), in which I collected together all the questions contained in these two celebrated works, accompanying such questions with the choicest answers. I followed these up with the *Durar al-Ghurar* (*Pearls for the Forehead*), into which book I wove the pearls of the *Anba' Nijaba' al-Abna'* (*Notices of Remarkable Children*), selecting for it those most difficult to find and which shine with the light of philosophy or the beauty of literary form.

In the fourth place, I now offer him the present work, in which I propose to relate certain tales hitherto exclusive to the most celebrated monarchs of earth, who guarded them with great jealousy, not revealing them at any price. These tales I will relate as I have heard them, seeking to elucidate them through my language and exerting my imagination to add to their variety. Moreover, I propose to treat my subjects in such a manner that is not prohibited by the *Shari'a* or offensive to anyone's ear. I desire that the personages who have figured in them as new moons should come forth resplendent as full spheres, and that those who have appeared as sapling shoots should develop themselves into noble palm-trees laden with fruit. I would breathe upon their appearances the spirit of their noble souls, and attire their persons in the mantle of regal bearing; bind their temples with the garland of their lofty thoughts, and suspend from their shoulders the sword of their warlike achievements.

I shall preface each book with a few verses of the immutable revelation, and with some traditions of the Chosen Prophet, upon whom be peace and the blessing of the Most High. I will then add some old wisdom on the same subject, both in prose and rhyme, the maidens and spouses of literature; lastly, I will open a garden for the delight of the heart and ears, and an arena for the exercise of the intellect and character.

I have titled this book *Sulwan al-Muta‘ fi ‘Udwan al-Atba‘* (*Consolation for the Ruler During the Hostility of Subjects*). The term *sulwan* is the plural of *sulwan*a, a shell Arabs believe that can gather water. If a person who is in love drinks from it, he will immediately recover.

The *Rajiz* has said: 'Not even were I to drink the *sulwan*, should I find peace. Not even were I rolling in wealth, could I live without you.'

The wealth of which I speak is five-fold: first, trust in God; second, fortitude; third, patience; fourth, contentment; and fifth, self-denial.

I look to God to grant me His aid for the attainment of my objective, and to support my work, for the benefit of those who worship Him – for He alone can will and execute. He is the Mighty One. Power and goodness dwell in Him alone.

Trust in God

Verses From the Holy Qur'an

God, whose name is blessed, has said:

It may well be that you dislike a thing which God has meant for your own abundant good. (4:19)

And again:

But you may hate a thing although it is good for you, and love a thing although it is bad for you. God knows, but you know not. (2:16)

With these words, God seeks to restrain those who are aware from following their own inclinations and indicated His approval of those who place their faith in Him. The wise person defers his own judgment into the hands of He who knows the true way of salvation.

The exhortation to implicit trust contained in these two verses will be clearly understood when one considers how frequently that which is repugnant to one's propensity serves to bring about that which one desires; likewise, the converse. It is the duty of the clear-sighted not to have confidence in that which is evil because of the pleasure that it may offer, nor to despair of that which is good because of the evil that, at first sight, one discerns in it. One must commit this selection to God, and not seek to make it himself. Such is the boundless trust of the person who prays to God for the removal of some calamity or who implores his clemency under adverse circumstances.

Pharaoh and his Kinsman

Behold God's dealings with a believer, of the royal blood of Egypt, who put his whole trust in Him. This is his narrative. The believer was a relative of Pharaoh, one of his closest friends and a follower of Moses. When the viziers and courtiers found out that the believer was a Jew, they informed the king, who, moved by the love he bore his kinsman, refused to believe them. However, when the miracles that God wrought through Moses were beheld even in the chief city of his kingdom, Pharaoh called a council of all his viziers and courtiers — amongst whom was this believer — to deliberate. They all agreed that Moses should be banished from the Kingdom. Yet, after the magicians had been summoned, ostensibly to test their supernatural capabilities against those credited to Moses, it occurred to Pharaoh to rid himself of the prophet by sentencing him to death; of which our Lord, whose name be glorified, informs us in the following words.

> Put them off awhile, him and his brother [they replied], and send forth heralds to the cities to summon every skilled enchanter to your presence. (26:37)

Pharaoh replied:

Let me slay Moses, and then let him invoke his God! I fear
that he will change your religion and spread disorder in the
land. (40:26)

Seeing that such was the king's opinion, none of his
ministers ventured to dissuade him, so great was the fear in
which he was held. Nevertheless, the believer — who was
grieved at the king's intention to harm Moses — lost patience
and, no longer able to conceal his deeply felt concerns,
exclaimed, as the Lord has revealed unto us:

Would you slay a man merely because he says: 'My Lord is
God'? (40:27)

He then interceded repeatedly on his behalf, admonishing
Pharaoh to use caution and to abstain from rash action,
quoting the Lord:

If he is lying, may his lie be on his head; but if he is
speaking the truth, a part at least of what he threatens will
smite you. (40:28)

When Pharaoh heard these words, he was very troubled.
He threw his kinsman into prison and, having laid the matter
before his viziers and courtiers, sought their counsel. The
consensus was to torture him before sentencing him to death,
as a warning to those who might be inclined to hold similar
views. Pharaoh would not consent to this advice because the
believer was one of his relatives. Instead, he commanded his
viziers to attempt to persuade, admonish and entreat the
believer to remain obedient to the ruler and, lastly, to

threaten him with severe punishment were he to persevere in his obstinacy.

The believer, on the other hand, having listened to the admonitions, sought to convert them over to the true faith, reminding the ministers of the miracles that their own eyes had witnessed. He further warned them not to forfeit the blessings God had bestowed on them, nor to incur his displeasure, as is revealed to us in the following words:

'He who was a true believer said: "I warn you, my people, against the fate which overtook the factions: the people of Noah, Ad, and Thamud, and those that came after them. God does not seek to wrong His servants." I warn you, my people, against the day when men will cry out to one another, which you will turn and flee, with none to defend you against God. He whom God confounds shall have none to guide him. Long before this, Joseph came to you with veritable signs, but you never ceased to doubt them; and when he died, you said: "After him God will never send another apostle." Thus God confounds the doubting transgressor. Those who dispute God's revelations, with no authority vouchsafed to them, are held in deep abhorrence by God and by the faithful. Thus God seals up the heart of every scornful tyrant.' (40:30–36)

The viziers and courtiers related to Pharaoh how the believer persisted in his affront, as well as disobedience, and how their admonitions produced no other effect than to make him adhere more obstinately to his own views.

This news sorely grieved the king and he wished to be left alone, absorbed in reflection. One of Pharaoh's daughters sought him out to tell her what had so disturbed him. He related to her all that had happened, and the maiden replied thus: 'If it rested with me to rescue you from this perplexity, I would surely counsel you to refrain from injuring your most trusted friends and kindred. Doubtless, your kinsman has no wish other than your own. But seeing how boldly Moses dares to resist the sovereign beneath whose sceptre he dwells, he concludes that it is impossible to publicly execute him and, therefore, has created a stratagem to uphold the doctrine which thus offends you — for the sole purpose of deceiving Moses. All that you have seen and heard is but a fraud devised against Moses. If the believer abstained from disclosing it to your ministers when they went to counsel him, he did so because he knew them to be shrews and full of envy and malignity, who would have never seconded his counsel nor aided in the execution of his purpose.'

When Pharaoh heard his daughter's words, he rejoiced, as God softened his heart to believe them. It is said that it was Aisha, the Pharaoh's wife, who had bidden the maiden to give such counsel to her father. Pharaoh then summoned his kinsman to his presence, showed him great honour, excused himself for mistreating him, and said: 'I now know your design, and the purpose of your actions; speak, therefore, as you will, act as it may please you, for I mistrust you no longer.'

And God, whose name is praised, speaks thus:

God delivered him from the evils which they planned, and a grievous scourge encompassed Pharaoh's people. (40:45)

Which signifies that God dispensed the punishment they intended to inflict upon the believer. Verily, temporal punishment has nothing in common with eternal punishment, as the following expression attests:

But evil shall recoil on those that plot evil. (35:43)

Meanwhile, be it known to you, reader — and may God show mercy on both of us — that the true meaning of the word *'tafwid'* is implicit confidence in the wisdom of the All-wise. The Lord has clearly revealed it to His Elect Prophet Muhammad, peace be upon him, when he said:

Say: Nothing will befall us except what God has ordained. He is our guardian. In God let the faithful put their trust. (9:51)

The foundation of boundless faith, and the reason that should lead us to it, is the certain belief that nothing, whether of good or evil, can come to pass but what He wills, and that man can never repose implicit trust in God if he does not hold this belief steadfastly and in full faith.

Tradition Concerning the Prophet Muhammad

This was a truth that the Prophet, upon whom is the blessing of God, earnestly strove to set forth clearly and render conspicuous, when he spoke to 'Abdallah ibn Mas'ud:

'Say within yourself, that which is foreordained will befall you, and that which is not foreordained will not befall you. Know, moreover, that if all created beings were to unite in an attempt to obtain for you a blessing which God had not inscribed in the book of fate, they would be unable to effect it; and that were they to endeavour to afflict you with some evil which God had not decreed, neither would they have the power to bring it to pass.'

In this tradition, the expression, 'say within yourself,' contains a command to trust in God, whereas the remainder illustrates the reason why men of understanding should commit themselves entirely into his hands.

It is likewise related in Muslim's (817–875) *Musnad* that, on one occasion the Prophet, conversing with Abu Huraira, said:

'When any unpleasant event befalls you, do not say, "If I had but acted thus and thus"; rather, say: "Such is God's decree; may His will be done." For the "if" opens the breach to Satan, and assuredly does not lead either to trust in God or resignation to His will.'

All thus perceived that the Prophet forbade the expression 'if' because it rejected implicit trust in God, and was conducive to opposing His decrees and resisting His will.

In his *Sahib*, Muslim relates, on the authority of Bara' ibn 'Azib, another of the Prophet's sayings, as follows:

'When you go to bed, perform the same ablutions as you do before your prayers; then lie down on your right side and say "Oh, my God, unto you I do commit my soul; unto you I look up with longing and fear; with you alone I can find refuge. I believe in the book of your revelation, and in your Prophet whom you have sent."' And so on to the end of the tradition.

Philosophical Maxims on Trust in God

If a sick person defies his physician, he must bear the suffering.

He alone is shrewd and subtle who commits himself into the hands of the Almighty.

For it is impossible to oppose destiny; and human diligence is one of the forces that assists the restless course of fate.

When an issue is uncertain, commit yourself into His hands as He governs destiny.

Amongst the arguments that prove man to be a passive being, subjected to rule and governance, is this: in many cases his judgment is obscured as he loses sight both of the right path and of the goal which he desires to attain. Therefore, if he follows his own guidance, he hastens to his ruin; if he trusts his own cunning, it leads him to certain destruction; and if he but moves, he perishes.

It is said that al-Hajjaj ibn Yusuf al-Thaqafi composed the following verse when his mind was torn by various conflicting opinions:

'Suffer this daughter of heaven to go forth and run the way of fate, and corrupt her not by the counsels of your foolishness.' To which I add: 'In moments of perplexity, you who trust your own counsel and provide for yourself, if the case is doubtful, commit it to Him who sees that which you cannot see. You shall find yourself guarded by love that preserves you from ruin and by goodness, that shortens your path to the end which is foreordained. Seeing you are ignorant of the end, and have neither liberty nor power to follow your own pleasure, why do you annoy yourself? What are you contented of? What do you fear or desire?'

Moreover, I add: How many are they who rejoice and are ruined? For they have embraced a counsel that will prove their destruction. How many are they who gasp for power? For, when attained, it will work their misery in this world and the next. The knowledge of the future is concealed by a veil that we endeavour to part in vain. He who seeks to resist destiny by cunning devices has chosen a narrow and perilous path. Therefore, be yourself frankly and believe that which is sure, and throw into his crucible the clipped coin of uncertainties.

Who holds trust in God has the best profession of the unitarian faith of Islam, and resistance to that which is foreordained is the guilt of polytheism.

Dialogue Between al-Walid ibn Yazid and a Poor Dweller

When al-Walid ibn Yazid ibn 'Abd al-Malik was informed that his uncle, Yazid ibn al-Walid ibn 'Abd al-Malik, became alienated from his people, he levied troops in Yemen to shake the foundations of his throne. He orchestrated a phony attempt on his life, fled from the company of his most intimate friends and did not wish to be seen by his trusted associates.

One evening, when a fit of melancholy was upon him, he called one of his servants, and said to him: 'Disguise yourself, and go forth from the palace; take up your post on a street corner, where you may carefully note all passers-by. When you cross an elderly man of a squalid appearance walking slowly and in silence, as if absorbed in thought, greet him and whisper in his ear, "The Commander of the Faithful desires to meet you." If he readily complies, then bring him to me. But if he seeks to excuse himself, or hesitates, or refuses, let him go and seek another, until you find one as I have described.' The servant went forth and returned to the Caliph with precisely such a man as was required.

When the man entered the dwelling in which al-Walid was seated, he saluted the Commander of the Faithful as it was customary to do, and remained standing until the Caliph asked him to approach and be seated. Al-Walid began talking to the man with so much deference that his fear dissipated and his spirits regained their composure. He then inquired whether the man was pleased to converse with a Caliph.

'Most assuredly, O Commander of the Faithful,' replied the man.

Al-Walid then resumed: 'Since you take delight in such conversation, tell us what you know of it, and what does it consist of?'

'It consists, O Commander of the Faithful,' replied the man, 'in discoursing with the prince when he is silent; in being silent when he speaks; and in conversing on subjects that are suitable and not ordinary.'

'You have answered well,' said the Caliph, 'and we are satisfied with the trial we have made of you. Now, therefore, speak and we will be silent and listen.'

'There are two kinds of conversation, O Commander of the Faithful,' continued the stranger, 'as a third cannot exist. The first consists in relating that which may be useful to know; the second, in discussing that which may tend to the furtherance of a proposed object. Now, in the capital of the Commander of the Faithful, I have heard no tale of any description. Therefore, instead of a tale, I will relate a similitude, and instead of pointing out the path to the Commander of the Faithful, I will approach it and pause on the brink.'

'It is well said,' replied al-Walid, 'and we will therefore point out the path and put you on the track so that you may follow it up. We know that one of our subjects has risen up against our authority, and is now pursuing his objective to our great injury and detriment. Have you heard anything of the matter?'

'Yes', replied the stranger, and al-Walid resumed: 'Speak of it, therefore, according to your knowledge, and set it forth in whatever form you may think best.'

Adventure of the Umayyad Caliph 'Abd al-Malik ibn Marwan and 'Abdallah ibn al-Zubayr

O Commander of the Faithful, I have heard it related that the Caliph 'Abd al-Malik ibn Marwan, having raised an army against 'Abdallah ibn al-Zubayr, and advancing upon Makka (may God defend it), desired to take with him 'Amr ibn Sa'id ibn al-'As, a man regarded with mistrust, suspected of cherishing sinister intentions and aspiring to the Caliphate.

'Abd al-Malik ibn Marwan was well aware of these aspirations but had spared 'Amr's life, given his clement disposition, and in consideration of blood ties by which they were united.

When the Caliph was several days into the journey, and fairly engaged in the enterprise, 'Amr ibn Sa'id requested permission – under pretext of illness – to return to Damascus. 'Abd al-Malik consented, and no sooner had 'Amr entered the capital then, ascending a pulpit, he harangued the masses. He spoke against the Caliph and exhorted the people of Damascus to depose him. The masses applauded this proposal, proclaimed 'Amr caliph and took an oath of allegiance to him. Having thus gained control of Damascus, 'Amr proceeded to fortify its walls, make preparations for the defence of the surrounding country, strengthened the frontiers and distributed largesse. News of these events reached 'Abd al-Malik while he was still on the march against

Ibn al-Zubayr. The Caliph further learned that the Governor of Hims had renounced his allegiance, and that people in neighbouring regions were on the verge of rebellion.

With this information, the Caliph entered the tent within which his ministers were assembled and, pointing with a wand first to his right and then to his left, he informed them of the facts: 'Here', he said, 'is Damascus, the capital of our empire, already occupied by 'Amr ibn Sa'id. Here 'Abdallah ibn al-Zubayr has made himself master of Hijaz, Iraq, Egypt, Yemen, and Khorasan. Here Nu'man ibn Bashir, Ruler of Hims, and Zafar ibn Harith, Ruler of Qinnisrin, and Na'il ibn Qays, Ruler of Palestine, have all renounced their allegiances. They have all hailed Ibn al-Zubayr as Caliph. Meanwhile the inhabitants of the border country are vacillating, and the Egyptians girding on their swords to avenge the massacres of Marj Rahit.' On hearing these words, the ministers lost their composure, and were persuaded that resistance was impossible. They bowed their heads and remained silent.

'What ails you all,' resumed the Caliph, 'that you are so dumbstruck? Give me your advice, for I sorely need it at this hour.' Then the wisest amongst them answered: 'What measures can we advise you given that all is lost? I wish I were a chameleon, living in the trunk of some tree in the Tihama, until these calamities end.'[1]

---

1. Muhammad ibn Zafar writes that this chameleon is a small reptile, less than a span long, with four feet and a head like a calf. At sunrise it crawls on a branch, a clod of earth or a stone, and, fixing its eyes on the sun, contemplates it steadily without ever removing its gaze. When the sun has reached its zenith and its rays fall perpendicularly upon the head of the chameleon, the reptile, no longer able to gaze at it, writhes, struggles and strikes the roof of its mouth with its tongue

(continued...)

Perceiving from this answer that he could hope for no assistance from his ministers, 'Abd al-Malik commanded them to remain where they were and walked out. He immediately mounted his horse, giving orders that a squadron of the bravest and most experienced of his horsemen should arm themselves, mount, and follow him closely to carry out any of his orders. In this guise, he left the camp, the escort following him as he had directed.

'Abd al-Malik rode on until he came upon an infirm old man, clad in worn garments and gathering sumac. After greeting him, the Caliph made a few observations on trifling subjects before inquiring, at some length, whether he knew anything concerning the position of the army. 'They are encamped in such a place,' replied the old man, 'this much I know.'

'And have you heard,' resumed the Caliph, 'what people are saying of the expedition?'

'What is it to you?' answered the old man.

The Caliph replied, 'I am inclined to enlist in the army and seek my fortune.'

'Is it possible!' exclaimed the old man, 'So richly attired as you are, and of high rank as you appear to be? Moreover, why do you ask my advice on a matter which you have already decided?'

Indeed, I have great need of it,' replied 'Abd al-Malik.

(...continued)

> as a man does when urging on a donkey; this it continues to do until the sun begins to decline. Then the chameleon, turning round to the other side, again fixes its eyes on it until it sets below the horizon. When the creature can no longer see it, it goes forth to seek pasture during the night, recommencing the same procedure the following day. The minister would have liked to be even as this chameleon, to escape from impending calamities.

The old man resumed: 'Well, then, you must give up this plan, to which you have taken so great a fancy, for the prince whose service you desire to enter is in such dire conditions that his power is crumbling, his followers disbanding and all his affairs becoming involved in confusion. And a falling monarch is like a tempest at sea: best witnessed from afar.'

'Old man', replied the Caliph, 'there is no consideration of prudence sufficiently powerful to restrain me, once a desire has taken possession of my soul. I feel irresistibly attracted to follow the fortunes of this prince, and follow them I will. Meanwhile, you would do me a favour if you would tell me what, in your opinion, are the steps the Caliph ought to take in the present crisis of his fortunes? I could suggest your advice to him, that might serve me as a recommendation and, perhaps, afford me the means of ingratiating myself with him.'

'There are disasters', rejoined the old man, 'in which the wisdom and power of God prevent every possible way of escape against the intellect of man. But the misfortune which has befallen the Caliph does not appear to me such as to defy human wisdom to apply a remedy, or human counsel to bring it to a prosperous conclusion. Moreover, as you have inquired of me, I should be sorry to disappoint your expectations. I will, therefore, give you such an answer as you desire, although I do not have entire confidence in my own judgment, for the case is one of great danger and the remedy to be applied is consequently of equal importance.'

'Speak, and may God reward you,' exclaimed 'Abd al-Malik, 'even as I trust that He will aid you and put you in the right way, and lead me to safety through your means.'

'The Caliph', continued the old man, 'is gone forth to fight his enemy; but it has since become evident that this undertaking is contrary to the will of God. It seems that God does not behold with favour a war against Ibn al-Zubayr because he has stopped the Caliph's advance by causing a rebellion to break out in the very heart of his empire, where 'Amr ibn Sa'id has dared to assume his seat, seduced his people, seized his treasures and even threatened the throne. I therefore would advise you to investigate minutely the position of Ibn al-Zubayr, and wait to see what he will do. If you see the prince pursue his enterprise and persist in his design of attacking Ibn al-Zubayr, then you should know that he will not succeed. Leave him; he must inevitably fail, because God has indicated His will. Although God has discouraged him from pursuing this undertaking, he nevertheless persists only more obstinately. But if you see him turn back and give up on the enterprise, then hope that he will escape, for he will thus show himself both penitent and anxious to amend. And God, whose name be praised, is accustomed to forgive the sins of those who implore His pardon, and to have mercy on those who return to Him.'

'But does it not come to the same,' interrupted 'Abd al-Malik, 'whether the Caliph returns to Damascus or continues his march against Ibn al-Zubayr? Is not the will of God as clearly demonstrated by the alienation of his subjects at Damascus, and by their stretching forth their hands to swear fealty to another? Surely it is the same thing, whether he goes forward against Ibn al-Zubayr or turns back against 'Amr ibn Sa'id, for both have strengthened themselves with the power of a mighty kingdom and a subjected people.'

'You do not perceive', replied the old man, 'the significant difference that exists between these two cases, and which I will now explain to you. 'Abd al-Malik, in advancing against Ibn al-Zubayr, does so in the character of an unjust aggressor, because the latter never swore allegiance to him, nor has he attacked any country belonging to him. But in advancing against 'Amr ibn Sa'id, on the contrary, 'Abd al-Malik appears in the light of the injured party, 'Amr having broken his oath of fidelity, abused the confidence reposed in him by the Caliph, distanced his subjects from their ruler by exciting them to rebellion and treason and assaulted the capital of a kingdom that neither belonged to him nor his forefathers, but to 'Abd al-Malik and his ancestors.

'Hence, 'Amr ibn Sa'id is a usurper and ravisher of a sovereign power, and it is said that 'he who has become rich through pillage shall waste away; he who rules by treachery shall be expelled; the army of the unrighteous shall be defeated, and the noose of tyranny shall be broken.'

'I will now relate to you a parable which shall be as succour to your soul, dispel its doubts and insert into it various philosophical epigrams that may sharpen your intellect, awaken your mind and unleash truth.'

The Two Foxes and the Serpent

A fox called Zalim ('Wicked') possessed a burrow in which he dwelt in great ease and comfort, for one more spacious could not have been found. One day, he stepped out in search of food and upon his return, found it occupied by a serpent. Zalim, therefore, waited for its departure. The vigil was in vain, however, because the venomous animal had appropriated the hole as its own dwelling. For the serpent has no lair of its own, and is therefore accustomed to enter other animals' dwellings, take possession and drive away their owners.

Thus the *Rajiz*, seeking to illustrate the injustice of a wicked man, said:

'You are as the viper that burrows not, but seeks out some careless one, and establishes itself in his den.' And hence the proverb: 'This one is more wicked than a serpent and the serpent's wickedness is this.'

Realizing that the snake had taken up its abode in the hole, and not being able to share it with him, the fox went in search of another shelter and wandered about until he saw a very inviting dwelling. It was excavated in firm soil in the midst of a fertile country abounding with trees and watered by numerous rivulets. Zalim, struck with admiration, inquired to whom the hole belonged and was told that it was owned by a fox named Mufawwad ('Trusting'), who had inherited it from his father. Zalim then called Mufawwad.

The latter came forth to meet him, received him with great courtesy and invited him into his abode, asking him what he desired. Zalim, thereupon related his adventures, lamenting over the misfortune that had befallen him. Moved by compassion, Mufawwad addressed him thus: 'I think that you ought not to abstain from attacking your enemy, but should use every effort to drive him out, and put him to death.'

Thus it was said: 'He who suspects his enemy is almost as far advanced as he who leads forth an army against him.'

'Cunning often ensures victory over a powerful tribe.'

'It is better to die in a fire than to live in dishonour.'

'But if you would employ force against your enemy, do not attack him unless you know him to be weaker than yourself; and if you would rely on ruse, never estimate him too highly, whatever may be his power.'

'Therefore', said Mufawwad, 'let us proceed to your former dwelling, of which you have been deprived by violence, and let me examine it carefully. Perhaps I may be able to devise a stratagem by which you may recover possession. The best measures are those grounded upon mature deliberation.'

It was said that all enterprises are ruined by three causes: First, a plan fails if it is imparted to several individuals before it is fully divulged; second, everything is spoiled if those in the secret are rivals, or envious of one another, because love or hatred entered their calculations; third, if the direction of an enterprise is assumed by one who has not been on the spot from the beginning, but rather by someone who came in at a later time. Then the old leader will be jealous and envious of the new one.

Therefore, if a man embarks on any undertaking according to hearsay, he will build upon possibilities; but if he regulates it according to what he sees with his own eyes, he will build upon certainties.

The two foxes went together towards Zalim's hole, which Mufawwad examined minutely. Having seen all that he required, Mufawwad turned to Zalim, and said, 'I have seen enough to enable me to devise a stratagem, and to identify the enemy's weak point.'

'What, then, do you think we ought to do?' asked Zalim.

And his friend answered: 'The counsel devised at first sight is worthless.'

It was said that 'counsel is the mirror of the intellect.' If, therefore, you would like to know the capacity of anyone, ask for advice.

It was also said: 'The best counsel is that which has been proven by reflection, and adopted after mature deliberation.'

And: 'Counsel is the sword of wisdom. If a sword is the keenest and has been sharpened with the best care, and its blade most diligently polished, then surely the counsel which has been the most frequently deliberated and the longest weighed will be better than all others.' And, 'The counsel which is delivered in haste is worthless.'

Mufawwad then said, 'Come with me, therefore, and lodge with me tonight. I will reflect upon all the stratagems that I can think of.' They did so, and while Mufawwad was taxing his brains, Zalim busied himself in minutely examining his host's dwelling. It appeared to him spacious, well situated, defended, and so abounding in comforts and conveniences that, becoming more and more attracted to it, he was seized with an earnest desire to possess it. He thus devised a stratagem by which to attain his wish and drive away Mufawwad.

Verily, the wicked man is like fire. If you feed him, he blazes up. He is also like wine, which makes a prey of he who loves him; and a slave of he who pursues him. Therefore, natural malignity cannot be conquered by sheer profits. He is a wise man who places trial before intimacy, examination before choice and confidence before love.

In the morning, Mufawwad said to Zalim: 'I have noticed that your hole is situated at too great a distance from trees and cultivated ground; give it up and take heart, and I will help you dig another in this pleasant and fruitful neighbourhood.'

'That is impossible,' replied Zalim, 'for such is my disposition that, were I to leave my dwelling, I should die of grief, and although I might find a resting place, I should not obtain rest.'

It was said that a well-conditioned mind is illustrated by seven qualities: filial piety; love of kindred; love of nation; the wish to live in tranquillity; self-reproach for youth wasted in vain; the habit of wearing worn-out clothes; and the patient endurance of evils and the infirmities of age. Likewise: exile is a state of living death; the shadow remains, but the soul is gone.

Mufawwad responded with the following words: 'He who gives counsel ought to be acquainted with the circumstances of the one asking, for otherwise it might only lead to greater evil. A physician should prescribe the proper remedy for a given complaint after knowing the age and constitution of the patient, or the diet and medicines to which he is accustomed, without taking into account the immediate causes of the illness, the time of year and the air of the neighbourhood. Only when the physician is persuaded that he has dispensed the proper remedy should he portion its strength to that of the disease.

Now, it is by no means impossible that if your disposition corresponds with your name, "the Wicked", you may be suffering the penalty of some sin, or of some oppression that you have practised towards others. If it is so, your anxiety to escape from your present distress would not be more successful than the struggles of a wild beast which, finding itself caught in a net, begins to tear it furiously with its claws, and by this approach becomes even more entangled or even brings about its own death — which perhaps the hunter had not intended, desiring only to take it alive.

But even if you are not suffering the punishment of any misdeed, your case is still doubtful. Indeed, in doubtful cases, there is no better way than to commit oneself into the hands of Him who alone decrees and knows them thoroughly, and who manifests His wisdom by bringing them to pass.

And now I will relate to you a fable, in which you may both enjoy the beauty of elegant diction and gather the benefit of mature philosophy. In truth, a fable, so easily divulged, attracts our minds with the force of a magnet, for allegories have great power of touching us quickly. The maxims derived from these recur more frequently, even as the eye often fixes more readily a painting rather than the original object. In fact, we are more than willing to listen to the language attributed to brutes, than to the sayings of men of great genius.'

The Peacock and the Cock

It is related, whether true or false, that a man who was well-versed in the diseases of fowls and the modes of curing them had two pea-fowls – a cock and a hen – of which the former was named Zibrij ('Multicoloured'). Their master, who valued them both and was in the habit of frequently caressing them, perceived one day on examining the plumage of Zibrij that the bird was losing its colour, which indicated a certain impending illness. He also knew that the illness might he counteracted, and thus cured Zibrij by plucking the principal feathers of his wings, removing him from the company of the hen, limiting his food intake and infusing a drug of a very bitter flavour into everything which he either ate or drank. These measures led Zibrij to rage and despair. It was said: impatience of the evils which befall us, is blindness to the blessings which are left.

Impatience of calamity is, in fact, a third misfortune – third, because he who is impatient loses the merit of his tribulation in the eyes of God, and in the meantime irritates himself by his own struggles, so that he is the victim of three evils at once.

Zibrij, thus isolated, saw a cock called Hinzab, who belonged to the same master and was one of the most beautiful of its kind both as to form as well as to the colour of his plumage and crowing. This sight increased Zibrij's discontent, and what marvel is it if God, amidst the abundance of his miracles, should have granted intellect and wisdom to these two animals as he once did to Solomon's lapwing? It is therefore by no means impossible that Zibrij may have said to Hinzab: 'You, who can enjoy your liberty, have you the heart to feel for an unhappy creature who is separated from his companion, whose wings have been clipped and whose food is poisoned every day? If you pity his misfortunes, and will listen to his complaints, you might perhaps give him comfort, and devise for him some means of escape.'

'And what should hinder my doing so?' replied Hinzab. 'Do I not know that, amongst all the deeds that spring from a generous spirit, kindness to the afflicted is that which finds most favour in God's eyes?'

It was said that 'we are all united in a mutual bond of protection against the misfortunes that may befall any individual; and amongst those who are at ease, the most prosperous will be he who regards as his own the calamity that befalls his neighbour, and who assists him first by relieving him from his distress and afterwards by admonishing him to avoid a repetition of his fault and consequent return of the misfortune; so that the sufferer should always be grateful to him, and should be careful not to fall a second time into adversity.'

The value of good is never appreciated at the moment of its attainment and possession, but rather after it is lost, and when we desire it in vain. And how, indeed, can we feel properly thankful for it until we are acquainted with its worth?

It is said that a man 'will never be grateful for benefits in the four following cases: if he already enjoys them; if, by their means, he is able to throw off his subjection to his benefactor; if he hears too much said about them; and if he knows himself unable to respond to them with any adequate return.'

Hinzab continued, 'In the first place, it is our duty to recognize the superiority of man, ennobled as he is by the gift of intellect and the dignity of wisdom, and to acknowledge his right to exercise authority and dominion over us; and that it is but justice that for our faults he should do to us that which displeases us, or that, even without any fault of ours, he who knows what he is about should exert his power.'

'What you say is true,' replied Zibrij.

'Do you remember having committed any fault?' resumed the cock.

'No, never,' said Zibrij.

Hinzab replied, 'If the acknowledgment you uttered just now of your master's authority were sincere, you ought to submit yourself to him, and to give up all thoughts of resistance.'

It is said that if a slave is angry at his lord's commands, he thereby denies his authority and makes an effort to escape from his post. Likewise, to be indignant at the sentence of a judge is to accuse him either of tyranny or of ignorance.

He is not sincere in his allegiance he who does not willingly submit to an act of justice imparted by his superior that is painful to himself.

'Listen', continued Hinzab, 'to a tale which may, perhaps, relieve your mind, and lead you to hope and to contentment.'

The Two Ministers

It is related that a certain king had two ministers, each of them honest and faithful. One, a devout man, was versed in works of benevolence and the practices of piety, and abstained from many of the unbridled desires of the flesh. These two ministers scarcely ever agreed. Annoyed by their differences, the king was compelled to dismiss one of them.

Yet, to determine which minister should be fired, the king devised the following expedient. Having located a dwelling with a hiding-place, he commanded one of his most trusted servants to conceal himself there. He then informed the servant that he was about to imprison the two ministers and bade him to heed all their words and actions carefully. Then the king had the two ministers seized and taken to that dwelling where the door was walled up, leaving only a little window through which food and drink could be supplied to the prisoners.

The first day passed without either of them having uttered a word. In the evening, the least devout of the two asked his companion: 'How do you feel?'

The devout one replied: 'I have confidence in destiny, and commit myself into the hands of Him who foreordains all things, whose holy name be praised.'

'I, on the contrary', resumed the first speaker, 'feel my blood boil within me, and cannot rest in peace. For what cause has this misfortune befallen us?'

'I have reviewed the whole of my conduct,' answered the devout minister, 'and I cannot see that I have fallen into any error which could have displeased the king. As regards the army and the people, I have committed two kinds of injustice; that is, I have always defended the people against the soldiers, and I have also made every exertion to satisfy the latter. Lastly, I find my sins against God to be innumerable, although I have never failed to examine my conscience daily, both morning and night, and then to repent of my faults, implore God's forgiveness and make every effort in my power to expiate them. It appears to me, therefore, that I am now enduring the punishment of my sins against the Lord my God.'

'And I, on the other hand', replied his companion, 'believe that I have been vilified by such a one from envy of my influence with the king. What do you think?'

'I think', replied the devout minister, 'that both of us ought to resign to God's edicts, and have confidence in His good pleasure; for our calamity is a mystery, which if our intellect seeks to penetrate it will only grope in darkness and never succeed in doing so.'

'Nonsense!' responded the other, 'many better plans than that have occurred to me, but the only one which suits me is to write to the king, offering to give up all my fortune on condition that I am set at liberty, so that I may remain undisturbed in my own house to worship the Lord my God.'

'That would be a very undesirable expedient,' replied the devout minister, 'for it would give rise to many suspicions. It would open the path of injustice before the king, and would be to despair of the grace of God.'

They spoke no more that night. In the morning, a single loaf of bread was brought to them.

'Eat', said the devout minister to his companion.

'No', he replied, 'I am afraid of being poisoned.'

'I', said the other, 'will take my share, and commit myself to God.' Then taking one half of the loaf and beginning to eat, he found a magnificent ruby encrusted in it! The second night passed, and at daybreak a loaf of bread was again brought to them of which the devout minister took the half, and found another gem in it. The same thing happened on the third day.

The king then released them from prison, and his servant informed him of all that had occurred; upon which the king sent for the ministers, and questioned them closely as to their words and actions while in custody. They both told him the truth, and the devout one, producing the gems, added, 'I found these in my food, but it is not right that I should appropriate another's share.'

'By my faith', replied the king, 'it is God who has deprived him of them, and has provided them for you as a reward of your trust in Him. These gems alone were in the loaves, and I merely wished to ascertain, by experiment, what each of you would do when his own interests were at stake.

'I have thus discovered that your companion is possessed by devils, and infested with evil thoughts concerning his maker, against whom he rebels; while he suspects me of a design to tyrannize him, to despoil him of his substance, and to poison him. You, on the other hand, speedily resigned yourself, without striving to discover what steps could be taken in a case of which you neither knew the cause nor true circumstances; you surrendered yourself into the hands of God, and in all your conjectures never sought to blame anyone but yourself. I conclude that the Lord has chosen you to be our support and has pointed you out as the only one worthy to advise us and enjoy our favour. Give thanks to Him, who has been your guide, trust him more in the season of calamity, and commit yourself into His hands in the doubtful events of life.'

Thus the king took him to be his only minister and sent away the other in dismal plight.

End of the Tale of the Two Ministers

In completing his tale, Zibrij commiserated with his master, whose counsels he first resisted, because he was not satisfied to have made his point. In fact, he did not care to cure diseases according to their symptoms, but sought to accomplish much more. The master rewarded him abundantly.'

End of the Tale of the Two Foxes

When Mufawwad understood Zalim's intentions, he said, 'We should go find a stick and tie two scraps to it, light a fire and proceed to your hole; there, we will place it at the entrance. If the serpent comes out, it will burn; and if it stays put, the fumes will kill it.'

Zalim said, 'Very well, we will do so.' The two foxes proceeded to execute their plan. At night, as nearby campers lit a fire, Mufawwad jumped onto it to light the scraps. Zalim, meanwhile, used one of the scraps to seal the entrance, reasoning that Mufawwad would not be able to enter his own dwelling, thus claiming it for himself. Little did he realize that his decision prevented him from seeing the folly of the step he had just taken, and from understanding that he was exposing himself to the same fate which Mufawwad had destined for the serpent.

It was said: 'Guard yourself from your own designs against your enemy, as carefully as from one against yourself.'

'Many have perished in attacks and ambushes planned by themselves; many have fallen into their own traps, or have wounded themselves with their own weapons.'

Returning with the brand and not finding Zalim, Mufawwad fancied at first that, perhaps to save him trouble, the latter had laden himself with both scraps, believing that he was able to bear the burden. Moved by this thought, Mufawwad endeavoured to reach his den, by overtaking Zalim. He therefore flung down the brand, but fearing that the wind would make it burn away — forcing him to fetch another — he placed it in the mouth of his hole for shelter. Coming in contact with the wood, the scrap caught fire, and Zalim, entrapped in his own snare, was burned within the den.

Mufawwad, realizing what had just occurred, exclaimed: 'I have never seen a weapon which injures those who wield it so severely as does injustice. Hence it is said that the unjust man goes of his own accord in search of the knife which slays him, and his own feet bear him to the brink of the abyss into which his evil conduct will precipitate him.'

It was said: 'Sovereignty and injustice cannot share a throne, which cannot be left vacant.'

'Every sinner will find one to pardon him, except the unjust, in whose fall all rejoice with one accord.'

'As much as injustice gives you, so much does it take from you.'

'Having waited until the fire was burnt out, Mufawwad entered into his den, threw out Zalim's carcass and continued to dwell there in wakefulness and vigilance, being always on his guard against the machinations of traitors.'

End of 'Abd al-Malik's Adventure

'Now this history,' resumed the old man, 'closely resembles the revolt of 'Amr ibn Sa'id, as far as his injustice is concerned, of his treachery against 'Abd al-Malik and of his having entered the capital of the Caliph to strengthen himself there during 'Abd al-Malik's absence. Still, 'Abd al-Malik, in advancing to fight Ibn al-Zubayr, increases 'Amr ibn Sa'id's power and leaves sovereignty to his family while wresting it away from Ibn al-Zubayr. For the power of 'Abd al-Malik is henceforth the power of 'Amr, and his kingdom, the Kingdom of 'Amr, neither looks with favour upon 'Abd al-Malik's campaign nor assists him in it, although it would turn to his own ultimate advantage. Thus, 'Abd al-Malik is acting as Zalim acted towards Mufawwad.'

'Abd al-Malik, having understood the parable and reflected on the moral contained therein, was greatly pleased. 'You may reckon upon a handsome reward from me,' he told the old man, 'for you have already acquired much influence over me. Consider this, therefore, as an agreement between us. And do not fail to remind me of it a few days hence so that I may acquit myself of my obligation.'

'I do not understand,' replied the old man.

'Abd al-Malik replied, 'I hope that your counsel will do me good service with the Caliph, and that I shall then be able to reward the assistance for which I am indebted to you.'

'And I', responded the old man, 'make a vow to God that I will never pray for one who is avaricious.'

'How do you know that I am avaricious?' asked 'Abd al-Malik.

'Can you be otherwise,' was the reply, 'if you delay giving me this present and reward when it is in your power to do so at once? What should prevent you from bestowing upon me some of the expensive weapons and garments that you are wearing?'

'By God, I had not thought of that!' answered the Caliph. Ungirding his sword, he said, 'Take this, for it is worth twenty thousand dirhams.'

'No, I accept no gifts from the oblivious,' said the old man. 'Let me go, for my Lord God is sufficient for me: He who neither keeps a grudge nor forgets.'

The Caliph, perceiving the sincere piety of his companion, exclaimed, 'I am 'Abd al-Malik! Depend upon me, and tell me what you want.'

'Unhappy that we are, oh, 'Abd al-Malik,' cried the old man, 'let us both hasten to lay our wants before Him whom we both serve.' The Caliph departed. He followed the old man's counsel, and was well pleased that he did so.

Conclusion of the Dialogue of al-Walid

When al-Walid ibn Yazid heard this discourse, he was struck with the talent and broad-ranging erudition of the stranger, and inquired his name. Having heard it and realizing that it was unknown to him, the Caliph was overcome with shame. 'Assuredly', he said, 'that prince must be walking in darkness who has among his subjects a man like you and is not aware of it.'

'Oh, Commander of the Faithful', replied the stranger, 'those are only known to kings who present themselves before them, and station themselves at their gates.'

'In God's name', resumed the Caliph, 'seek not to offer excuses which we do not deserve.' He then gave him an expensive present, made out a written order enabling him to appear at court at all times and received the counsels dictated by his wisdom and experience with great attention until what happened to him came to pass, which is known to every one.

Al-Ma'mun and the Old Persian

It is related that when the Commander of the Faithful, Muhammad al-Amin, desired to deny his brother 'Abdallah al-Ma'mun — then Governor of Khorasan — succession to the Caliphate, he summoned him to his presence. Al-Amin informed his brother that he needed to confide on a matter of great importance. He therefore required him to set out immediately for Baghdad, leaving in his stead in Khorasan a man capable of governing the province with a firm hand. Simultaneously, al-Ma'mun's spies in the capital reported that al-Amin wished to deprive him of the succession and declare his own son, Musa, presumptive heir to the Caliphate.

Having received this news, al-Ma'mun took counsel with his ministers, who endeavoured to amuse the Caliph and gain time by pretending that the vast territory of Khorasan — surrounded as it was by infidel nations constantly on the watch for an opportunity to attack it — prevented his immediate departure. Finally, by pleading that he did not know whom else to trust, al-Amin wrote again to urge al-Ma'mun to come at once, adding that he would keep him but a very short time in Baghdad and only required him to benefit from his counsel on a matter of such importance that he could not commit it to writing. Al-Ma'mun showed these letters to his advisors and, having consulted them as to his course of action, was struck by their silence. Al-Ma'mun replied much to the same effect as before.

Meanwhile, al-Amin's spies in Khorasan sent word that al-Ma'mun, perceiving the snare, was prepared to repel force by force and maintained a defensive posture, with all his ministers agreeing on the need to resist. Al-Amin, therefore, despairing for not being able to ensnare his brother, cast into prison as many of al-Ma'mun's household, partisans and friends as were in Baghdad, and seized whatever of their fortune he could find.

When al-Ma'mun heard what had transpired he was much troubled, and again summoned a council of his advisors. The latter persisted in the advice they had given him earlier, encouraging the ruler to stand firm and wait for better days. He followed their counsel. Al-Amin, concluding that his brother was so determined to resist, summoned his subjects to pay homage to his infant son Musa — who received the surname of 'al-Natiq bil-Haq' ('He who speaks according to Eternal Truth'). (As some learned men have observed, Musa could speak neither truth nor falsehood.) The Caliph's subjects all acquiesced and swore allegiance to the child.

Al-Amin committed the education of his child to 'Ali ibn 'Isa ibn Mahan, who had been Governor of Khorasan for a long time. Having ruled well and ingratiated himself with the nobles through liberal policies, he retained a considerable following in the country. When the Caliph questioned him about the state of Khorasan, Ibn Mahan informed his ruler on the subject and concluded by saying that if he, 'Ali, had gone thither, no two men in Khorasan would have refused to obey the Caliph. Al-Amin thereupon named him Governor of Khorasan (and of all the other countries he could occupy), entrusted him with large sums of money, the greater part of his forces and arms and ammunition to accomplish his objective.

Once informed of these preparations, al-Ma'mun hesitated, doubting that his forces could oppose 'Ali ibn 'Isa. He then mounted his horse and proceeded to a country residence where his ministers were deliberating on measures to adopt in this emergency. A decrepit old man, who was by birth a Persian and by religion a Zoroastrian, presented himself before al-Ma'mun to demand justice for some wrong that he had received. Moved to compassion by his advanced age, al-Ma'mun commanded that he should be mounted and follow in his train to the country residence, where he should be brought into his presence.

When, therefore, al-Ma'mun gathered with his ministers in the hall of council, the old man was conducted thither and the prince asked him to sit on the cushions. Turning to his counsellors, he informed them of the steps taken by al-Amin: the imprisonment of his adherents, seizure of his property and mission of 'Ali ibn 'Isa ibn Mahan. Al-Ma'mun spoke freely, assuming the old man did not understand Arabic and that, moreover, being advanced in age and anxious to settle his own affairs he would not have cared to listen to those that occupied the council. The ministers, meanwhile, concluded that al-Ma'mun entertained no suspicion of this stranger and felt free to discuss their views openly.

They debated measures to be taken. One minister said: 'For my part, I think that we ought to levy foreign troops against 'Ali ibn 'Isa.

'I think,' said another, turning to al-Ma'mun, 'that you ought to instantly send off express messengers to ask the Caliph's pardon and submit yourself to his will today, looking for God's help tomorrow; for if it is obvious to everyone that you are compelled to yield your right to succession, and will have incontestable proof upon which to rest your claims whenever you may be able to do so.'

'My advice,' said a third, 'is, to assemble all your faithful partisans and, to obviate their scruples, lead them to attack one of the infidel kingdoms around us, where if we fight resolutely we may hope that God will grant us victory. When we have thus made ourselves masters of a powerful state — which will serve as a sure refuge — all those inclined to our party in the empire of the Caliph will align themselves to us, and we shall be able to continue the holy war until God's objective is accomplished.'

Another said: 'Let us shut ourselves up in a fortress from where we can defend ourselves, and await our opportunity.'

Lastly, another suggested: 'In my opinion, O Emir, the best plan would be to take refuge with the King of the Ottomans, and ask him for protection and assistance against a false and treacherous brother. Do not all princes act thus when they are threatened by dangers from which they see no escape?'

This expedient pleased al-Ma'mun much at first sight; he was about to adopt it, but paused to reflect. 'Shall I thus be the first to open a path to the Ottomans, to make war on Muslims?' he exclaimed, then asked his counsellors to leave him.

Al-Ma'mun, turning towards the old Persian, called on him to approach. Requesting an interpreter, he inquired with much kindness who he was and what he wanted. The old man, however, replied in Arabic, 'O, Emir, I came before you on business of my own, but I have found here more important business worthy of greater attention.'

To which al-Ma'mun replied: 'Speak freely of all that is in your mind according to the rules of wisdom.'

'O Emir,' resumed the old man, 'when I presented myself before you, I could by no means have been mistaken for an admirer; but since then God has filled my heart with great affection towards you.

'It is said that affection is of three kinds: the first and most comprehensive that embraces man is that which springs from our origin, namely, love of God, the Maker and Creator of all things. The second is the result of benefits, namely, that which is felt towards a benefactor. The third is the offspring of coincidence, and is, in turn, of two classes: friendship, closely resembling original love in that it embraces the inward and outward man, and love of the subject for his sovereign and of the slave for his master. Now, be it known to you, O Emir, whom I pray God to exalt, that I feel myself bound to you by three kinds of affection: that which embraces the inward and outward man, that which springs from benefits received and that which arises from coincidence.

'If you will accept my affection, fulfill my hope, gratify my desire, clothe me with the mantle of your confidence and honour me with the privilege of being numbered amongst your intimate friends, you will do so out of pure generosity and without having any need of me. Yet your servant hopes to be able to repay your benefits by his gratitude, and your condescension by his sincere affection and truthful counsels.'

'What religion do you practice?' inquired the ruler. 'I am a Zoroastrian,' replied the old man, who thereupon observed al-Ma'mun bend his head and ponder his words. 'Do not scorn me, O Emir,' he continued, 'either on account of the lowliness of my station or of the abhorrence in which you hold my faith.

'It was said: Never refuse a partisan, whomever he may be, because he will be able to serve you. He can either be a noble or a man of low station. If the former, he will be an ornament to your dignity. If the latter, he will defend your life and wealth.

'Moreover, when I spoke of my low station compared to you, I did not mean this to apply either to my character or to my origin. As to my character it rests with you, O Emir, to test it whenever you please. As to my origin, you should know that I am a Brahmin, of the race of Brahman, Prince of the Kings of Persia, and holding an intermediate place between them and the Great First Cause. My words were merely intended to express that my religion may appear contemptible in your eyes, and that I live under the yoke of vassalage and as a tributary in an inferior station.'

'We feel no aversion towards you,' replied the Emir, 'and if you choose to pass from this condition of vassalage into our faith, we will find an appropriate station for you.'

'I sincerely desire that which you propose,' replied the old man, 'but not at present. Perhaps I may at a later date. In the meantime, if you will allow me to comment on the subject which you just discussed with your counsellors, I may be able to shed light on it.'

'Speak', replied al-Ma'mun.

'I have listened, O Emir, to all the counsels of your ministers. They have struggled to hit the mark, but none of their suggestions have satisfied me.'

'Let me hear yours, then,' said al-Ma'mun.

'Amongst the maxims that my forefathers inherited from their ancestors, I find this one,' said the old man: 'That the prudent man, when threatened by a danger so great that he is unable to avert it, ought to commit steadfastly to His wisdom because He divides every man's share equitably. Thus, if the prudent one does not obtain victory he will at least protect himself from blame.'

'Old man', interrupted al-Ma'mun, 'it is said that he who does not know the truth cannot give counsel. We have granted you our confidence without knowing you by experience, and this, not because we neglect the dictates of prudence, but because we give you a mark of our favour by speaking openly to you in pledge of your acceptance of our offer. We will now tell you, therefore, that the man sent forth against us, 'Ali ibn 'Isa ibn Mahan, has more power than we do in this country. Moreover, if we would, we could not possibly oppose him, as the necessary funds are lacking.'

'O Emir', replied the old man, 'you must banish all these thoughts from your mind, and give no heed to those who have suggested them. It is said: "He who has waged great injustice shall not flourish. He who is strengthened by malice shall not endure. He who is raised to the throne through violence shall not reign." I will now relate to you the history of one who reaped advantages that, if his example fits your case, you may likewise obtain.'

'Relate it,' said al-Ma'mun, and the old man continued.

The King of the White Huns and Firuz, King of Persia

Khush-nawaz, King of the Hephthalites, wished to set free Firuz, son of Yezdejird and King of Persia, whom he had taken prisoner. He concluded an agreement to the effect that Firuz should never fight him nor seek to injure him by treachery. He further placed on the Hephthalite border a block of stone, which Firuz bound himself by a solemn oath never to pass. Adhering to this compact, the king of the Hephthalites allowed Firuz to leave. However, no sooner had the latter reached his capital than, burning with shame and regardless of the treaty, he resolved to declare war anew against Khush-nawaz.

Having laid this proposal before his ministers, they warned him against any violation of the compact, arguing that he would draw upon himself the fate reserved for the unjust. These objections did not shake Firuz's goal and, when reminded of the conditions agreed upon with Khush-nawaz, he said: 'I swore never to pass that stone. Well, then, I will have it borne by an elephant at the head of my army, and thus not one of my soldiers shall cross it.' The ministers, seeing him so passionately bent on achieving his goal, concluded that Firuz's judgment was enthralled by covetousness. They remained silent, therefore, and vowed not to raise the subject any more.

It is said: 'He who is too fond of his own counsel shall err and he who exalts himself above others shall be humbled. Strong passions obscure one's judgment and prevent from reflecting on the truth.'

'Passion, before it reaches obstinacy, is like a high; but when it becomes obstinate, it is like reeling drunkenness.'

'He who is passion's slave cannot keep to the straight path, for the outbreaks of his covetousness and anger cast a veil over his understanding. Because passion, as the firmer tyrant, has a far stronger hold upon the soul than understanding, whose influence is acquired and more recent. Two reasons may impede understanding: covetousness and anger. If one is not obscured by both, it never fails to watch over passion, and even to control it. But if one is blinded by them, passion reaches absolute mastery, and requires special attention.'

'Firuz', continued the aged Persian, 'assembled his four military chiefs, each of whom commanded fifty thousand men and governed one of the four quarters of the kingdom of Babel. He ordered them to prepare for war against the Hephthalites. When the preparations were completed, Firuz advanced in person against Khush-nawaz with a powerful following. He believed himself invincible and, in fact, the king of the Hephthalites could not muster sufficient forces to oppose even one of Firuz's military chiefs. Nevertheless, the Hephthalites had obtained victory before through a stratagem that need not be related at this juncture.

'Meanwhile the Mobedan-mobed — title of the chief priest of the faith who was considered as a prophet by the Persians — seeing Firuz preparing for war against Khush-nawaz, had said to him: "O King, refrain from this enterprise. The Lord of the earth is tolerant with princes, so long as the abuses they commit do not shake the foundations of His holy laws. But He does not permit them to carry on with their wickedness to excess. The respect for conquests and the inviolability of treaties are part of the fundamental laws of religion. Beware, therefore, O King, of exceeding your authority."

'But Firuz ignored this admonition as well as the warnings of his most faithful adherents, and chose to act according to his own caprice.'

It is said that five indications presage the fall of a king: First, if he believes gossip and those who cannot foresee the consequences of actions; second, if he turns against those whom he ought to love; third, if his revenues are not sufficient for his station; fourth, if he favours one and dismisses another for capricious reasons, not upon reflection; and fifth, if he despises the counsels of men of wisdom and experience.

It is further said: 'He who will not listen to a faithful friend, makes himself an enemy.'

'A man will adopt or reject a prudent measure according to his capacity for reflection. He who has much, goes forward in the strength of reason, while he whose brain is weak is dragged along by the force of passion. And he who acts without reflection deserves to be counted among beasts.'

The aged Persian thus continued his narrative: 'Firuz, advancing against Khush-nawaz, reached the confines of his kingdom at the spot where stood the stone he had sworn never to cross. He ordered it removed and placed upon the back of an elephant that was to march at the head of the army. It was strictly forbidden for anyone to advance in front of it. Firuz had not gone far from the spot, however, when a servant informed him that one of his highest-ranking knights had, against all reason and justice, cruelly put to death a poor man.

'The man's brother appeared soon after, entreating and imploring Firuz to grant him the vengeance of the law against the slayer. The king commanded that a sum of money should be offered him as the price of blood. But the brother replied: "No, nothing but the blood of my brother's murderer can satisfy me." When Firuz dismissed him, the man sought the knight and rushed upon him with a *khanjar* (dagger) in hand. The knight turned and fled upon seeing the weapon.

'Firuz was informed of these circumstances. While he was considering them, the wisest of his ministers suddenly dismounted his horse and kneeled down before the king. When Firuz asked what he wanted, the minister implored a private audience on a subject of great importance. The king requested that a small tent be pitched immediately and, having dismounted and entered, he called the minister and asked that the matter be explicated.

"Most fortunate Prince", said the minister, "may you reign over the seven climates of the earth, and live the life of 'Umar Byurasib, with similar glory and power. The will of the Almighty is now manifest to you by the example that he has placed before your eyes. This brave knight turned to flight at the approach of a poor rascal armed with a *khanjar*. What could have caused his flight but the consciousness of his own guilt and injustice?"

"No", replied the king, "he did not run away because he feared his assailant, but because he feared us, who are not accustomed to leave such guilty deeds go unpunished."

"If it is so, O King", replied the minister, "I would suggest that you summon the knight to confront this man in single combat, assuring him full security. Were this poor devil to conquer, would you not consider it a warning sent to you by Him who sustains all worlds?"

"I will assuredly do so," replied Firuz.

Having summoned the knight, Firuz sought to encourage him, and commanded him to confront his accuser. A duel was proposed to the latter, who appeared pleased and eager for it. Bystanders sought to frighten him but in vain, saying to him: "Do you not see his coat of mail, his arms and his steed? Have you not heard the fame of his skill in horsemanship, of his courage and of his enthusiasm in combat? You are committing suicide and going in quest of your death. We wash our hands of your fate."

But the poor man replied, "Leave us alone to deal with one another, for he is mounted on the steed of vanity, I on that of truth; he is clothed with the mail of doubt, I with that of confidence; he brandishes the sword of evil, I that of justice."

"In truth", said the minister, turning to the king, "this man's words are an example and a warning more obvious than even his anticipated victory in the duel. I entreat you, therefore, to retain your knight and save his life. Do not expose him to perish in the encounter with this poor fellow.

"As for him, O King, persuade him to accept some compensation for his brother's death; and if he will not consent, then do justice yourself with your known impartiality. You may thus obtain remission of the punishment destined you by the Almighty, in consideration of your readiness to render the justice which gains His approval, as much as every deviation from it excites His wrath."

But Firuz replied, "The single combat must take place. You will see how it will end if this poor man is still willing to abide by the trial."

A duel was, therefore, once more offered to the poor man, who desired it as ardently as before. Although it was repeated that he was going to meet his own death, these attempts to alarm him only increased his courage and eagerness for the contest. "Forward, then", cried the bystanders to the knight, "fear him not."

The two men advanced against each other, and in the first encounter, the foot-soldier seized the bridle of the horse. The horseman was about to deal a blow with his sword when the poor man avoided it by stooping his head, and the weapon barely inflicted a very slight wound on his back. Then, springing on his adversary, the poor man thrust at the horseman's throat with a *khanjar*, seized him, dragged him from his mount and, stretching him on the ground, dealt him a second blow that drove some of his coat of mail links into his stomach. The horseman was thus killed.

Firuz spent the whole night on the spot, reflecting upon what had occurred. Nevertheless, he convinced himself to be guided by passion, and proceeded with his plan.'

It is said that 'passion starts easy but ends miserably;'

'Passion is a tyrant that slays those whom it governs. It is like fire, which, once thoroughly kindled, can scarcely be quenched; or like the torrent, which, when it is swollen, can no longer be restrained within its banks;'

'A man is a prisoner if he has been put in fetters by his enemy, or if his own passions overpower him, hurrying him to destruction.'

'Khush-nawaz', continued the old man, 'having heard of Firuz's hostile movements, regained his composure and committed himself into His hands — who is the beginning and the end of all things — imploring him to vindicate the treaties, the sanctity of which Firuz had violated, mocking the consequences his treachery would entail. Simultaneously, Firuz took all the necessary prudent measures to strengthen his confines, assembled his forces and ordered the necessary preparations for war. He then waited until the enemy, having scoured the greater part of his territories, reached the very heart of his kingdom, sacking and spoiling so as to rouse the hatred of his subjects against the invaders. Then Khush-nawaz, leading his army, caught Firuz unaware; joining him in battle, he defeated Firuz and put him to flight. Khush-nawaz liberated the occupied provinces, slaughtered Firuz's followers, seized their wealth and pursued Firuz on his track. He overtook him, put him to death and captured his family along with his chief adherents. Khush-nawaz thus concluded the campaign with complete victory.'

Conclusion of the Adventure of al-Ma'mun

Al-Ma'mun, appreciating the example laid before him by the old Persian, cheerfully replied: 'Your discourse is graceful and pleasant to our ears, and we thank you for it. What do you think of the hint we gave you, to lead you to confess the unity of God, who has enlarged your understanding; opened your mind to reflection; loosed your tongue to utter words of wisdom; and taken from you every pretext for remaining in ignorance of His revealed will by sending Muhammad upon earth (upon whom, as well as upon all those who are his disciples, be the peace and blessing of God)?'

'That there is no God but God, and that Muhammad is His Messenger,' replied the old man.

Al-Ma'mun, delighted by this conversion, loaded the old man with gifts, gave him an honourable post in his own palace, numbered him amongst his most intimate friends and wished that he should be always present at his court. A few days later, the old man was summoned by the Lord. Al-Ma'mun − having followed his counsel − prospered as God rewarded him with his wishes to ascend to the throne of the Caliphs.

2

Fortitude

Verses From the Holy Qur'an

Amongst the most noted chapters of our Lord's revelation is one titled 'The Confederate Tribes,' that contains several marvellous verses concerning the subject of this chapter, namely, consolation to princes in times of public calamity. Praise be to God, who has guided and directed our minds towards these verses. In allusion to those who sought the destruction of His vicar (the apostle of His doctrine and counsels) on earth, and to the instability of Muslims whose eyes were dimmed and minds polluted by evil thoughts concerning God, the divine author thus writes:

They attacked you from above you and from below, so that your eyes were blurred, your hearts leapt up to your throats, and your faith in God was shaken. There the faithful were put to the proof; there they were severely afflicted. (33:10–11)

And when hypocrisy unveiled itself, and hypocrites (beholding the faithful in this strait and confusion) boldly manifested that which they had concealed, God said:

The hypocrites and the faint-hearted said: 'God and His apostle made us promises only to deceive us.' (33:12)

And, again, addressing those who refused to defend the faith and abandoned those who were willing to doing so:

God well knows those of you who hold the others back; who say to their comrades: 'Join our side,' and seldom take part in the fighting, being ever reluctant to assist you. (33:18)

Likewise,

Others said: 'People of Yathrib [Madinah], you cannot stand much longer. Go back to your city.' And yet others sought the Prophet's leave, saying, 'Our homes are defenceless,' while they were not defenceless. They only wished to flee.' (33:13)

And concerning merchants who seek their profit in war and are ready to follow everyone who speaks, and to support every new leader, God has said: 'Had the city been entered from every quarter, and had they been roused to rebellion, they would have surely rebelled. But they would have occupied it only for a little while.' (33:14)

And concerning the inability to resist the power of fate, God has said:

Say: 'Nothing will your flight await you. If you escaped from death or slaughter, you would enjoy this world only for a little while.' (33:16)

Say: 'Who can protect you from God if it is His will to scourge you? And who can prevent Him from showing you mercy?' They shall find none besides God to protect or help them. (33:17)

All these verses touch the conditions of those tested by great tragedies. But God has pointed out a path to those thus troubled, through the teachings of his apostle. God has said:

There is a good example in God's apostle for those of you who look to God and the Last Day and remember God always. (33:21)

As fortitude was one of the virtues enjoined on the apostle, the most sublime of authors addressed him in the following words:

We know too well that what they say grieves you. It is not you that they are disbelieving; the evil-doers deny God's own revelations. Other apostles have been denied before you. But they patiently bore with disbelief and persecution until Our help came down to them; for none can change the decrees of God. You have already heard of those apostles. (6:34)

God, whose name be praised, told His apostle that, if he lost courage and ceased to exhibit this virtue in all his actions, nothing that he undertook would ever succeed; and He said:

If you find their aversion hard to bear, seek if you can a chasm in the earth or a ladder to the sky by which you may bring them a sign. (6:35)

And the Lord made him understand that it was his duty to endure the injuries of unbelievers with unflinching fortitude, saying:

Had God pleased, He would have given them guidance, one and all. Do not be foolish, then. (6:35)

And afterwards,

Those were the men whom God guided. Follow then their guidance and say: 'I demand of you no recompense for this. It is but an admonition to all mankind.' (6:90)

This, then, is a subject that admits no doubts. It is related that the Prophet was accustomed to saying, 'God has instructed me and I have been taught a great lesson.' And this lesson, this positive precept, was fortitude, such as we have set forth.

Traditions of the Prophet Concerning Fortitude

'Look at those who are beneath you, not those who are above you, for we should not despise God's blessings.'

These words of the Prophet have been handed down to us and they apply exactly to the present subject. Yet to understand them properly, we must not confine ourselves to the letter of the precept and neglect its spirit or its general applicability. It is assuredly of general application, since it enjoins one to turn his eyes upon those less fortunate; and to one who is afflicted, to consider those troubled with a worse calamity. Thus, there is little doubt that the less fortunate are more oppressed by poverty.

Whoever enjoys a larger share of fortune's favours, or of any kind of personal and social advantages, is happy. Likewise, in adversity, one is fortunate if his lot is less severe than that of another, and if he is exempted from harder trials to which another is subjected. Such considerations tend to inspire fortitude by familiarizing the individual who suffers from every calamity to compare his burdens to those of others. Thus not only will his misfortune appear less terrible, but he will even be awakened to gratitude towards God, who has spared him additional miseries. Such a feeling is of a higher order than simple fortitude, that neither entails the satisfaction of thankfulness nor gives rise to the confidence founded on an appreciation of happiness, but leads merely to endurance. The fortitude inculcated by the aforementioned tradition is that which gives birth at once to endurance and thankfulness.

Philosophical Maxims Concerning Fortitude

Fortitude is misfortune's heaven; the virtue of noble men.

Fortitude serves as a stepping stone to patience, even as despondency leads to perdition.

Let him who has understanding consider this world's wealth as borrowed goods, which must be restored; as treasures held in trust, which may be reclaimed. If he does not consider them as such, he will be weighed down with grief at their loss and will stigmatize the sovereign benefactor who deprives him, as a tyrant.

Let him not forget that all men have a right to share in the goods of this world and to enjoy them in turn. If riches should therefore pass from his hands into those of others, let him not complain of those who accept that which falls to their destiny. But let him take comfort, and endure their good fortune with the same patience with which they formerly beheld his wealth and their own poverty.

And to that end the Qur'an recommends alms-giving, lending, hospitality and all the various kinds of assistance which may be rendered by means of wealth, power, or influence. For the good of the benefactors who, by sharing a part of their possessions with neighbours, secure the rest.

There are several philosophical maxims herein, for those who choose to meditate upon them, as assistance must be sought from God alone.

A king once shared the following verses during a period of great tribulation:

'Behold us in your company, O sage, who has received instruction from the smiles and frowns of fortune; although our race is illustrious and powerful.'

'Ours is a lofty spirit, accustomed to the vicissitudes of fate; so that it can find comfort even when it appears as though all consolation were denied us.'

Then, during one of his periods of sorrow, he recited these verses:

'Fortune smiled upon me. But it did not inspire me to remain long her friend.

'She then turned her back upon me. But it could not overpower me, as her cruelties failed to draw one word of lamentation.

'Let us praise God for His wisdom.'

Then, turning to me:

'Now complete that verse,' he said; and I rejoined:

'For my strength is in Him, and from Him are derived my powers of action.'

Another day, when I was arguing a proposition on fortitude, he recited several more verses and I, in turn, added the following, written by the poetess al-Khansa':

'Never shall I be able to forget you, O Saqr, until I bid farewell to life and go to visit my tomb.

'The rising sun reminds me of Saqr, and I remember him every time that I see it set.

'Had I not been surrounded by so many who wept for those they loved, I should undoubtedly have slain myself with my own hands.

'Alas! None of those whom they bewailed resembled my brother; yet by fortitude I have lightened my sorrow for his loss.'

'These verses,' said the king to me, 'are more appropriate than those of Taylasan ibn Hirb. Listen.' Then he recited the following verses:

'We roll onward in waves of plenty like the Nile; our advance is like the clash of swords.

'And if some heavy calamity befall us, we endure it with fortitude, as is the duty of lofty souls.'

Sapor, King of Persia, and the Roman Emperor

It is related that Sapor ibn Hormuz ibn Narsi ibn Ardashir, known as Sapor al-Aktaf, resolved to enter the Roman Empire in disguise to explore it. His more faithful counsellors sought to dissuade him, arguing that he ought not to hazard his own person in an enterprise that might be undertaken by others. Sapor, however, rejecting their counsel, ordered them to keep his design secret and prepared to carry it out.

It was said that no one is to be pitied more than ministers serving underage monarchs or old men in love with maidens.

It is hard for the young to advance from the blindness of passion to the straight path of counsel, for two reasons: first, because their desires exercise a despotic power over them; second, because experience has not yet settled in to control their energies and teach them to resist passion's influence, as do the wise.

The reason why anger and desire have so much power over the mind, is because they accompany it from the hour of birth. This is not the case with understanding, which is bestowed upon the mind at a later period. As a latecomer, understanding has much more difficulty gaining mastery over the mind. Therefore, he who seeks to give advice to a man inflamed with anger or desire will have little success, because the haze of these two passions obscures understanding's light, just like drunkenness.

Sapor, preparing for his journey, selected as his companion a counsellor who had earlier served his father. He was a man of mature years; astute; firm; clear-sighted; experienced in business; a theologian; and well-versed in languages, literature, science and the stratagems of war. Sapor ordered him to prepare everything he needed in order to undertake the journey – although he wished the advisor to travel separately, remaining nearby to watch over the ruler's safety by day and night.

They set out on their journey towards Damascus. The counsellor, who spoke the language of Galicia, disguised himself as a monk and, having some knowledge of surgery, carried a certain Chinese balsam which, being applied to a wound, caused it to heal instantly. Several witnesses have declared that they have seen the efficacy of this remedy, and one in particular related that in order to test it, the counsellor had on one occasion inflicted a very slight cut upon himself. On anointing it with this balsam, the wound healed immediately.

During his journey, and even after crossing the confines of the Roman Empire, the counsellor had cured several wounded persons merely by applying to their wounds a little of this balsam, which instantly produced its healing effect. If those he cured were men of fortune, he took still greater pains to attend them and, having done so, refused to accept any reward. He thus gained good will and earned the reputation of a pious and learned man.

It was said: 'He who plants the seeds of knowledge, shall reap fame; self-denial will lead to glory; reflection to wisdom; gravity to reverence, caution to security; pride to hatred; avarice to contempt; ambition to shame; and envy to a crumbling heart.'

It was said: 'Notwithstanding the differences of time, place, and creed, all nations prized four virtues: learning, self-denial, generosity and honesty.'

Sapor and his counsellor reached Constantinople separately, as the latter was watching his sovereign with utmost vigilance. In Constantinople, the counsellor sought an audience with the Patriarch, the religious head of the city and, having obtained one, explained that he had left Galicia to obtain the privilege of entering his service. Simultaneously, he offered the Patriarch a costly present with which the latter was greatly pleased. The stranger was granted much courtesy, as the Patriarch bestowed upon him his friendship, lodged him sumptuously, admitted him amongst his intimate associates and, appreciating his intellectual capabilities, held him in the highest esteem and admiration. The counsellor, for his part, applied himself to study the Patriarch's character to further ingratiate himself by propitiating his taste with wares for which it would afford a useful outlet and which his dupe – the Patriarch – would readily swallow.

It was also said: 'If you wish to ingratiate yourself with a great man, first take notice of what may serve to attract him and to find favour in his eyes. Once you are prepared to practice them and he has received you honourably, take courage and set to work. Otherwise, remain cautious until the right moment when you are sure to secure the prize. Then strike the blow.'

Having studied the Patriarch, the counsellor concluded that his weak points were commentaries on canon law, but that he was also enthralled by narratives of marvellous adventures. So he began to dazzle him with abundant tales and curious anecdotes. The counsellor had little trouble gaining the Patriarch's good will and close affection.

Meanwhile, he continued to practice surgery for free, which increased his reputation with the public at large.

It was said: 'If it is true that we are naturally inclined to love our benefactors, then that love is a form of servitude because bondage is repugnant to free men. In truth, he who delivers himself from his benefactor's affection may consider himself free. By striving to the utmost of his ability to compensate for such subjugation, and even if his powers are not sufficient to affect this change, the pains he has taken to do so will free him from all blame.'

The counsellor continued without fail to exert himself for the sake of his prince. When it was announced that Caesar was planning a great banquet to which Roman citizens were invited, Sapor wished to attend as well. He hoped to meet Caesar, become acquainted with the regulations of the court and appraise the splendid decorations of the palace. The counsellor endeavoured, but in vain, to dissuade him from exposing himself to this new peril. Sapor assumed a disguise, insisting it would be impossible to recognize him, and presented himself at the palace along with other guests. It should be remembered that Caesar, having heard of the singular gifts which God had bestowed upon Sapor — sagacity, magnanimity and courage, all earned from childhood — had long been on his guard. Caesar had even sent to the capital of Persia a skillful artist to draw Sapor's images on various occasions when he had been able to observe him, such as when seated in his palace, on horseback and in other similar circumstances. Caesar had authorized the reproduction of these images on carpets, curtains, plates and goblets.

Sapor entered the palace and was seated at a table with several other guests. After the meals were served, drinks were handed to each guest in goblets of crystal, gold, silver and solid glass. Amongst those present was a Roman of much wisdom and penetration and an excellent profiler. Seeing Sapor, and not knowing him, he began to examine his features, demeanour and general appearance. The Roman thought he perceived in him something of a princely character. This induced him to scrutinize Sapor more closely. He kept his eyes steadfastly fixed on him until, as the goblets were carried round, one was handed him, which carried the portrait of the King of Persia. The profiler examined it closely and, struck by the resemblance which it bore to the stranger's features, he became convinced that the latter could be no other than Sapor himself. He thus remained for some time holding the cup in his hand.

Then, raising his voice, he declared: 'The likeness that is sculptured on this goblet has imparted to me a marvellous piece of news.'

'What is it, what is it?' asked everyone, and the Roman resumed:

'This portrait informs me that the original is here amongst us, seated at table.' He fixed his eyes upon Sapor. At these words, Sapor's facial appearance changed. The profiler mingled with other guests, convinced of the truth of his suspicions, and repeated his charges so as to be heard by Caesar. Having summoned him to approach, the Roman affirmed to Caesar that Sapor was there in his presence and pointed him out. Caesar, therefore, ordered the stranger to be arrested and interrogated. As Sapor endeavoured to elude inquiry under various pretexts, the profiler kept repeating: 'Do not believe him, for he is Sapor; there is no doubt about it.' Caesar then ordered Sapor to be put to death, which terrified the Persian into finally acknowledging his identity.

It was said: 'A ruler's understanding penetrates mysteries in the twinkling of an eye. For first indications uncover ultimate consequences.'

Likewise: 'As the eye is a mirror upon which objects are etched, so the mind, if unsullied by the weight of passion, is a mirror upon which are similarly imprinted the images of many things that do not fall under the recognition of the senses.'

Amongst the arguments that prove God sometimes reveals to the human intellect that which is to come, may be this one: When a man expects something he neither desires nor abhors, he frequently sees it materialize nearly as he had envisaged it. The same thing occurs when, at first sight, we are conscious of a feeling of affection towards one who has done us no good, and of aversion towards one who has done us no harm, and that in time we do, in fact, receive a benefit from the one and an injury from the other.

Sapor acknowledged the veracity of the profiler's assertion and Caesar had him imprisoned, though treated with respect. Caesar then gave orders for the construction of a machine in the form of an enormous bull, to be made of seven coats of hide, with a small window underneath and a trap door in the back by which to go in and out and deliver food to anyone within. The wrists of the prisoner were then fettered with a chain of gold that hung from his neck but, being wrought in links, did not prevent him from making use of his hands to feed himself or for any other purpose. Sapor was thus lodged in the hollow interior of the bull.

Caesar, meanwhile, had assembled his forces in preparation for war against Persia. He assigned Sapor's custody to 100 of the strongest and most valiant men of his army, who were to carry this singular litter. A corporal was placed over every five men, and the whole party fell under the authority of the Metropolitan.[1] Sapor's bull was to be borne before the very eyes of the Metropolitan when the army was on the march. When it halted, it was to be placed in the midst of the encampment with a hut erected over it to conceal it from view. Fifty men of the guard, with their corporals, were to keep watch over the tent, with the remaining fifty to occupy ten other canopies pitched in a circle around it. The tent of the Metropolitan was to be placed beside that of Sapor; lastly, an awning would be spread near the circle to serve the whole party as a kitchen, where various meals would be prepared according to each individual's rank.

Everything concerning the guard was defined with the most rigorous precision. Caesar set forth, expecting to throw Persia into confusion and subdue it so effectively that not a vestige of the kingdom would be left − for, as was well known, it had no ruler to defend it.

It was said: 'To hide from an adversary while wind and fortune favour him is rationalized prudence. Likewise, it is considered foolishness to let slip an opportunity when fortune turns her back upon an opponent and the wind fails him.'

'The king who wallows in pleasure and allows opportunity to escape him will never attain success in state affairs.'

Kings should be distinguished from their subjects through merit rather than splendour. There are five virtues in which princes ought to excel all other men: paternal mercy, which should extend to all their subjects; vigilance, which should embrace and watch over them; courage, to defend them when

---

1. A title that signifies the ruler of a province but is confined to Orthodox ecclesiastics and, accurately speaking, means the vicar of the Patriarch.

attacked; sagacity, to delude their enemies; and prudence, to take advantage of every opportunity. As for superior luxury, it may be displayed by kings in the splendour of their dwellings, the elegance of their attire, the value and rarity of their jewels, the gaiety and brilliance of their feasts and the beauty and measured steps of their horses. All these luxuries will be, in their ways, superior to those of others. But they will only exalt the respective merits of the palace, the garment, the jewel, the kitchen, or the stable. They cannot confer greatness upon their possessor.

Caesar having set forth, and Sapor in the plight described, the counsellor addressed the Patriarch as follows:

'Most reverend Father, I sought to approach you, and to enter your service on account of my eager desire for good works. But is there any work more meritorious than to lighten the burden of the afflicted, and afford assistance to those who stand most in need of it? You know, O Father, that I am not unskilled in the treatment of the wounded, and my soul longs to follow Caesar on this expedition, for perhaps it might please God, through my means, to save some good Christian from death so that I might afterwards obtain divine mercy for his sake; that my heart might be sanctified by the service rendered him and that through him, I might be preserved.'

This request greatly displeased the Patriarch. 'You know,' he said, 'that I cannot bear you to be absent from me one moment, and yet you come and ask me to let you go upon so distant a journey. Indeed, I did not think that you would ever have wished to displease me, and to lay upon me a burden, which I cannot sustain; nor did I believe that you would have preferred anything in this world to my friendship and my company. You have now altered the good opinion that I had of you.'

The counsellor remained steadfast and persuaded the Patriarch to grant him all that he desired. Not only did he let him accompany his party, but he even provided him with all his needs for the long journey. The Patriarch even wrote a letter to the Metropolitan, to the effect that he was sending him the apple of his eye and, therefore, he was to hold him in the highest honour and to have recourse to his counsel in every obscure matter.

In time, the counsellor presented himself to the Metropolitan, who treated him as he was duty-bound to and lodged him in his own tent. The astute counsellor proceeded to draw from his stores such wares as he knew the Metropolitan would most appreciate, and began to propitiate him by adapting himself to all his tastes. Every evening he entertained him with amusing stories, raising his voice so as to be heard by Sapor. He thus provided his prince diversion, while at the same time he wove into these stories such information as he desired him to receive, including secrets he deemed necessary to impart. By doing so, he consoled the prisoner. The counsellor, those sole object was to effect his master's liberation, had already devised many intrigues for this purpose, all of them based on the Metropolitan's esteem.

It was said: 'The king who believes that the minds of princes are superior to those of counsellors has fallen into great error. If he gets into the bad habit of contradicting a wise and faithful counsellor – without manifest reason – it is certain that he will never prosper. For counsellors have in general more shrewdness and penetration than princes, as the latter have only to attend to the management of their subjects whereas counsellors are obliged to devote attention to both sovereign and people at once. Thus, kings resemble those animals trained to the chase that, indeed, pursue and seize their prey. But they are hunted in turn by more ferocious animals which may be more skilled in guarding themselves from danger, tracking their victims and capturing them in their clutches.'

It was said: 'The counsellor who best understands his duty is the one who prepares for any consequences that, when they present themselves, he can deal with. Likewise, the worst counsellor is the one who, trusting his wit, the power of his cunning and his management experience, deems himself secure with no need to prepare ahead of time against any contingencies. He thus acts like a person who trusts his speaking skills, thinking capability and facility to improvise, who neglects to prepare an oration and to polish and study it beforehand. When he finds himself tongue-tied and unable to proceed in some academic session, he fails. Likewise, when a warrior, trusting his tried valour and the strength of his arm, frees himself from the weight of his armour, he is overcome and conquered by the enemy in a surprise struggle.'

One of the counsellor's artful devices was to refuse to dine with the Metropolitan, insisting that he would only eat the food furnished him by the Patriarch at the commencement of his journey. Moreover, he pretended to gain great spiritual benefits from this diet. When the Metropolitan's meals were served, he consumed a portion of his provisions, which he ate without ever partaking of anything else.

Meanwhile, Caesar entered the Persian dominions with his army, deluged the land with blood, dragged women into captivity, contaminated its waters, cut down trees and razed forts and villages to the ground. Without once pausing in his onslaught, he advanced straight to the capital to conquer it and, in one blow, arrest all its leaders. Caesar feared that his actions would induce them to appoint another ruler, who would be able to unite and defend them all against the invader. In the event, the Persians fled before the enemy reached the capital, and barricaded themselves up in their fortresses.

Caesar reached Sapor's city and capital of the empire, called Jundi-Shahpour. He laid siege to it and directed his catapults against the city. The town nobles could devise no other means of defence except to strengthen city walls and defend it from its elevated hills.

Sapor was soon acquainted with these events by deciphering the hidden communications he received from his counsellor, through various hints, enigmas and allegories interspersed throughout his tales (given that he had not spoken to him in person since his capture). On hearing that Caesar was already ruling the people of Jundi-Shahpour, that his catapults had breached city walls and that the conquest of the capital could no longer be delayed, Sapor's patience gave way. Mistrusting even his own counsellor, and in despair of ever escaping from his plight, he said to the keeper who brought him his food: 'This chain torments me so much that I can endure it no longer. Therefore, if you do not wish to kill me, loosen it a little, and tie some pieces of silk around my neck and wrists. You may fasten it around them.' Sapor sent away the keeper with the food, who showed it to the Metropolitan and repeated Sapor's words. The counsellor, who understood the despair and mistrust of the king, guessed his intent and applied himself to its execution.

That night, as the counsellor was seated with the Metropolitan and his companions, he said: 'This evening a marvellous tale recurs to my memory, that I have known for many years, and which, before my departure, I had meant to relate to the Patriarch.'

'Oh! Then, my judicious hermit, I beseech you to relate it to me,' replied the Metropolitan.

'As you will,' answered the counsellor and, raising his voice so as to be heard by Sapor, he began.

'Ayn Ahlih and the Old Woman

There lived in Galicia a young man and a young woman both of exceeding beauty, liveliness and intelligence. The young man's name was 'Ayn Ahlih ('Eye of His People'). The young woman was known as Sayidat al-Nar ("Matron of Fire"). Loving each other with tender affection, it appeared as if nothing in the world could have induced either one of them to leave the other.

One day 'Ayn Ahlih was sitting with a party of his friends when the conversation turned to women. Someone began to relate the wonders, beauty and vivacity of a woman whose name was Sitt al-Dhahab ('Matron of Wealth'). 'Ayn Ahlih, smitten with a fancy for her, asked his friend where she lived and, learning that her dwelling was in a neighbouring village, decided to look her up. He turned away from his wife, as his heart was filled with longing after this new love.

It is said: 'Understanding is unto the husband as the will is unto the wife and the body unto their dwelling. When understanding is an absolute master of will, the latter devotes its attention to provide for the good of the body to protect it from injury even as the woman, who is dominated by her husband, attends to herself, her children and her home, by which means they all prosper. But if, on the contrary, will prevails over understanding, its conduct will be evil, and its demeanour reprehensible, as is the case when a wife dominates her husband.'

'Ayn Ahlih hastened to Sitt al-Dhahab's village where he searched for her house with diligence and, once he located it, waited to spot her. He was struck with admiration and amazement at her beauty although she was not, in truth, more attractive than Sayidat al-Nar. Yet, it is said: 'One of the most irresistible impulses of the soul is to seek a change of condition. Change is introduced into a being, largely due to circumstances, but evolves into corruption through greed. A person who embarks on one change and effortlessly crosses into the other, must attain the condition most suitable in the intermediate state — between the starting point and the goal — if he is to prosper.'

Egged by his desire to contemplate Sitt al-Dhahab, 'Ayn Ahlih endlessly circled the house, looking for her. Naturally, his presence drew the notice of her husband, a Galician of fierce, rugged and violent disposition named Ad-Dib ('Grizzly'). The jealous husband surprised 'Ayn Ahlih, sprang upon him and slew his horse, ripped his garments, seized him by the throat and cruelly beat him. He then called for some of his friends, with whose assistance he carried 'Ayn Ahlih into a house, where the victim was bound to a pole supporting a tent. Ad-Dib consigned the stricken lover to the care of an old woman of sinister appearance who had been deprived of a hand, eye and her nose.

At nightfall, the old woman kindled a fire near 'Ayn Ahlih and sat down before it to warm herself. The poor youth, meanwhile, reflecting on the tranquil and happy life that he had hitherto led, sighed deeply, upon which the old woman asked, 'What sin is it that has driven you into the path of degradation and misery?'

'I am not aware that I have committed a sin,' replied 'Ayn Ahlih.

'Ah!' rejoined the old woman, 'it is thus that the horse once answered the wild boar but he would not believe him. When the horse had related all that had befallen him, he pointed out a circumstance of which the horse had never thought, so that at last he led him to confess his error.'

'If you would tell me how this came to pass, you would do me a great favour,' said 'Ayn Ahlih, and the old woman continued.

The Horse and the Wild Boar

It is related that a brave warrior owned a stallion that he fancied, and upon which he lavished much care, riding it on his most arduous journeys. The horseman could not bear to have the stallion out of his sight. Each morning, he would lead it to a meadow, where he took off its saddle and bridle, loosened its halter and let it graze and roll upon the grass until sunset, when he would again return it home.

One day, having gone out with the horse as usual, he dismounted and had scarcely set foot on the ground when the horse bolted and ran away with all its gear. The horseman could not stop it, notwithstanding his efforts to do so. Finally, having lost sight of it, he returned home, weary and despairing of ever recovering his horse. The animal, meanwhile, perceiving that he was no longer followed, stopped. As it was growing dark and as he started to feel hungry, the stallion attempted to graze but found that the bridle prevented him from doing so. He tried to roll on the ground but could not do so because the saddle prevented him. He endeavoured to lie down on his side but was obliged to give that up because of the stirrup. Needless to say, the stallion passed a comfortless night.

In the morning, he dashed off at full speed, hoping to free himself from this discomfort, when suddenly he stumbled upon a river. He was therefore forced to enter the water to reach the other bank. As the bed of the river was deep, the stallion was compelled to swim. Given that the girth and saddle were made of leather, and because he was insufficiently dressed, he was exposed to the rays of the sun after coming out of the water. The leather items shrank once they dried, squeezing the poor beast so much as to cause his flanks and shoulders to swell. This suffering added to his hunger pains, further weakening the animal in just a few days. Consequently, he was no longer able to walk, and came to a complete halt.

Just then, a wild boar came up to the stallion that, at first, appeared inclined to strike him. But the boar was moved to compassion by the horse's miserable plight; he asked him what the matter was. The horse recounted the tortures he'd endured from the bridle and saddle. He then entreated the wild boar to free him from them, for the love of charity, in return for which service he would become his servant. When the wild boar asked to know what crime had entailed such sufferings, the horse protested that he had committed none.

'No', resumed the wild boar, 'one of two things must be the case. In asserting your innocence you are either a liar or are ignorant of your guilt. Now, if you are a liar, it is not my duty to break your bonds. Moreover, I can do you no kindness or accept you as a retainer, if that is the case.'

Thus it was said: 'When I beheld the soul of the liar, it was absorbed by the world of corruption — which is congenial to it — because its ingredients are corrupt. Indeed, it is so because the liar's soul harms him, avoids the truth and inclines the absolute nothingness. It gives a form of existence to nothingness, and reality to vanity, and thus depicts them in the minds of those who allow themselves to be deceived by it and who rely upon it.'

It was said: 'Avoid individuals with evil dispositions, lest your own character contract some taint of theirs, without your knowledge.'

It was said: 'The most arduous task of a man is to associate with a companion he cannot trust.'

It was said: 'Seek not to correct the evil man, and enter not into connection with him, for he will cleave to his own nature rather than to you, and will never give it up to you.'

'But', continued the wild boar, 'if you are ignorant of that which has afflicted you enduring this punishment, know that ignorance of your faults is a greater evil than the fault itself. Because he who does not know his own guilt will persist in it and can never hope to free himself from it.'

It was said: 'Be on your guard against an ignorant man because he sins against his own soul nor can he hold you in any esteem.'

It was said: 'Nothing resembles falsehood as much as ignorance. For the liar feigns ignorance of the facts and objects that may be perceived by the senses. By imagining a lie, which is in direct opposition to the facts, the liar abandons the true way for the false one. The ignorant man sees things in a different way, for he beholds ugliness in beauty, and beauty in ugliness. Thus the only difference between him and the liar is that the latter lays before you that which he knows is false, while the ignorant does so unknowingly. Yet, the ignorant man commits a greater sin against himself and against his neighbour, than does the liar.'

'Nevertheless', replied the horse, 'you ought not abstain from doing good to your neighbour.'

'I have no intention of doing so,' returned the wild boar. 'Still, it was said that "the wise man does not do good indiscriminately, even as the propagator does not take up indiscriminately the seeds which are to be sown upon good ground." Endeavour, therefore, to relate to me all that has befallen you, and to explain the original cause of your troubles, as well as the condition in which you formerly lived so that I may see whence the stroke has come.' The horse, thereupon, related to him everything, without omitting to mention the kind treatment he had received at the hands of his master, nor the manner in which he had left him, nor the misfortunes he had encountered before meeting with the boar.

'I now conclude', said the latter, 'that you are ignorant of your own mistakes, although you have committed six faults. The first is having rejected the nobleman who desired to hold you in readiness to serve him at his need. The second is your ingratitude for his benefits. The third is the trouble you caused him in running after you. The fourth is your appropriation of that which did not belong to you, namely the saddle and bridle. The fifth is your sin against yourself, because you sought a wild life to which you were not born and which you could not endure. And the sixth is your obstinacy and persistence, for you might have returned to your master and begged his pardon, pleading profound ignorance before the bridle had nearly reduced you to die of hunger and the girth and saddle inflicted such torture upon you.'

'Very well', replied the horse, 'now that you have pointed out my faults and opened my eyes to that which I did not perceive — blinded as I was by the veil of ignorance — let me go free, for my state of exhaustion gives me a right to demand it.'

'Now you perceive what you have done,' said the wild boar, 'and having reflected upon it, acknowledge that you deserved this punishment for your folly, and are willing to follow the dictates of the wisdom I have identified. Therefore, you are worthy to receive assistance. It is said that Father Luke wrote this sentence above his door: "One may only benefit by our wisdom if one knows himself and is able to confine his desires within the limits of his ability. If you are such a one, enter, but if not, return when you have become one."'

'The wild boar then broke the headstall of the horse, freed him from the girth and restored him to life.'

'Ayn Ahlih, having listened to the story, understood the parallel conveyed to him by the old woman; he turned to her and said: 'You have spoken the truth, and in this parable have clearly set forth my own case; you have taught me many maxims of unparalleled wisdom, taught me a lesson which I will not forget and an admonition by which I shall not fail to live.' He then related to her all that had befallen him, and entreated her to have compassion, show him favour and set him at liberty, even as the wild boar had done to the horse.

'That is too simple,' she said, 'and you should not reflect upon existing circumstances when you ask me to do that which I cannot possibly undertake at present. Nevertheless, perhaps I may be able to discover the means of granting you relief – and even some way of escape – but you must have patience.' And having said this, she held her peace.

At this juncture, the counsellor turned to the Metropolitan and complained of a great pain in his head. Because he was in such pain, he told him that he could not possibly finish his story that night. He added that he hoped to relate the rest of his tale during their next meeting – on the following evening

— if he felt better and stronger. Thereupon he took his leave and retired to bed.

Sapor, thinking about his counsellor's tales and the many allegories, understood that he was 'Ayn Ahlih (being King of Persia), the eyes of his people, and the tool of their visual powers. That Sayidat al-Nar alluded to his own kingdom of Babel, whose inhabitants worshipped fire. That Sitt al-Dhahab, referred to the Roman Empire, on account of its wealth. That Ad-Dib, Sitt al-Dhahab's pretended husband, was well suited to the Roman Emperor on account of his fierce cruelty towards Sapor, whom he had seized and imprisoned. Sapor's desire to behold that empire with his own eyes was represented by that of 'Ayn Ahlih to contemplate another's beauty. Likewise, his arrest was clearly illustrated by the capture of the youth.

Under cover of philosophical examples, the counsellor had sought to rebuke Sapor for his covetousness and rashness (in exposing himself to danger), and for his opposition to his most faithful counsellor. Lastly, to portray himself and the life he led, his grief, impotence, and the degradation to which he consciously submitted by becoming a servant of the Metropolitan, the counsellor had imagined a crippled, one-eyed and noseless old woman with a repulsive and sinister look. The counsellor had sought to give notice to Sapor that he was unable then to expedite his freedom, but was exerting himself for that purpose. The king, having reflected upon all these developments, calmed down as his confidence in the counsellor was restored. He breathed the sigh of relief as he anticipated the following day and night.

At dusk, the Metropolitan hastened to the usual meeting, and turning to the counsellor, said: 'Learned hermit, pray tell what happened to 'Ayn Ahlih, how his misfortunes ended and whether the old woman succeeded in liberating him from Ad-Dib's chains. I am very curious to know all about it, and you look the picture of health this evening.'

'To hear your words and to obey your commands are one and the same thing,' replied the counsellor, and resumed his narrative.

'Burdened with grief and bound all night, 'Ayn Ahlih was confronted in the morning by Ad-Dib, who threatened to kill him but only added cumbersome chains to his body and went away. 'Ayn Ahlih spend the day counting each hour with hope. But as night came, he became overpowered with gloom and anxiety, weeping and sobbing. The old woman, returning to light a fire, sat nearby and turned to him. "Be steadfast and patient. Think upon the tribulations of those worse off, which should comfort you. Moreover, do not forget that while you are alive, a great blessing remains in you."

"Alas!" replied 'Ayn Ahlih, "he who said that the miseries of a captive appear light to those who are free was right."

"Oh, young man," she interrupted, "how many truths does your age prevent you from perceiving! Come, will you listen to a story which will give you some comfort?"

"Willingly", replied 'Ayn Ahlih; "I entreat you to relate it to me."' And the old woman began.

The Gazelle and the Antelope

A wealthy merchant had an only son whom he loved with tender affection. One of his friends gave the boy a little gazelle with a white forehead, for which the child conceived such great fondness that he could not bear to be parted from it a single moment. The house staff made a handsome collar for the gazelle and brought a sheep to suckle it until it was fully-grown and its horns began to sprout. The child then anxiously inquired what was happening to the head of the gazelle. Once informed, he could never weary of admiring the black polish of the little horns; he was told that they would become much longer.

The child, therefore, expressed to his father a great desire to see an antelope with fully-grown horns. The nobleman sent forth his hunters, who soon procured him a two-year old specimen that had attained its full vigour and with which, needless to say, the child was delighted. The entire household, likewise, adopted it. They placed a collar around its neck, endeavoured to tame it and succeeded in doing so. The antelope, moreover, became friends with the gazelle, on account of the similarity of their species.

One day the gazelle said to the antelope: 'Before I saw you, I did not believe that any animal resembling me was to be found upon earth, but now I understand that you cannot be the only one.'

'Assuredly not,' replied the antelope, 'there are a great number.' When the gazelle asked where the other animals were to be found, the antelope confided that they led a wild and wandering life in deserts, escaping man. Moreover, the antelope informed the gazelle of what they ate and drank, and of their loves and other features. The gazelle's eyes sparkled with joy on hearing all this, and it conceived an eager desire to see its kind and live amongst them.

'No', replied the antelope, 'such a desire will do you no good. You have been brought up delicately, far removed from all perils, and know nothing of any other life. If, therefore, you were ever to obtain your wish, you may regret it.'

It is said: 'There are three species of creatures, that, if you do not lodge and nourish them as befits their worth, will immediately turn their backs and break with you: these are kings, men of letters, and worldly riches.'

It is said: 'Hope gives comfort in affliction, but in prosperity – like a fiery horse – it obtains the upper hand. Therefore, the sage cannot follow the impulses of his feelings, except inasmuch as they may dissipate his sadness and lighten his grief. To tolerate such impulses is to allow them to become absolute masters over us. This would be similar to allowing persons of low estate – who count heads for tails and tails for heads and labour to overthrow the aristocracy and to chance the established forms of society – to rule.'

'Nevertheless', replied the gazelle, 'I must go and seek my kind; I must do so at all costs.'

The antelope, finding that it would be impossible to dissuade the gazelle from its intention, and fearing lest it should meet with some disaster before it could attain its object (for the gazelle was but a simple little creature quite unable to guard against the snares of any other creature), perceived that it would be necessary to accompany it as companion and guardian. Having chosen a favourable opportunity for flight, they both went forth from the house, towards the desert. When the gazelle saw the desert, it was unable to contain itself with joy and started off at a speed that nothing could stop until it fell into a narrow ravine, hollowed out by a torrent, and there found itself a prisoner. The gazelle hoped that the antelope would immediately come to liberate it. When the latter failed to appear, the gazelle remained where it was.

When the child woke in the morning and did not find the two animals, he became inconsolable for their loss. The father, taking pity on his son, sent for all the hunters that could be found in the neighbourhood, and having related the circumstance, dispatched them in search of the two little fugitives, promising a handsome reward to whosoever should find them. The huntsmen immediately set to work scouring the hills and plain.

The merchant dispersed his household to the gates of the city to see which of the huntsmen would return first. He then mounted his horse and, with two slaves, took the direction of the desert. There, at a distance, he saw a man bending over some object that lay at his feet. Hastening forward, he soon reached him where he beheld a sportsman who, having bound an antelope, was about to cut its throat. The merchant examined it closely, and recognizing his own antelope, immediately took it from him. He also ordered his slaves to search the sportsman. They discovered the animal's collar on him. The merchant asked the sportsman how and where he had found the collar, to which he replied:

'Last night, I went into the desert to hunt, and having spread a net, I crouched down near it. Towards dawn, an antelope and a gazelle arrived. The gazelle galloped at full speed in another direction. I lost sight of it. But the antelope, advancing at a foot's pace, fell into my net, so I caught it and was about to take it to the city. When, however, I had come thus far, I thought I was acting foolishly, as I could probably get into trouble on account of the ornaments that were round the antelope's neck. I therefore resolved to cut its throat, and take it into town as venison. This is my entire story.'

'You see,' said the merchant, 'how you have been deprived of your reward? This would not have happened had you let the antelope go when you knew that it belonged to a master. Now you have lost the antelope, and are brought into difficulties by its collar.' He therefore, was in the right, and said:

'He who follows the paths of covetousness will end up in an unlawful deed. He who chooses avarice will have anguish. And he who, out of greed, swallows more than he can chew, exposes himself and will have to regret it.'

The merchant sent the antelope to his son with one of his slaves. He then turned to the sportsman and said: 'Come with me and show me which direction you saw the gazelle vault, and I will reward you.' They set forth together in that direction, and the sportsman began to search every place and ascend every rising ground while the merchant followed slowly behind him. At last, they heard the *nazib*, which is the cry of the gazelle. The little animal, recognizing its master's voice, brayed in reply, so that the merchant, following the sound, could locate the place where it was caught in a ditch. The merchant extricated the gazelle, and having called the sportsman and given him a dirham, dismissed him. He returned home with the gazelle to please his young boy, but when the gazelle saw the antelope, it turned away.

If by chance the gazelle found itself near the antelope, far from resuming their former intimacy, it would fly away at full speed. This greatly distressed the child. His attendants did all in their power to reconcile the two animals, but in vain. Then one day, when the gazelle was asleep in a corner, the antelope, drawing near, began to reproach it for withholding friendship and flying its presence. 'Have you then forgotten your perfidy?' asked the gazelle. 'Did I not stand in the utmost need of you when I was in that strait? Did I not feel the firmest confidence that you would hasten to my rescue?'

'But I neither betrayed your confidence nor abandoned you,' replied the antelope. 'It is you who, from thoughtlessness and want of experience, are accusing an innocent being. If I did not hasten to free you from the peril into which you had fallen, it was because I was prevented by a power superior to my own.' The antelope then related its own adventures, and how it had been caught in the huntsman's net. The gazelle concluded that the antelope was not to blame as their mutual friendship was restored.

Conclusion of 'Ayn Ahlih's Tale

From this narrative, 'Ayn Ahlih concluded that the old woman was unable to liberate him at the present time. He ceased to reproach her.

At this point, the counsellor stopped. 'Well my learned hermit,' exclaimed the Metropolitan, 'why do you pause? Do you plan to put off again how the matter ended? Whether 'Ayn Ahlih had to endure any further outrages from Ad-Dib and what service the old woman succeeded in rendering him?'

'I would willingly relate it all to you,' replied the counsellor, 'were it not for a feeling of general debility that has come over me.'

'Nay, do not leave us thus,' resumed the Metropolitan, 'for it would vex me more than I can say. Take courage, O philosopher, for I have a longing desire to hear you, and am filled with admiration of your narratives!'

'And I', returned the counsellor, 'will proceed, because I would like to please you. If you knew, O Metropolitan, what marvels and what adventures I have in store for you, they would indeed, fill you with amazement!' Having said this, he resumed his narrative.

'Ayn Ahlih was deeply impressed with the allegory conveyed by the old woman. He had resigned himself to hold his peace. Nevertheless, he passed a miserable night and at daybreak, Ad-Dib again attacked him with insults, ill treatment and death threats, warning him not to look for assistance nor to hope that any human being could deliver him out of his hands. The young man began anew to reproach himself and to despair. Towards evening, he abandoned himself to still more violent grief, and, bursting into tears, waited impatiently for the old woman to come and sit beside him to divert his mind with her narratives.

But that evening she kept constantly going back and forth in and out of the tent, without ever staying put. This behaviour increased the prisoner's alarm, who took it for granted that his end was at hand and that Ad-Dib would infallibly come that very night to kill him. He had thus passed several hours in tears and terror without uttering a word, when, turning to the old woman, he said: 'What ails you this evening, and why do you not come and sit by me as usual, to divert my mind with some of your stories?'

'Let us see', she declared, 'if I were to tell you of a woman who has been deprived of a hand, her nose and an eye, and is, moreover, deformed and reduced to the lowest depth of misery, whether such a story would give you comfort, restore your composure and lead you to praise and give thanks to God, who has kept you alive and spared you a calamity worse than your own present condition. Let us see whether, after that, you will venture to repeat that 'the woes of the captive appear light to him who is free. Ah, had you only been able to judge my mental condition from my outward appearance, which should have convinced you that my fate was more intolerable than yours. Listen, to me, then, young man, and I will relate to you my own story.'

'You should know that I was the wife of a chief warrior in our country, from whom I experienced nothing but tenderness and attention, and with whom I lived happy and most joyous years. I bore him sons and daughters who grew up in the midst of plenty. But the king became angry with my husband, put him and our sons to death and sold my daughters and me as slaves after separating us from each other.

'This warrior who has dealt so harshly with you purchased me and brought me to this village. Given his savage and brutal nature, he abused me, demanded an amount of labour that I was unable to perform and overwhelmed me with undeserved punishment. In vain, I attempted to appease him; in vain, I sought the intercession of his friends and of those individuals whom he held in high esteem, to induce him to lighten my lot or at least sell me again. All this rendered him harsher and unfeeling towards my sufferings.

'After leading such a life for seven years, I ran away. But this too was in vain, for he pursued me and, having recovered me, cut off my nose and began anew his oppression and torments. I thereupon resumed my entreaties and intercessions, but having failed in deterring him from his evil practices, at the end of seven years I fled again and was captured once more. He then deprived me of an eye and continued to afflict me as before. This I endured for another seven years, at the end of which I once more escaped, but was retaken. After this third attempt at evasion, he cut off my hand and said to me: "Now the only members you have left which can be employed in my service are an eye and a hand. Give heed to my words. Should you attempt to escape again, I will cut off both your feet and continue to make use of your eye to watch and of your hand to work."

'He accompanied his words with a terrific oath and, from that time forward, he has done nothing but trample upon and torment me more cruelly than ever. But now I am resolved to cut loose your chains and then slay myself with my own hand to escape from my sufferings. That is the reason why you have seen me constantly wandering in and out. The prospect of death appalled and troubled me. Now, however, I have no desire but to die.'

She then unfastened the chains that held 'Ayn Ahlih, cut the cords which bound him, and was grasping a dagger to kill herself when the young man exclaimed: 'If I see you slay yourself, I will be an accomplice in your crime.' Wresting the dagger from her grasp, he shouted: 'Come with me and we will escape or perish together.'

'How can I follow you, oppressed as I am with age and weakness?' replied the old woman.

'It does not matter', answered 'Ayn Ahlih, 'the darkness favours us, a place of refuge is at hand and my arms are strong enough to carry you.'

'Oh', said the old woman, 'since you have thought of this, you should know that I have no need of anyone to carry me as long as my life lasts.'

Thus they went forth and reached a safe haven before the night was over. 'Ayn Ahlih liberally rewarded the old woman, adopted her as his mother and obeyed her implicitly as long as she lived. This is all that I know of this story.

Conclusion of Sapor's Adventure

'This is indeed an admirable tale,' exclaimed the Metropolitan. 'In truth, most learned friar, I would not wish to be absent from you, and I even desire the prolongation of our campaign so that I may have more time to enjoy and benefit from your company. I would almost consent to abandon both kindred and country to be near you.'

They thereupon rose to retire. Sapor, pondering over the interpretation of the allegory, perceived himself to be represented by the gazelle, and the counsellor by the antelope. Their going forth to the desert and the fall of the gazelle into the ravine referred to his own journey with the counsellor until he became Caesar's prisoner. The gazelle's aversion to the antelope referred to the suspicions he had entertained of the counsellor because the latter delayed his liberation. He, moreover, gathered from the rest of the story that the counsellor was already preparing to free him, to take him – by night – to the capital, which was close at hand, even carrying him on his back should he be unable to walk. He thus concluded that escape was a certainty.

Accordingly, the next night, the counsellor entered the tent that served as a kitchen and added a powerful soporific to the food prepared for the Metropolitan and for all of Sapor's guards. When the Metropolitan's table was spread, the counsellor, as usual, ate some of his own provisions separately. Scarcely an hour had elapsed before all the others, overcome by the strength of the drug, fell into a deep sleep. Not wasting a single minute, the counsellor opened the trapdoor at the back of the bull, assisted his sovereign to come forth, loosened the chains from his neck and hands and stealthily and silently made way out of the Roman camp.

Sapor and his counsellor finally reached the walls of the city, where they were challenged by sentinels. The counsellor stepped forward, commanding the guards not to raise their voices, and making himself known, informed them that their king was safe. The two men were instantly admitted into the city, where their arrival infused fresh courage into all. Sapor, without loss of time, assembled his forces, supplied them with arms and commanded that every man should equip himself;

that, at the first sound of the trumpets they should approach the Roman camp, prepare for battle, and stand ready to attack; and that, at the second sound of the trumpets, they should launch a general assault. When he had thus fully instructed them as to the part they were to take in the encounter, Sapor selected a powerful body of the bravest and most stalwart knights in Persia and took up his station against Caesar's tent.

Accordingly, when the second watch was sounded, the Persians charged on all sides while Sapor advanced straight upon the tent of the hostile sovereign. The Romans, believing the besieged were discouraged and believing that they would not venture beyond the gates of the city, were off their guard and in disorder. They were taken completely by surprise. Caesar fell into Sapor's hands and was made prisoner; the camp was sacked, the treasure seized and only those who fled escaped from the general slaughter.

Sapor returned to the seat of his empire, divided the booty amongst his soldiers, distributed largesse to all citizens, conferred honours and favours upon those who had governed the kingdom in his absence and committed the whole direction of public affairs to the counsellor who had freed him from his captivity.

Then he summoned Caesar to his presence, and treating him with great honour and courtesy, he said: 'I will spare your life, even as you spared mine, and will not inflict upon you the kind of cruel imprisonment to which you subjected me. I demand nothing of you except to repair the damage you have inflicted throughout my dominions; to rebuild the edifices which you have destroyed, to plant an olive tree from your country in the place of every palm tree that you have cut down in mine; and, lastly, to release all Persian prisoners in the Roman Empire.'

Caesar accepted these conditions and proceeded immediately to carry them into effect. When it came to the restoration of the damaged walls of Jundi-Shahpour, the Persian sovereign wished that they should be repaired with Roman cement. The necessary orders were given by Caesar for a quantity of that cement to be brought to the capital of Persia. Thus the work was completed. Sapor then sent his prisoner back to his own country in freedom and honour. Addressing him a last time, however, he warned: 'Now, make haste to take up arms, and make all your preparations for war, for I shall assuredly come and attack you within a short period of time.'

The author, may God have pity on him, concludes: 'I have accomplished in this second *sulwan* the goal that I had set for myself; and praise be to God for the truths which He has revealed to us on this subject.'

3

Patience

Verses From the Holy Qur'an

Lord God, whose name be blessed, speaking of His elect favourite, the Prophet whom He loves, has said:

> Be patient, then God will grant you patience. Do not grieve for the unbelievers, nor distress yourself at their intrigues. God is with those who keep from evil and do good works. (16:127–128)

This saying alludes to the secret council held by the persecutors of the Prophet who plotted a treacherous scheme against him, as is explained in the following verse:

> Remember how the unbelievers plotted against you. They sought to take you captive or have you slain or banished. They schemed – but God also schemed. God is most profound in His machinations. (8:30)

Attempt on the Prophet's Life

The chiefs of the Quraysh were assembled in the hall of council to determine how to banish the Apostle of God. Iblis presented himself before them in the form of an old Badu. When they wished to expel him from the council, he said: 'I am from Najd and I am not here as a spy. I know the purpose for which you are assembled and my presence may possibly prove beneficial to you.' Then each began to state his opinion.

'I think', said 'Utba ibn Rabi'a, 'that we ought to send him into banishment. If, after this, he should succeed in his undertaking, his victory will turn to our benefit; and if he should perish, it will satisfy our objective as well as if we had slain him with our own hands.'

Iblis replied: 'That will not do. Have you not heard the eloquence of his words and the power he exercises over the minds of men? How would you fare if he were to fall in with some powerful Arab tribe? He would mesmerize them and lead them against you.'

'For my part', urged another, 'I would arrest him, throw him into prison and leave him there to perish.'

Iblis responded: 'That will not do. Are you not aware of the number of his friends and kinsmen who would not accept such treatment? It would kindle a war amongst you; your strength would be exhausted, and the wheel of fortune may turn against you.'

Then Abu Jahl ('Umru' ibn Hisham ibn al-Mughira al-Makhzumi al-Qurashi) spoke: 'Let us take a gallant youth from each tribe within the Quraysh and give every one a sword. They shall then go and strike Muhammad while he is asleep. The guilt of his blood would thus be divided between all the tribes. Consequently, his family will not be able to exact vengeance from all of them.'

'Here is one who has hit the mark,' exclaimed Iblis. All agreed to Abu Jahl's proposal, and the assembly was dissolved.

Yet God, through a revelation, forewarned His apostle of this conspiracy and commanded him to take refuge in Madina.

The assassins assembled in front of Muhammad's home at an early hour of the night. The Prophet, meanwhile, commanded 'Ali to lie on his bed and cover himself with Muhammad's green mantle, assuring him that he would receive no injury from the Quraysh. 'Ali obeyed, and Muhammad opened the front door of the house – where the assassins were keeping watch – reciting the Holy Qur'an ('I swear by the wise Qur'an that you are sent upon a straight path' [36:1]). He then took a handful of earth, sprinkled it on the assassins' heads and thus, unseen, walked forth and left for his cave. The heathen assassins, meanwhile, looked inside the house and saw 'Ali lying in bed covered with the green mantle. They believed him to be Muhammad sleeping and waited for daybreak. At dawn 'Ali rose from bed and the assassins asked where Muhammad was. 'I do not know,' replied 'Ali; 'you bade him to leave, and he is gone.' Thereupon they seized 'Ali and imprisoned him for an hour inside the mosque before setting him free.

Sayings of the Prophet Concerning Patience

The Prophet, peace and the blessings of God be with him, has said: 'The believer has knowledge as his friend; prudence as his counsellor; understanding as his guide; activity as his governor; benignity as his father; piety as his brother; and patience as the captain of his armies. Be content to be distinguished for a virtue that holds command over all the rest.'

He did not mean to imply that patience is a greater virtue than knowledge, understanding and other qualities but, rather, that none of these can be firmly rooted without patience that includes firmness, moderation and perseverance. A man who is fortunate to have any one of the aforesaid virtues – but has no patience – will, because of this deficiency, be as if he possesses no virtues. Indeed, patience rules over all virtues even as a ship is governed by a captain who is never absent from duty, and who does not neglect the comfort and security of his men.

Philosophical Statements Concerning Patience

It is related that 'Ali, peace be unto him, once said: 'Patience is a stallion that never stumbles.'

It is also said that amongst the sentences inscribed on yellow leaves suspended in the great temples of Persia was the following: 'Even as the iron cleaves to the magnet, so does success to patience. Endure, therefore, and you shall conquer.'

And you should know, reader, that the shadow of patience endures forever, and that he who loses it remains in anguish. Patience is the stair by which we reach contentment. And the least of patience's benefits is this: that by it you embitter the triumph of your enemy, who exults with insolent satisfaction upon seeing your affliction.

There are two kinds of patience: that which is universal and governs the body, and that which is individual and governs the mind. This distinction was set forth by Habib ibn 'Aws al-Ta'i in the following verses:

'Patience is a coat of arms, and he who wears it in adversity puts on an excellent armour.

'And there is the patience of the mind, whose virtue is well known; the patience of kings, which does not show itself in the body.'

And in the following verse as well:
'When you see how a man takes courage and endures, then you may know the quality of his mind.'

The poet Nahshal ibn Harri has sung:

'On a day of scorching heat, which well may have burnt us up – although no flames rose from the furnace;
'We endured until it wore away; and thus patience alone can wear away days of adversity.'

And I have written the following verses on the same subject:

'Man's fate is in accordance with his worth. A man may be known by his patience in enduring calamities that befall him.
He has little to hope for from fortune who has little patience to support him.'

And another poet has said:

'He who in adversity clings to patience, will always prosper.
Endurance is the most effective remedy for the infirmities of the valiant; it behooves him to keep away from impatience.'

'Umar Dhu'l-Kalb has said:

'Many woes surrounded me; and I was trapped in their midst, like the string of a sandal caught between toes. Nevertheless, I stood my ground; and while cowards disbanded and fled, I, like a faithful brother, fought to defend

my people. Meanwhile, the hand of death was upon me —
death that one of these nights will bring to me.'

These are examples of maxims concerning patience in
general. This virtue is of several kinds, but one kind alone
pertains to the subject of my book, and that is the patience of
kings.

The patience of kings is composed of three elements. First,
that of forbearance, which gives birth to clemency. Second,
watchfulness and foresight, which result in the prosperity of
kingdoms. Third, courage, which leads to two goals: one is
embedded in the king's character as firmness; the other, in his
defence of the kingdom through his readiness to take up
arms. This should not to be understood as readiness to fight
with his own hand — for this in a king would be rashness,
thoughtlessness and vanity — but in the poise that causes him
to be the keystone of an army in battle and a rock of refuge in
defeat. This can be accomplished if trusted men can defend
his person, repulse attacks directed against him and preserve
him from all injury.

The Poise of Chosroes Anushirvan

Persians relate that once during the mating season, an
elephant entered Chosroes Anushirvan's palace in its fury, for
during this season the elephant no longer obeys its driver and
overthrows and tramples those who try to stop it. The
elephant made its way to a hall where Chosroes was seated
with his courtiers, all of whom fled as the infuriated animal
approached. Chosroes alone remained seated on his throne.
With him was one of his favourite knights, who positioned
himself in front of the king, brandishing an axe. The elephant

rushed upon him, but the knight did not move. He waited for the animal to strike him with his trunk, before striking it with his axe. The strike was so severe that the grievously wounded elephant turned away. During the whole time, Chosroes did not rise to leave the hall, nor did he alter his composure.

This is the highest degree of courage that is required from a king. But if the sovereign does not find trusted men to defend him, it is well that he should then defend himself, either by confronting the enemy if he deems he can repulse him or by flight, if he perceives successful resistance to be impossible and fears that his subjects may be injured by his death.

An Example of 'Abbasid Caliph Musa al-Hadi's Valour

The Caliph Musa al-Hadi was riding an ass in his garden one day, unarmed and surrounded by servants and courtiers, when his chamberlain informed him that a Khariji — whom the Caliph had wanted in custody — had been arrested. Musa ordered that the man be immediately brought to him. Accordingly, the prisoner, led by two soldiers who held him by the wrists, appeared. But no sooner had the Khariji entered than suddenly he disengaged his arms from his keepers, and snatching a dagger from one of them, sprang upon the Caliph. The servants and courtiers dispersed in the twinkling of an eye, leaving al-Hadi alone. The Caliph stood firm until the Khariji was actually upon him and, just before the latter could strike, he exclaimed: 'Now, my lads, off with his head!' At these words, the assailant turned to look behind him. This allowed the Caliph to leap from his saddle, fall upon his attacker, throw him to the ground, grasp his hand and wrest away the dagger before slaying the Khariji. When done, he remounted the ass. His followers, servants and courtiers rushed back into the garden, all eagerly unsheathing their swords, filled with shame and terror at what had just occurred. The Caliph did not say a word, but from that day onward he never appeared without his sword, nor rode any animal other than a horse.

This anecdote illustrates that strength of mind, a quick eye, sagacity, courage and personal vigour are the gifts that God bestowed upon Musa al-Hadi.

Chosroes Anushirvan's Campaign in India

Chosroes Anushirvan had heard of a famous land bordering India adjoining the Kingdom of Babel, which was celebrated for its scenic beauty; mildness of climate; the sweetness of its waters; the abundance of its fruits; the number of its towns and villages; the vast amount of its revenue; and the strength of its fortified places. Moreover, its inhabitants had been represented to Chosroes as being a tall and vigorous race, yet dull and of limited understanding, submitting patiently to social discipline, obedient to their sovereigns and very easily governed. Chosroes, hence, decided to conquer the country and to use the nation to his own benefit.

It was said: 'Indulgence is the most heinous of all vices. Avarice is the father that begets it; transgression the son to which it gives birth; greed of that which belongs to others is its brother; and servility its companion.'

It was also said: 'He who desires too much will obtain that which he abhors.'

And: 'Indulgence is a vice that has its origin in nature and is provoked by greed.'

Chosroes's heart being set on gaining possession of that country, he inquired about its ruler and learned that it belonged to one of the most powerful princes of India, a young man enslaved by his passions and addicted to a voluptuous life, but who adhered strictly and unswervingly to the path of justice. He practised liberal policies from which he never deviated, and his mildness had gained the hearts of all his subjects, whose hopes were fixed upon him alone.

Chosroes, therefore, dispatched to the court of this prince one of his most trusted retainers, who had studied the science of government and courts. The man was cunning and quick-witted, prudent in design and well-versed in geography. He became acquainted with the roads, frontiers and fortresses of the kingdom, in order to discover its weak points; and inquired into the character of both the sovereign and the people. Chosroes entrusted a letter to his messenger addressed to the Indian prince, demanding tribute and warning that in the event of a refusal he would feel compelled to launch an assault.

The messenger soon reached the court of the Indian prince. The latter lodged him sumptuously and provided him with several garments and other articles of luxury. At the same time, he took every precaution to deny him information and prevent all contact with the citizenry. He himself never received the messenger in an audience, nor demanded his credentials, nor even inquired for what purpose he was there. Lastly, he entrusted one of his most astute courtiers to keep watch over him, charging him to acquaint himself – as far as possible – with the envoy in order to discover what his designs were and with whom he associated.

The courtier-spy set to work at once, and began by hiring a shop opposite the envoy's dwelling that he stocked with earthenware. He then took up his post as if for the purpose of selling his goods, and observed a servant — whom the messenger employed to run his business and errands and wait upon him at home. The spy began to make advances to the servant, always asking whether he could render him any service. The unsuspecting youth soon struck up a friendship with the Indian spy and began to frequent the shop, where he would sit and sometimes ask favours. The spy and the servant continued to converse for a long time without ever discussing the envoy.

When the spy believed that the young man was lulled into perfect trust, he said to him, 'Well, now, tell me who you are, and whom do you go to visit in that house?'

'You have been associating with me for a long time and you do not yet know who I am?' replied the youth.

'No, indeed I do not,' answered the spy.

'I am in the service of Chosroes's messenger,' replied the youth, 'and my master lives there.'

'Who is this Chosroes, and who is his envoy?' asked the spy.

The servant answered, 'Chosroes is the king of Babel, and has sent my master to the king of this country.'

'The name of Babel,' resumed the other, 'is not new to me, for in my youth I was in the service of a native of that country.'

This said, he held his peace and for several days did not ask the youth any other questions.

It is said: 'Diligent search leads to discovery. Inquiry makes even the cunning waver.'

It was said: 'Shame on you if you hold for a fool he who bestows his confidence too readily. For a babbler, he who cannot keep a secret without revealing it. For a deceiver, he who gives counsel when not asked. For an evil-minded person, he who seeks to discover what is withheld from him.'

The spy then said to the servant, 'Can you point your master out to me when he steps out from his house?'

'But he never goes out,' replied the servant.

'Is he sick?,' inquired the spy.

'No,' responded the servant, 'but your king chooses that he not leave his house, nor that anyone enter it.' On hearing this, the spy began to weep.

'What is the matter?' asked the youth; and the former replied,

'I am moved to tears by compassion for the life your master leads; for I know something of it by experience. I was once cast into prison for debt, where even my wife was forbidden to come to me; and if God had not in his mercy granted me the company of another prisoner – who afforded me some solace by his conversation and his friendship – I should undoubtedly have died of grief. I suppose, of course, it is you who entertain your master by your discourse?'

'I do not know how to do so,' replied the youth, 'nor do I have anything to relate to him.'

'Am I not here to help you?' asked the spy. The young man willingly accepted the offer, and the spy continued: 'Well, then, when you go out, try to visit the city a little and take notice of what meets your eye. If you see a group of people talking together, seek to join them; sit down amongst them, and hear what they are talking about; then, when you return to your master, relate: "Today I have seen so and so, and have heard such and such discourse." Through this, your master's mind will be diverted, and some amusement afforded him in his solitude, and you yourself will rise in his favour.'

The young man followed this counsel to the letter. No sooner had Chosroes's messenger heard him that he asked: 'Who was it who gave you this idea?'

'It came into my head, and so I did it,' was the answer.

'Not so,' returned the envoy, 'you do not have the brains for that. Come, tell me who suggested it?'

'A neighbour of ours who sells earthenware,' replied the servant, 'and who is the most ignorant simpleton I ever saw.'

'And why do you think him such a simpleton?' inquired the messenger.

'Because,' replied the servant, 'I had been acquainted with him for more than a month before he knew who I was, or who my master was. Besides, when I talked to him of King Chosroes, he did not even know his name.' These words awakened the ambassador's suspicion, leading him to think that the earthenware dealer might be a spy sent to watch him, feigning excessive ignorance and simplicity.

It was said: 'He who goes too far forward is no better than he who lingers behind; and he who strives to send an arrow to too great a distance shoots below the mark.'

And: 'Nothing can reveal the circumstances in which a man is placed more plainly than his own words.'

And: 'If your ears do not enable you to know a man when you are absent, neither will your eyes do so when you see him face to face.'

The envoy listened to his servant and told him: 'Bring this man to me tomorrow. Perhaps his sight may be a relief, and I may derive some benefit from his stories.' The following day, the young man went in quest of the spy and informed him of his master's wish. After some false pretence, the spy acquiesced.

Once the ambassador spoke with the spy his suspicions were confirmed. He sought, therefore, to attract him and draw him out, making himself out to be as foolish and ignorant as possible. He entreated the spy to visit him often. The spy latched on to the envoy, kept a record of all their conversations and, when he believed he had ascertained as much as was necessary, he went to his sovereign. The spy told the Indian Prince that Chosroes's messenger was a clod and an ass, without the slightest wit or penetration, skilled in horsemanship and the use of arms, brave, proud and nothing more. The prince, trusting this report, pictured the envoy such as the spy had represented him.

It was said: 'Do not listen to the first informer nor trust the first who joins your company.'

And: 'As truth and falsehood may occasionally bring you the same tale, it is foolish to accept or reject it without examination.'

And: 'What entails the truthfulness of the message is the veracity of the messenger.'

The interpretation of these maxims is this: that the truthful narrator, if he has no understanding, is liable to be mistaken. Even if the messenger is trustworthy and refrains from distortion, his understanding may not be infallible. A truthful but unobservant man, fixing his eyes upon the sun, may tell you that it does not move; or, looking at the moon when clouds are sweeping across it, may assert that it is proceeding with augmented speed upon its course. Likewise, gazing from the deck of a vessel under sail, he may think it is the sea that flows from beneath it; or, being in the presence of a sorcerer, his statement of what he has seen will differ widely from reality. Even as, hearing the voice of a parrot behind a curtain, he would maintain that he had heard that of a man. Thus he will fall into falsehood, not by voluntary misrepresentation of the truth, but by his incapacity to perceive it correctly.

Blindly trusting the spy's report, the Indian prince summoned the messenger to his presence and bestowed upon him great honour, conversed with him courteously and presented him with costly garments and other splendid gifts, pleasing him immensely. Simultaneously, he authorized him to travel as he pleased and allowed him to visit whomever he wished. Thus, lavishing gifts and favours upon him, the Indian Prince kept Chrosroes's envoy at his court for a whole year. He then sent for him, received his credentials and entrusted him with magnificent presents for Chosroes. It is said that amongst them was a dagger five spans in lengths made of red copper, and of such exquisite quality that it would cut through iron as an ordinary sword might cut through lead. There was, likewise, a small turquoise plate able to contain a measure (100 pounds) of corn, a chrysolite (topaz) cup that could hold a *ratl* (20 pounds) of liquid and a chandelier of crystal, in which was encased a ruby as large as a dove's egg. A lamp reflected its rays on every object presented in a cone of red light that one would have believed them to be red too. He added one thousand large pearls, and a great quantity of perfumes, small arms, shields and other similar articles. Lastly, he bestowed upon the envoy himself gems and other valuable gifts and sent him back to his sovereign.

The messenger returned to Chosroes, who questioned him as to the result of his mission. He described to the king the beauty of the country, the precious things that abounded therein, its manifold advantages and the strength of its borders; he added that for those who would seek to attack it, its only weak point was the simplicity of the inhabitants. They were easy to dupe and devoid of any foresight. This simplicity rendered them tractable to any authority that they were accustomed to obey. It also gave reason to hope that it would be easy for another authority to alienate them from their sovereign. By dispersing emissaries – who would win them over through an artful system of proselytizing – an outside authority would be able to attract the population. The people thus shaken in their allegiance towards their prince, the latter would have no means of resistance as his only strength consisted in the loyalty of his subjects, who granted him a rich harvest in peace and weak soldiers in war.

Chosroes read the Indian prince's letters and concluded that they were written with great courtesy. He could not but acknowledge the dignity and gentleness with which peace and friendship were requested from him. Nevertheless, he called a council of his advisors and informed them that he was not disposed to grant such peace. Their views were not favourable for war. Notwithstanding the advice of his ministers, Chosroes was determined to send back the presents of the Indian monarch. This done, he summoned men skilled in the art of proselytizing in favour of new sovereigns, and of paving the way for dynastic changes. He provided them with money and provisions, along with minute instructions concerning the course they should pursue, as he initiated the task of corrupting the Indian subjects.

Several of these men entered the kingdom, established themselves in various cities – as Chosroes had directed – and set about performing their tasks with diligence. Within two years, their tasks were accomplished both in the capital as well as in smaller cities, villages and fortified places. Whereupon, they wrote Chosroes who, in turn, charged his four *Marziban*s (satraps) to start necessary preparations to march towards India. For the kingdom of Babel was divided into four provinces, each governed by a *Marziban* (satrap) who commanded a force of fifty thousand soldiers.

When the satraps began to levy troops and prepare for war, the spies kept in Babel by the Indian prince informed their sovereign of these developments. Simultaneously, the king learned that rumours of war were rife amongst his own subjects, that infiltration from abroad was frequent and that disaffected voices were being heard among the masses. Thus roused from his lethargy, the Indian prince inquired into the real state of affairs and soon discovered the truth.

It was said that revolutions are aimed against sovereigns whose crown was a hereditary right. Brought up in the midst of plenty, most are inclined to sloth and are persuaded that their capacity to govern is inherent in them. Moreover, most believed that the virtues of their illustrious ancestors applied to them, without any necessity for exertion on their parts.

The Indian government was administered by five persons, namely, four ministers and the chief priest (Magus) who presided over the temples of the Sacred Fire. Having assembled these five, the prince shared the news he had received — of the disaffection of his subjects, and of the military preparations of the satraps — stating, in conclusion, that he needed their assistance. During a council discussion, one of the ministers advanced the following assessment:

'It seems to me that the King ought to endeavour to appease his subjects, to fill their pockets with wealth and their hearts with hope so that those who have fallen prey should return to the straight path and those who behave wildly should be tamed. The enemy, perceiving this, will either refrain from attacking us, or if he does so we will be strong enough – with one mind and with united forces – to oppose him.'

'That,' replied the chief priest, 'would be a very good plan if the disaffection of the subjects were the result of tyranny, or even of any misconduct on the part of the government; for then, the cause of evil would be removed and all would return to their duty. But the king's subjects are not in such a case. Their discontent arises from ignorance of the immutable principles of truth and justice, and from the arrogance engendered by a long period of prosperity.

'It is said that four kinds of people, when spoiled by arrogance, will become worse if they are treated with mildness: children, wives, servants and subjects. This has passed into proverb.

'Likewise, the four most ignoble passions of the soul overstep in their ardour the limits of propriety, and these are: anger (when it crosses the bounds of valour and indignation against vice); sensual pleasure (when it does not confine itself to that which is required for the recreation of the mind after the exertion of profound study); greediness (of wealth exceeding need); and idleness (extending beyond the rest required for a body weary of its efforts to secure the comforts of life). These four passions, when they overstep their limits, will never be tamed by gentleness and kindness. On the contrary, they will become more violent and impetuous. Those who are afflicted by such plagues can only be cured by fire and steel.'

'The sage is right,' replied the Indian prince.

Another minister advanced: 'Let us rather employ the subjects who remain faithful to us in restraining those who are gone astray, and bring them back by force into the right path so that we may be safe. Then we will advance against the enemy with loyal troops, for we shall assuredly be compelled to fight. We are dealing with a foe who will not be content until he has taken from us all that we possess and leave us bereft of everything.'

The high priest of the Magi replied: 'This would help the enemy more than all his hosts, and would procure him partisans far more numerous than his emissaries can succeed in gaining. We know that amongst the people there are able men but, at the same time, they are the poor, whose fears alone have hitherto prevented them from joining the fighting. Now, if the king should act according to your counsel, it would place swords in the hands of those who would assuredly fight, not for us, but against us. The masses would follow their example, owing to the natural feeling that causes kings to be regarded with envy, and the unfortunate with favour.

'Moreover, it would divide the populace as merchants, artisans and servants join military groups; whereas their bosoms are not filled with that enthusiasm which leads a soldier to sacrifice his life to enhance the glory of his sovereign. That is why monarchs strictly restrain their subjects, each one within the limits of his own social stratum, to prevent uprisings.

'Philosophers have said that there are four things that will cost you your life if confronted by violence: A king in his anger; a torrent that has burst its banks; an elephant during mating season; and masses in a state of excitement and tumult. They have said, moreover, that the measure which most resembles the forcible repression of the masses — when people rise in their fury — is that of treating smallpox with an ointment when it breaks on the skin.'

'The sage is right,' replied the king.

A third minister then ventured: 'In the first place,' he said, 'we ought to scrutinize the masses to acquaint ourselves with those who are dissatisfied and to separate them from the rest. We will then look into each suspect's condition and, whether he is poor or rich, noble or of low standing, powerful or of no account, we will then adopt measures that may be most fitting.'

'We have reached such a point,' said the high priest of the Magi, 'that an inquiry of this kind would lead to great danger; for those repulsed by suspicion would be so alarmed by it as to instantly join the enemy. In turn, they would then assist the enemy with counsel and information, revealing our most vulnerable points, and would fight for him with a zeal far exceeding their own. Individuals filled with suspicion would do anything to return to their country, their families and their property, but these inducements are altogether lacking in the foe.

'Moreover, in cases of civil dissension, those who are offended by suspicion do not in general go over to the enemy, but resist us without leaving their own homes. Or else, they discover themselves more openly by increasing, to our detriment, the number of their fellow-subjects who are declared rebels. They give them assistance without necessarily sharing their views but rather from love of class. (There are those who hate the government because of some rebuff that they have experienced and punishment inflicted. Then the lower classes in general abhor the military, at whose hands they are frequently subjected to outrage and oppression. But if the latter are treated with kindness, the whole nation finds fault with the sovereign. If he seeks to punish the wicked, the upright fear that the punishment may extend to them, and join forces with those that oppress them).

'Likewise, we may see two angry dogs lay aside their own quarrel, though excited against each other, to meet the challenge of a wolf. Together, they rush on the wolf, helping each other like good friends and regardless of whatever they may share with the wolf. Only the wolf's peculiar qualities, his wildness, evil odour and ferocity, preoccupy the two dogs. Thus the masses do not look upon the king as a member of the human family, but consider only his peculiar characteristics: his isolation, dignity and the elevation of his office; therefore, they turn against him and unite with those who are on par with themselves (as, for example, in ignorance and other similar qualities.) Moreover, among the masses may be a blind fanatic who, purporting to defend religion, oversteps his bounds and rules the people with authority more absolute than the sovereign himself.

'Wise men have said that there are three kinds of human beings against whom, if tested, you could lose. These are the pedagogue (if you seek to test his learning while you are not a scholar); an intimate friend (because you would take advantage of him); and a woman (if you would marry her when you are advanced in age). These have given rise to the saying, "like those who test the stomach of a convalescent with heavy food".

'Now, to place your subjects on trial under the present circumstances would precisely resemble the aforesaid tests. The wise have said, moreover, that governments – like individuals – may be stricken with diseases that threaten their dissolution. The chief perils that they have to encounter are four in number: pride; the ire of the king (that so disturbs the march of government as to cause the monarch to overstep the bounds of policy); rapacity (that leads to abuse of power and violence on the part of the monarch); and rebellion on the part of his subjects.'

The king answered, 'The sage is right.'

Then the fourth minister, who was esteemed above all the rest for his far-sightedness and sagacity, said: 'I will only relate to the king a story which I learned from my mentor, and which was the last lesson that he imparted to me, adding, "Save it in the lowest depths of your heart and hope that you may not live to see the day when you will have need of it." But that day, I believe, is come.'

'Speak, for we are listening,' responded the king. And the chief priest of the Magi added: 'What acuteness of understanding!'

'Very true,' replied the three other ministers with a single voice, and the fourth continued thus:

'We are as the fingers of the hand, which have need of one another for mutual assistance; but we all obtain light from the understanding of our serene prince, upon whom our eyes are turned, even as the most brilliant stars derive their radiance from the sun. For we all have need of the king, and derive our prosperity from him.'

'Oh, faithful minister,' said the king, 'proceed, for your words are welcome to our ears, and likewise those of any one who shall speak through you. We receive assistance and upright counsel from you, even as does the soul from the five senses.'

At these words all bowed down before the king, and the minister continued.

The Rat and the Gerbil

My mentor imagined that a wealthy merchant had in his house a room with a loft where he occasionally went. The empty space between the roof and the ceiling was inhabited by a number of rats who led the most prosperous and jovial life that could be, in the midst of safety and plenty. All day long, they enjoyed themselves quietly. At night, they came down from the roof and dispersed throughout the merchant's warehouses as well as the servants' apartments, gnawing and carrying away whatever they chose.

The merchant was displeased at this annoyance when, one day, he lay down in the room to reflect upon his affairs. The rats, meanwhile, who were amusing themselves above the ceiling, started to sprinkle down some dust through the fissures of the boards. The angry merchant ordered his servants to remove all the furniture from the room, then asked them to tear down the boards of the ceiling. This done, the rats dispersed throughout the house, where they all met cruel deaths. Two rats, a male and a female, who happened to be absent, survived.

Returning to their 'home' and seeing the devastation of their colony — with rats lying dead throughout the house — saddened them both grievously. The male rat turned to his companion, observing, 'The wise man was right when he said, that he who is wrapped up in the things of this world and places his trust in them is like one who lies down to sleep in the shade before the sun has reached the meridian. As the shadows dissipate, they leave him exposed to sun-rays until, scorched by the heat, he can find no trace of shade.'

'Very true', replied his companion, 'but what do you propose doing?'

'I propose not to remain where this fearful catastrophe has occurred. To leave man to his fury more terrible and cunning more subtle than that of any other animal.'

'I will go with you,' said the female rat.

Eventually, they reached an area inhabited by various animals in the midst of a valley carpeted with green pastures and little lakes inhabited by frogs and tortoises. Struck with admiration at the scene, the two rats examined the valley in search of a spot to make their home. Having reached a knoll that rose at its centre, flanked on either side by water beds, they burrowed a hole at the foot of a slope where they made their abode.

One day, they came across a gerbil peering out the mouth of his hole, on top of the hill. The gerbil welcomed them and inquired as to their whereabouts. The two rats thereupon related their adventures up to the time when they had come to inhabit the hole at the foot of the hill.

'If', said the gerbil, 'those who take it upon themselves to give advice to others did not, in general, excite mistrust, I would give you a warning.'

'We have no need of your warning,' replied the rats; and the gerbil resumed:

'It was said that there are four undertakings in which one should not venture without taking the advice of experienced persons: First, do not go to market without first asking whether business is brisk or people idle. Second, do not ask for a woman in marriage without first inquiring about her family and disposition. Third, do not start a journey without ascertaining whether the road you plan to travel on is safe or hazardous. Finally, do not settle in a country without ascertaining its advantages, learning about the conduct of its sovereign, deciphering the divisions that may exist between its inhabitants and identifying the visible or hidden strengths of the nation.'

It was said: 'Attend to one who offers you advice. If the advice he gives would injure others without serving you, then conclude that he is a villain. If it injures others, but is beneficial to you, then conclude that he is an ambitious man. But if it is beneficial to you, and hurts no one, then listen to the counsellor and trust him.'

It was said: 'If a man gives you advice, and you do not allow him to help you, he will be a man attempting to straighten a warped beam before it was fitted into its correct position.'

It was said: 'If you would like to know whether good or bad prevails in the mind of a man, ask for his counsel. The advice he gives you will reveal his true light.'

It was said: 'Amongst the varieties of character that are to be found amongst men, the worst is that which is assumed where it does not exist. Because, through this assumption, you only increase your own faults, as is the case when the weak man endeavours to feign strength, the ignorant learning and the poor man wealth.'

It was said, moreover: 'When you need counsel in any matter of business, seek shrewd and experienced persons in your own profession. Take heed that you do not ignore them. Living in a different world that knows nothing of the peculiarities of your condition, their advice would distance you from your own sphere, allowing you to reach solid judgements.'

'You should know', continued the gerbil, 'that I share your instincts. Both of us burrow holes for our homes, even if I excel in the art, but I have more experience of this country. And there is a saying that a country spells the death of he who does not know it. But he who knows it can do with it what he pleases. Thus, I say to you, give up this hole of yours and seek another spot in which to take up your abode.'

The two rats strolled away laughing and mocking, accusing the gerbil of stupidity. They returned to their dwelling where they lived for a long time and reared several young ones. One day, however, when the male rat was attending some business in the countryside, the valley was inundated. On his return, he saw that the water had surrounded the knoll. It had risen so high that the knoll appeared to be standing in the midst of a raging sea. The poor wretch stopped on the edge, loudly bewailing his misery, as he watched his dwelling go to ruin, the destruction of his mate and offspring at hand along with the waste of the provisions which he had laid up.

Then he saw the gerbil standing safely at the top of the knoll; the latter called out to him: 'Hello, you rat! What do you think of the fruit of your imprudence, which made you despise the advice of an upright and experienced person?'

'That it is very bitter,' replied the rat. And the gerbil resumed:

'Do not distress yourself too much on that account, but stop your lamentations. The good fortune of being alive is greater than the calamity that has bereft you of your family. If you seek to allure her through gratitude, good fortune will come to you, and you will enjoy her favour.'

It was said: 'There are three things you should meet with a smiling face: a friend, a debtor and good fortune.'

It was said: 'A lofty spirit will not forget to be grateful whatever wrong he may receive from one to whom he owes a benefit.'

It was said: 'If a man has helped you and then turns his back on you or even injures you, do not on that account break with him. Continue to show him gratitude and affection. Such conduct on your part will prove the most powerful intercessor on your behalf.'

'I am unhappy,' replied the rat, 'that I did not listen to, and withdrew myself from you! It is rightly said that he who has understanding should associate with the wise, who observe the precepts of philosophy and conduct themselves prudently. If I had been reasonable, I would have understood that you, O sage gerbil, burdened as you are with age and infirmity, would not have exposed yourself to the trouble of ascending and descending this steep hill had you not been prompted to do so by wisdom and the counsels of prudence.'

He then waited until the waters subsided before ascending the hill to find a hole close to that of the gerbil where he lived in happiness and security.

'This', said the minister in conclusion, 'is what my mentor related to me.'

Continuation of the Enterprise of Chosroes

'O faithful minister,' replied the king, 'your words are true, your advice to the point; the course you propose is straight and your diction elegant, compelling the attention of all who hear it. But now, seek to find the hill up which we may willingly ascend to establish our abode at its summit, taking courage to endure the fatigue of the ascent and the weariness of the isolation we shall experience there. We will be deprived of the pleasures to which our soul has been accustomed in the world of delight in which it has hitherto frolicked. So that we might thus find, in the midst of this flood of rebellion, the same safety which the gerbil attained.'

And the minister responded: 'O serene prince, may the loyalty of the faithful save you from tribulation and death and may you live as long as it pleases you to obtain all that you desire. Marvellous is the prudence with which you grasp this solution that we have set before you and that is assuredly yours. Your own rekindled wisdom is great. I know of a fortress in one of the provinces of your kingdom, from which you can look down upon all the nations of earth, even as Saturn exalts himself above all the stars; a fortress that neither the most piercing glances nor the most ambitious thoughts can reach. Moreover, this fortress enjoys the purest air, and waters like those of Paradise. It encloses within its limits gardens shaded by tree groves and every aspect of luxury. One of your earliest ancestors, most serene prince, devoted much care to it and would have completed its fortifications, but his hopes were cut short by his untimely death. It would now be an admirable expedient for the king to complete the work of his predecessor and safeguard his treasure there, strengthening the fortress's defences. He might then go forth to meet the enemy, should they advance into the kingdom. But if any signs of treachery should appear in the army, he might take refuge in this stronghold with all who remained faithful and loyal to him, there to wait patiently for his opportunity.'

The prince was happy to listen to his minister. He mounted his horse, and with a following of courtiers and trusted supporters proceeded forthwith to the said fortress. When he beheld it with his own eyes, he realized that it was superior even to the description given by the minister. He found solid foundations already laid with stores of earthenwork placed by one of his ancestors. Thus he immediately sent for engineers, artisans and superintendents, charging them to use their utmost diligence to complete the fortifications. Meanwhile, he began transporting all that he dearly valued of his treasures, military equipment and most precious possessions. He also demanded from his subjects a sufficient supply of rice, both thrashed and un-thrashed (the latter, because rice in the husk will keep for a longer period). In short, he made every preparation for residence in the fortress, ordered the requisite supplies to be collected in the provinces throughout the kingdom, summoned troops to take up arms and erected strong defences at key points.

Three months had elapsed since the Indian prince's spies had first noticed the satraps's hostile preparations. The latter assaulted the Indian borders with a large, fully equipped army. Simultaneously, Chosroes's name was being proclaimed throughout the province amongst inhabitants already corrupted by Persian emissaries. Rebels occupied the whole of the surrounding country soon thereafter. As they marched, the satraps entrusted local affairs to prefects, in whom they placed implicit confidence. Cities and villages were garrisoned with mixed forces composed of soldiers and inhabitants of the country. Then, penetrating further into the interior of the kingdom, the satraps confronted the Indian army, whose ranks fought with great valour. Given such well-prepared treachery, the Indian army was routed as it fell into the hands of Chosroes's men. The lives of prisoners were spared, but their goods were seized and, continuing their advance, the satraps occupied the entire country.

On the first day of battle the Indian prince had sent his family and court to his fortress, and, assembling the principal citizens of the capital, reminded them in grave and earnest terms of the many benefits they had received from him. He spoke of the rebellions that he had detected, but added that this was not the time to examine his subjects and punish the guilty. On hearing these words the citizens repented and solemnly swore to be faithful and obedient.

Yet the prince interrupted them: 'It is not for this that I have summoned you. I have no intention of turning my back on the enemy. Nor do I despair of overcoming him and obtaining a complete victory. Much less do I relish suspicions against any of you. But one of my most trusted advisors has reminded me that one of my ancestors had undertaken the construction of a fortress upon which he had bestowed many pains, when his death prevented its completion. Hence the minister exhorted me to carry out that which my ancestor had begun. According to the saying of the philosopher, that the most pious prince is he who executes the purpose of his ancestors and the most evil-minded, he who suffers it to fail. I have thought fit to lay up my treasures and supplies in this fortress in accordance with another wise saying, to the effect that the most prudent amongst rulers is he who deliberately provides for every contingency that the mind of man can foresee.

'The philosophers have likewise said: 'It is the king's duty to ensure five things for himself. First is a faithful counsellor, from whose advice he may seek assistance in good as well as in adverse fortune; second is a sharp sword, to defend himself against his enemies; third is a stallion, whose speed he may rely upon when further resistance is impossible; fourth is a beautiful woman, whose love may preserve him both in thought and deed; and fifth is an impregnable fortress, in which to take refuge when surrounded by an enemy.

'In order, therefore, to sustain the full splendour of the monarchy, I have resolved to take up my abode in the aforesaid stronghold. I have already sent hither my treasures and all that I hold most highly. Those who are firmly resolved to imitate my example may follow me.'

Having thus concluded his speech he dismissed them, and all those amongst them who had either sense or experience adopted the measure proposed by the king. They dispatched their families, goods and provisions to the fortress.

Chosroes's satraps, meanwhile, were scouring the Indian kingdom and occupying it even as the weather turned inclement. Every hostile force was defeated. Having reached the capital, they encamped at a distance of three miles, not venturing to assault it. The Indian prince had commanded his citizens to go forth into battle. Accordingly, a great number had done so, with the sovereign at the head of four thousand combatants, officers of the court, other faithful partisans and slaves. The prince took up his post near the city, not allowing his immediate followers to mingle either with the army or the urban militia. He then placed the elephants in battle mode and marshalled his forces one last time.

In the capital, two of Chosroes's emissaries sought to take advantage of what appeared a favourable opportunity – the absence of the king – and as soon as he was gone, raised a tumult. Followed by their partisans they seized the king's lieutenant and killed him, took possession of the capital and fortified themselves within it. The prince was in the camp when he saw the chief priest of the Magi running barefoot, his head uncovered, tearing his hair and smacking his face. The ruler immediately asked him to mount his elephant and, interrogating him, discovered that the capital had fallen and that people had revolted. The prince and his followers immediately turned towards the secure fortress, with many loyal and faithful subjects following his track. Apprised of this movement, the satraps sent several squadrons of cavalry troops in pursuit. They overtook the Indian prince, who repulsed the attack and continued his march until he reached the citadel.

Meanwhile, the satraps who advanced on the capital entered it, appointed an administrator and then moved with their armies in the direction of the stronghold where the Indian ruler had sought refuge. There, Chosroes's men concluded that the splendid and imposing fortress was impregnable. It was so formidable that the satraps pitched their camps at a certain distance from which they could cautiously keep watch. In the end, they wrote a letter to the Indian prince couched in respect and reverence, proposing surrender terms. These would have granted the Indian prince full and honourable restitution of his throne and kingdom, provided he would recognize the supremacy of, and swear allegiance to, Chosroes.

The messenger who delivered these terms to the Indian prince was not granted an audience; nor was the letter received. Instead, the prince sent the messenger back, and the satraps lost all hope of persuading the Indian to surrender.

It was said: 'If you so much as bestow a glance on your enemy, you lose your advantage. And if you listen to his words, you submit yourself to him.'

It was said: 'By demonstrating friendly approval to the enemy, you expose yourself to the risk of being submerged in his world, and of falling into his schemes.'

It was said: 'When a man bows to listen to his enemy, what good does it do if he obtains nothing in exchange?'

It was said: 'He who cannot resist the temptation to gossip with the enemy is incapable of guarding himself against its stratagems.'

The satraps then returned to the capital. One of them wrote Chosroes, informing him of his success but warning of his fears. Chosroes ordered him to hold the places he had occupied and defer an attack on the fortress until such time as it appeared that troops guarding the besieged prince were beginning to lose courage. Chosroes further commanded a strict watch over the fortress, surrounding it on every side with advanced posts. These orders were punctually executed by the satraps.

The Persians grew insolent in the conquered kingdom and treated its people with harshness and violence totally foreign to the Indian character. Hatred began to fester in the hearts of the citizenry. They became jealous when they saw how revenues derived from their soil were taken out of the country; foreign interests rather than native labourers reaped its fruits. Once again they learned to appreciate whatever advantages they had enjoyed earlier, as the contrasts made their current predicaments intolerable. They began to complain boldly. The Persians experienced the wrath of the Indians; city inhabitants took courage in voicing their displeasure, and the conquerors began to fear the people's alienation if they were further repressed.

It was said: 'Subjects first shake their tongues and then their fists. Rulers cannot control their tongues unless they master their whole bodies, nor will sovereigns remain in power unless they can win the hearts of the masses. But these hearts will never cleave to a sovereign if he does not administer justice impartially (applying similar measures to high and low), lighten taxes on provisions and labour and exempt his subjects from excessive taxation. These three causes are in fact those that generate hatred amongst the upper classes and propel the lower ones to long more ardently to rise to their level.'

There are three kinds of subjects. The first are worthy individuals who are faithful and who recognize the superiority of the ruler. They acknowledge the importance of the care that is devoted to him, and feel the burden of his responsibilities. Their affection towards the ruler may be recognized by their graciousness and courtesy. The second group includes good and bad individuals who must, therefore, be held in check by a combination of gentleness and severity. The third is the populace that always supports those who advocate causes without questioning either their words or actions. They side without knowing friend from foe. They must be governed through fear, without harsh treatment, and tough punishment without excessive rigour.

To neglect the repression of slight faults is to encourage additional crimes. Thus the dishonour of a woman has its origin in a flattering word, the restiveness of a horse in an unchecked leap.

Well established in the fortress, the Indian prince consulted his ministers on his actions. They recommended him to be patient; fight depression; execute strict justice; secure the roads near the citadel; protect whomever should seek refuge; conciliate the alienated affections of his subjects and always practice generosity and clemency. He observed these precepts with precision as if they had been those of holy law. His fame increased, and his subjects grew fond of him and blessed him.

Meanwhile, a prefect appointed by the satrap in one of the border districts was accused of unbecoming conduct. A local chief went to warn and admonish him with friendly advice. The prefect took umbrage and falsely accused this individual, insinuating that this person opposed the government and stirred up the masses. Naturally, the satrap commanded that he should be sent to him, in chains. As the prefect ordered the man seized and bound, and as preparations were underway to send him to the satrap under an infantry escort, a group of daring youths attacked the convoy, slaughtered the escort and liberated the prisoner. The latter, a man of great power and influence in the community, thereupon presented himself before the prefect and told him what had occurred. He further confessed that he had not been able to prevent the attack. In response, the prefect commanded the man's head to be cut off. But when the sentence was executed, the people of the city rose in rebellion, slew the prefect and most of his soldiers and prepared to defend themselves.

Rebel ranks soon swelled both in the city and in the fortified places in the vicinity with those who held similar views of authority. Letters were sent to neighbouring provinces, where many imitated this example and expelled their current prefects. Thus in a very short time several provinces of the kingdom had renounced their allegiance to Chosroes. These developments filled the satrap with terror and amazement. He assembled his slaves, increased supplies into his strongholds and wrote Chosroes requesting assistance.

There was in the capital a vicar of the chief priest of the Magi, who had been elected by the people when the chief priest had followed the prince to the fortress. This vicar, a man universally loved, saw that the satrap was filled with alarm and mistrust and determined to seek him out.

The satrap's men in the capital had begun to molest citizens whom they most feared, with all manner of punishment and oppression. 'I came,' said the vicar, 'to inquire after a well known development.'

'What is it,' replied the satrap? The vicar continued:

'I have been informed that, amongst the maxims bequeathed in his testament by Ardashir, son of Babak and king of Babel, is the following: "The severity of a government often drives subjects to revolution, of which they had otherwise not thought."

'Elsewhere in the same testament is written: "Let him who has seized the territory of another never forget by what means he succeeded in gaining possession over it. He should know that he who does not rule over it in a manner pleasing to the Almighty Lord, this kingdom shall be taken away from him in precisely the same manner, and in the same conditions, that he used to gain its possession. Because both are recorded against him by eternal justice, and his conduct confirms the decree enjoining the liberation of the country from his hands." It is related that this testament was written in the hall of state of the royal palace, opposite the throne, and at the spot where Ardashir imparted justice.'

The satrap understood the meaning of the Indian vicar but wished to see how far the latter would go. He merely replied, 'So it is, priest.'

'Since it is so,' replied the vicar, 'why do you not govern according to these principles? Why do you oppress the people with tyranny? This has already led a number of them to rebel, and will prompt others to follow suit. Do you not fear that this kingdom may escape from your grasp the same way it fell into your hands?'

On hearing these statements and questions, the satrap delivered a stern and menacing reproach. The elderly and infirm vicar swooned to the ground and was carried to his home, where he died a few days later. His death made matters considerably worse. People vented their frustration and displeasure and, setting aside earlier considerations, openly opposed the occupiers. The satrap summoned city elders, strictly admonished them and threatened them with the full weight of Chosroes's power. He tormented them, hinting that he would exterminate them all, but they managed to delay any responses while they escaped. Meanwhile, the rebellion throughout the provinces gathered strength and the satrap, preoccupied with security in the capital, could not take any measures to repress it.

Simultaneously, rebel forces dispatched a messenger to their rightful sovereign begging for forgiveness and requesting a distinguished leader who could rally the troops. The king, thereupon, granted them a general amnesty and appointed a prefect who received full support. Rebel units obeyed him implicitly and defended him with utmost zeal.

The satraps were thus compelled to dispatch troops against the rebellious provinces. They soon returned, defeated and demoralized, forcing them to lead fresh forces in person. Before leaving, the satraps appointed a governor – whom they believed to be capable – but the capital was largely defenceless. They then marched against the insurgents, but no sooner had they left the city than its inhabitants rose against the Persians, slaying some, arresting the rest and fortifying their positions throughout the capital. News of these developments reached the satraps who, cognizant of what was lost, abandoned the kingdom. They reached Chosroes defeated and as fugitives. The Indian prince, on the other hand, returned to his capital and henceforward governed according to the strictest rules of justice, displayed greater firmness in resisting his passions and practised the wisdom he had gained from this experience.

A Citizen of Madina Speaks to 'Uthman ibn 'Affan

I have read that 'Uthman ibn 'Affan, who was besieged at the time of the rebellion, turned one day to his companions and exclaimed: 'I wish that a man could be found who would speak frankly.'

Whereupon a young *Ansari* (supporter)[1] from Madina rose and said 'O Prince of the Faithful, I will speak to you. I say to you that you acquiesce and, therefore, they oppose you; that you cater to your urges and therefore, they ignore you; and it is nothing else than your excessive mildness that has rendered them so daring.'

'You have spoken the truth,' replied the Caliph, 'sit here. And do you know,' he continued, 'what kindles rebellion?'

'Doubtless, I know it, O Prince of the Faithful,' answered the youth. 'I once asked an elderly experienced man of the tribe of Tunukh, who had visited several countries and had learned many doctrines. "There are two causes," he revealed to me, "that give rise to revolutions: the first is partiality, that awakens hatred towards the great; the second, mildness, that encourages audacity amongst the populace."'

'And did you ask him,' continued 'Uthman, 'what should be done to crush them?'

---

1. The *Ansar*, or 'supporters', were the believers who received and assisted the Prophet Muhammad in Madina after his flight from Makka. They are sometimes more explicitly called *Ansar al-Nabi*, the 'Supporters of the Prophet.'

'Yes', resumed the youth, 'and he told me that sedition may be checked when it starts, by correcting the sovereign's own errors and by extending equally to all the nobles the favour that had hitherto been shown only to a few. But when a rebellion has gathered strength, there is no other remedy than patience.'

'And I', replied the Caliph, 'will wait with patience until God, the most righteous of judges, shall decide between me and my enemies.'

Sayings of a Philosopher to Yezdejird II

There is a tale related by the Persians concerning Yezdejird, son of Bahram. When a wise philosopher was asked what made good government, the philosopher replied: 'In benevolence towards subjects; in taking from them what is justly due without violence; in soothing their hearts through impartiality; in ensuring their security; and in rendering justice to those who were injured.'

'And who is a virtuous monarch?' asked Yezdejird.

'If the ministers are good, the king will likewise be good,' replied the philosopher.

'O Philosopher,' resumed the king, 'the masses have already embarked on the path of revolution. Explain to us how they arise and how they may be stopped once they are so motivated.'

'Revolutions have their origin in disappointment,' was the reply, 'and the audacity of the masses causes them to engage. The insolence of the great gives birth to revolutions (that are propelled by ideas), as well as the timidity of the rich, the confidence of the poor, the carelessness of those with plenty and the wakefulness of those who suffer.'

'And what is it that can quell the masses, O Philosopher!' added Yezdejird. And the philosopher answered: 'They may be quelled, O Prince, by providing in a timely fashion that which you have reason to fear; earnestly applying yourself to business, acting according to a steadfast purpose; arming yourself with patience; and resigning yourself to the decrees of Fate.'

'Well said,' concluded the monarch.

4

Contentment

Verses From the Holy Qur'an

God, whose name is blessed, has said of those who doubted his judgments and ordinances and ill endured the division of his ordained tithes and booty:

> If a share is given then, they are contented; but if they receive nothing, they grow resentful. (9:58)

Thereafter, he warned them of their discontent, with these words:

> Would that they were satisfied with what God and His apostle have given them, and said: 'God is all-sufficient for us. God will provide for us from His own abundance, and so will His apostle. To God we will submit. (9:59)

And for the virtue of contentment, God has praised his prophet, saying:

> God is well pleased with them, and they are well pleased with Him. (58:22)

Tradition Concerning Moses

O Reader, you may understand the pleasure that God takes in them, and they in God, by that which is related concerning Moses, upon whom be the peace of God. Moses exclaimed: 'Oh my God, show me some work by which I may find favour in your eyes;' and God, whose name be exalted and praised, answered, 'You cannot do it.' Then Moses bowed his head and humbled his soul before God. God answered him again: 'O son of Ibn 'Imran ('Amran), I shall be well pleased with you, may you be well pleased with my decree.'

Sayings of the Prophet on Contentment

The Prophet, upon whom be peace and the blessing of God, once said: 'Oh, my God, I ask of you the virtue of contentment after your decree.' It is maintained that he used the expression 'after your decree' because, before God's decree, contentment implied nothing more than being contented. A disposition to accept God's decree willingly, whenever it should manifest itself, is real contentment.

It has moreover been handed down to us that one day the Prophet met with one of his companions, who was complaining of his ailments and poverty. The Prophet admonished him, saying: 'Now what is the cause of this impatience in you?'

'It arises from suffering and need, O Apostle of God!' replied the other, and the Prophet resumed:

'Don't you know that I can teach you a lesson through which God will deliver you from these tribulations?'

'By Him who has sent you to reveal the truth,' resumed his companion, 'the only thing that gives me joy in the midst of my sufferings is to have fought together with you at Badr and at Hudaybiyya.'

'Don't you think,' continued the Prophet, 'that the same portion is allotted to the warriors of Badr and Hudaybiyya as to those contented and resigned.'

Philosophical Sayings on Contentment

The prince of the faithful, 'Umar ibn al-Khattab, may God be well pleased with him, wrote to Abu Musa al-Ash'ari:

'Without a doubt, all blessings are encompassed within contentment. Be content if you can, and if not, endure with patience.'

Abu Darda' has said: 'The ultimate happiness is to bear the powers of this world with patience and be content with the judgement of fate.'

When Sa'ad ibn Abi Waqqas reached Makka after the loss of his eyesight, people gathered to entreat that he would pray to God for them. 'Abdallah ibn Sa'id declared to him: 'Oh, my uncle, you always pray for others, and God hears you; wherefore, then, do you not implore him to restore your sight?'

Sa'id smiled, and replied, 'Oh, my nephew, God's decree is far dearer to me than my sight.'

And be it known to you, O reader, and may God be merciful unto you, that contentment consists in ceasing to demand from others that which is to our own advantage. Since destiny is inevitable, he who sets himself against it is a fool; he who is content with it shall be crowned with success; and he who lays aside all invocations shall be prosperous and happy.

It is better to govern contentment than be governed by it. Incline yourself to contentment before you are compelled to it by necessity.

Hassan al-Basri was interrogated one day as to where unhappiness originated. He replied: 'From the absence of contentment in God.'

And when asked further, 'where does this proceed from?' he responded, 'from lack of knowledge of God.'

I have composed the following verses on contentment:

Oh, you who are my refuge in the misfortunes that befall me, and have compassion for my bitter losses.
I feel in my heart the desire to gladly do whatever you wish.
If I appeal my fate to a judge who speaks plainly.
And reveals himself to all.

Oh, you who behold my fate;
And know that I cannot do other than be content with it;
You from whom there is neither refuge nor defence;
Do not let your power weaken those you protect.

But if it is your pleasure that I should perish;
Make me ready for whatever you may decide.
Your every admonition shall be sweet;
Save for my separation from you and the flames of hell.

When I am wounded by God's decree,
I never reject it with anger or bitterness.
Such patience undoubtedly comes from knowledge
As contentment springs from reverence towards his decrees.'

The Education of Yezdejird II's Heir, Bahram Gour

When Sapor Dhul-Aktaf's son Yezdejird was blessed with a son, Bahram Gour, he consulted astrologers on the powerful influence that presided over the birth of the infant and of prospects for his fate. The astrologers told Yezdejird that the empire would indeed come under Bahram Gour's rule, but only after painful vicissitudes, trials and long wanderings. Moreover, Yezdejird was told that his heir would be educated in a foreign nation, in the midst of a high-minded and generous people ― but of a wrathful spirit ― through whose assistance he would attain supreme power.

Yezdejird, thinking about the virtues and qualities of all nations, concluded that the Arabs possessed such assets as identified by the astronomers. He therefore chose them and wrote Nu'man the Great, son of 'Umru' al-Qays ibn 'Uday ibn Nasr the Lakhmi, to visit him. Yezdejird received Nu'man, along with accompanying Arab chiefs who were presented with splendid gifts and treated with great courtesy. Yezdejird proposed making Nu'man their leader ― which they readily accepted ― whereupon Yezdejird invested Nu'man with royal robes, placed a crown on his head and proclaimed him King of the Arabs. He then entrusted his son to be educated under Nu'man's supervision. Nu'man appointed four wet-nurses for the royal infant, two Arabs and two Persians, all of lively intelligence, lofty lineage, and even temperament to whom he prescribed healthy life-styles. Then, returning with Bahram to his own country, he build Khawarnak, a castle positioned in an area with pure air and excellent water sources as recommended by Arab physicians.

After four years, when Bahram was breast-fed, the nurses weaned him. He grew into a robust child, and was so precocious that he seemed to have reached adolescence prematurely, speaking fluent Arabic and Persian at an early age.

When he attained the age of five, Bahram told Nuʻman that he desired to be instructed in studies that were suitable for princes. On this occasion, a dialogue occurred between them, which I have recorded in my book *Pearls for the Forehead*, that contains an abstract on the *Notices of Remarkable Children*. Nuʻman thereupon wrote Yezdejird requesting for his son's further instruction several philosophers, jurists and religious figures from Persia; Yezdejird complied. Nuʻman seconded to the group a wise and learned Arab whose name was Jalis, a man who had studied politics and literature and was well-versed in the histories and biographies of kings and the war chronicles of the Arabs as well as those of other nations. Each of these individuals instructed Bahram in his own specialty. At the age of twelve, Bahram knew more than all of them put together; realizing that the young prince needed no further instruction, they considered his education complete.

Nuʻman then dismissed the instructors after bestowing great honour upon each one of them, retaining only Jalis, from whom the youth would not be separated. Bahram held Jalis in great esteem because of his dignity, refined manners, literacy, political and historical knowledge and analytical clarity. Bahram had not seen the totality of these qualities in any other individual. Simultaneously, Nuʻman asked Yezdejird for military instructors to train his son in the art of war, horsemanship and other disciplines. These men proceeded with Bahram's education for three additional years. During this period the young prince mastered several new subjects. Nuʻman then honourably dismissed these masters as well, again retaining Jalis because the young man bore great affection towards him.

When Bahram reached fifteen years, Nu'man requested and obtained Yezdejird's permission to return his son to him in person. Several Arab chiefs and lords accompanied him on his journey. The King of Persia was pleased to receive them. He lodged them sumptuously, showered Nu'man with presents and overwhelmed him with honours and distinctions. He then thanked him for his services and allowed him to return to his country. Bahram, however, would not be separated from Jalis, to whom he was closely attached on account of their friendship.

Yezdejird was a stern man, tough, proud, inaccessible and swift to shed blood and seize the property of his subjects, on which account he received the surname of al-Athim, or the Great. He treated his son with the harshness that was natural to him, and made him suffer innumerable vexations and hardships. He appointed Bahram 'Superintendent of the Drink', that annoyed the young man beyond measure. Unable to accept these conditions, Bahram complained to Jalis. The sage showed him compassion, and addressed him in these words: 'May God console your sorrow, exalt your glory, make you loved by your people. Make them bow down beneath your sceptre along with the kings of the Arabs, and the barbarians. You should know that the most capable in giving upright counsel is the one recognized as such, and if called and instructed to do so, he is the ruler.'

It was said: 'Good counsel is nauseating at first and sweet in the end. It is like medicine that disgusts you when you take it but causes you to rejoice after you experience its beneficial effects. When you first drink such medicine, you curse; but then laud the heaven for its positive results.'

It was said: 'The faithful minister stands beside the king with untiring zeal to serve him, and endeavours to give him sound advice; while the traitor seeks to win the king's favour through horrid flattery and exaggerated submissiveness.'

It was said: 'Sincere advisors do not find favour with the king, unless he is endowed with magnanimity; otherwise they will fail and the flatterers will succeed. This is the case because a truthful counsellor gives to others that which appears good in his own eyes and can only be understood by another lofty spirit.'

It was said: 'You will deserve severe blame if you withhold truthful counsel from the ruler who gives you his confidence, or if you conceal the best measures to be adopted after he has revealed his secret without reservations.'

It was said: 'Amongst the faithful and far-sighted counsellors, he is most deserving of attention whose prosperity depends on your own, and whose safety is tied to yours. He who stands in such a position, exerting himself for your interests, will likewise serve and defend himself while fighting for you.'

Jalis continued: 'I am grieved that the son of the King should be invested with such annoyance and vexation in submitting to his father's authority. For my part, I advise you to put up a good face in the matter, instead of exhibiting so much weariness and disgust. Once the King entrusts an office to an individual, it is as incumbent on that person to be gratified by it; for those who bear company to kings in a manner not pleasing to them only succeed in inflaming their rulers' anger against themselves. Nor do I mean to say, therefore, that we should assume an outward semblance contrary to that which we bear in our hearts. Because when we assume a nature foreign to our beliefs, the truth comes out, as is the case with hair tinged with a colour not its own. But, in the present case let the son of the King consider with an impartial eye the command that appears to him so grievous, and I am sure that he will acknowledge it to be good.

'In truth, the King has placed his son in charge of the consumption of certain drinks, that is to say, over his whole amusement, the only one in which his soul expands to joy and seeks recreation after the heavy responsibilities of government. Moreover, he has entrusted to his son the custody over his own life, and chosen him to watch over it in his most private affairs. During these amusements, he has committed to his son the safety of his person unreservedly, whether to protect him from the malice of his enemies (who might seek to poison his drinks) or from the perturbations of his mind (that might be caused by drunkenness and excitement). How, then, can so high and important a charge be considered unworthy of a generous and affectionate son? How would he feel if his father should entrust such a task to any other?

'Let the King's son reflect upon that which I have stated, and let him be persuaded that the responsibility is not only honourable and befitting of his stature, but may even be an enviable one. Let him submit contentedly to the arrangement that has been conferred upon him. Let him bestow his care and attention to discharge it well. He need not accept that which he abhors. Nor should he seek to be released from such duty, because that would be unsuccessful. After all, others would read into his behaviour, and their thoughts would guess what is in his soul, that which he was making every effort to conceal.'

It was said: 'Dissimulation is a mirage that only deceives short-sighted intellects but conceals nothing from those who can see through it.'

It was said: 'The power of dissimulation extends only over sight and hearing, the two senses that are satisfied with outward impressions, but that do not go beyond them. Its capability does not reach the intellect to which He, who is the Beginning and End of all things, reveals by His peculiar gift – things that cannot be perceived by the senses.'

'So it was with the bear,' continued Jalis, 'who, with all his stupidity, discovered that the monkey was acting a role.'

'Tell me how that came to be,' said Bahram, and the sage thus resumed his discourse.

The Bear and the Monkey

It is related that a bear, living in a marsh richly covered with fruit trees where a large tribe of monkeys also lived, admired the latter's agility as they ascended the trees, sprang from branch to branch and chose the most delicious fruits. The bear wished to catch a monkey to compel it to gather fruit for him. To this end he went to a place where a large group of monkeys assembled and began to climb up a tree, making them believe that he wished to ascend even higher. All of a sudden, he stopped his climb and fell, to show the monkeys that he could no longer hold on. Falling to the ground, he twitched his legs for a while and, at last, ceased to move. He opened his mouth and pretended to be dead.

The monkeys, thereupon, assembled around him. A shrewd monkey said: 'It is not at all unlikely that the bear may be practising some evil stratagem. Prudence dictates that we should not approach him and should remain on our guard.

But if we must go near him, let us collect some wood, pile it up around him, and set fire to it. Then, if he is only pretending to be dead he will be taken in, and if he is really dead there is no harm in burning him.'

It was said: 'Your enemy is your opposite. It is the nature of opposites to avoid each other, to turn their backs on each other and mutually do their utmost to increase the distance that separates them.'

It was said: 'Do not tread the same soil with your enemy unless you are armed and on your guard, and do not be deceived by the knowledge that he may have left. For, before his departure, he may well have spread a net to prepare his attack.'

It was said: 'Do not go against your enemy unless you are well-armed, and proceed with caution and vigilance. If he is unarmed, do not be deceived because not all weapons are visible.'

'Likewise', continued the monkey, 'the Hermit fell into the Scoundrel's trap, and suffered the consequences.'

'Tell us the story,' said the other monkeys, and the wise animal continued:

The Hermit and the Thief

It is related that a hypocritical monk retired to a hermitage at a certain distance from the city, where members of his flock would visit him frequently out of devotion and the wish to obtain the benefit of his prayers. The monk pretended that the miserable condition of the poor believers who frequently visited him wrung his heart. Still, he insisted that he could not give them relief. Thereupon, well-off devotees began to give him large sums of money to dispense to those deserving of charity, as he insisted he knew best to do so. The monk appropriated this money to his own use and customarily buried it, with the exception of a small portion that he actually distributed to the indigent to better impose upon faithful almsgivers.

It was said: 'The cheat is equal to the robber in villainy and superior to him in cowardice and shamelessness.'

It was also said: 'The rogue will suck blood under the semblance of charity, until the most simple-minded agree with his villainy. But when this has come to pass, all compassion will be withdrawn from him, leaving only hatred in its place.'

A thief, concluding that the alms collected by this hermit were substantial, was determined to rob him by scaling the wall of his hermitage. One night he set to work, scaled the wall and found the hermit saying his prayers in the chapel by the light of a lamp. Whereupon, he yelled out: 'Surrender yourself, old man, if you would not have me cut off your head.'

Turning round at these words, and seeing a young and strong man brandishing a smart dagger, the hermit realized that resistance would be vain. He interrupted his prayers and fled from the thief towards the side of the chapel. There was a niche in the wall, into which he thrust his head – placing his arms behind his back in the posture that a man is compelled to assume in order that he may be bound. The thief, thinking that he meant to surrender as vanquished and hiding his head from fright, sheathed his dagger and was preparing to seize him when all of a sudden the floor gave way beneath his feet and he fell into a pit with a violence that deprived him of all his strength.

The hermit looked at the thief and, seeing him defeated and his prisoner, said: 'So you are caught, you covetous villain!'

'Yes, you impostor,' replied the thief! 'Then lie there and die,' continued the monk. 'Do you think that, after having gulled donors of this money, I do not know how to secure it?'

'But I do not think,' replied the thief, 'that you can defend through prostration.'

'Fool!' retorted the monk, 'do you not see that the nets in which I enclosed it, and the snares in which I trapped and caught it, were no other than a few reverences with my face on the ground, a few tears, a few sighs, a few contortions, a few hours spent in prayer and in patching my friar's gown?' The thief remained there all night, unable to escape. At daylight, the hermit denounced him to the authorities and he was taken and led to execution.

The hermit had dug a deep pit in line with a niche and fitted a trap into it that gave way beneath the weight of any who pressed upon it, then covered it with a mat from the chapel. He himself, in escaping from the thief towards the niche, had taken good care not to step on it, but to pass by; while the other miscreant, who knew nothing about it and used no prudence, trusted the apparent surrender of the monk without perceiving that the latter may have prepared an invisible defensive weapon.

Continuation of the Fable of the Bear and the Monkey

The monkeys heard their sage companion's parable and took care not to approach too near the bear, but collected wood to burn him. A foolish monkey, however, who was neither present for nor heard this counsel, approached the bear and laid its ear on its mouth to determine whether he was breathing. The Bear, therefore, caught him. Having torn up a fibre from the roots of the *khayzuran* (rod), the bear tied one end around the monkey's body while he held the other. He compelled the monkey to climb trees, gather the choicest fruits and throw them down. This lasted the rest of the day. In the evening, the bear led the monkey to a cave, where he imprisoned him. Returning the next day, he dragged forth the poor little animal, carried it to the marsh, compelled it to spend the whole day gathering fruits and at night, again, imprisoned it in the cave. This behaviour continued for a long time. The Bear achieved his wishes while the monkey, thrown into the most deplorable condition, spent each day serving the bear and each night in prison.

It was said: 'He who volunteers to do that which is not his business will find grief.'

It was said: 'The passions of a man of reason are subordinate to his judgment. If a desire awakens his mind, he submits it to judgment, then examines its origins and implications before disposing of it according to the dictates of reason. But the judgment of the fool is subordinate to his passions. If a fool conceives a wish, he pursues it with all his might, as nothing in the world can restrain him.'

It was said: 'A trifle of food that you are compelled to carry on your shoulders to your enemy is a crushing weight. For it weighs upon the mind as much as upon the body, and hence its annoyance is overwhelming. It is the reverse, however, when the provisions are to be carried to a friend because the mind rejoices in the task and the body obeys the mind.'

Meanwhile, the monkey, reflecting upon his situation, concluded that the good faith with which he served the bear, prevented an escape from the latter's clutches. So, repenting of his uprightness, and convinced that only cunning could allow him to escape, he devised a clever trick to play on his master.

It was said: 'When the passions of a slave are muted, his understanding obtuse and his thoughts grovelling, then he will be true to his master. But if the slave is free from these poor judgements, his master will soon find that he must share him with others more powerful than himself. If a slave has any passions, he will not accept to be ruled. If his intellect is sound, he will exert it to find some alleviation of his sufferings, or to devise a method of escaping from his captivity or of defending his person. If the thoughts of the slave awaken, indignation, rancour and hatred will follow. In turn, these impulses will lead him where he prefers, not where his master pleases.'

Amongst the plots the monkey devised against the bear was that of feigning his sight to be much impaired. For this purpose, he began to throw him rotten fruits; upon which the bear reproached him vehemently. This did not produce any effects on the monkey. The bear then beat the monkey, but that did not stop his approach. After this behaviour continued for some time, the bear said: 'I am tired of reproaching and beating you, and I have decided to eat you, since you are no longer of any use to me.'

It was said: 'When you find your servants ill-disposed, you better serve yourself by ending their service. For the vexation that they will cause you is equal to the fatigue you would have to endure if you waited on yourself.'

The monkey replied to the bear's threat: 'I am not so ill-disposed as you may think, and if you were to kill me, you would have to repent as the miller did when he killed his ass.'

'Tell me that story,' said the bear, and the monkey started:

The Miller and the Ass

It is related that a miller had a little ass that turned his mill, and a misguided wife whom he dearly loved but who had a fancy for one of his neighbours. Nevertheless, the neighbour avoided the miller's wife and, indeed, hated her. One night the miller had a dream in which he was ordered to 'go and dig the circle around the mill wheel to find a treasure.' The miller hastened to share his dream with his wife, bidding her not to repeat it to any living creature.

It was said: 'He is a fool he who is relieved to trumpet his secret. For the labour of acting by yourself is less of an evil than to divulge a secret to others.'

It was said: 'There are two things that deprive a free man of his liberty — rendering homage to virtue and divulging a secret. The interpretation of this saying is as follows. If you hold another to be a just man, you will implicitly submit yourself to him. For a man becomes the servant of whomever he holds in great esteem. Likewise, if you communicate your secret to another, the fear that he may betray you will make you humble and reverent towards him.'

It was said: 'Women are gifted at keeping house, cooking, nursing children, maintaining household staff and exciting as well as soothing passions. He who asks them to take part in his affairs or imparts to them a secret cannot but otherwise be part of their world, since the capacity of women does not enable them to become part of his domain.'

No sooner had the miller related his dream to his wife that she hastened to communicate it to the neighbour whom she loved, hoping to gain his affection through this gesture. The neighbour promised to go with her that same night to the identified spot, where they would dig together. They did so, found the money and took it out. Then the neighbour said to the woman: 'What will you do with this money?'

She replied: 'We will divide it equally between us, and will each go home with our own share. You shall divorce your wife and I will do likewise with my husband. Then you shall marry me, and when we are man and wife the whole of the money will be united in our hands.'

'No', said the neighbour, 'I will be afraid that riches will make you arrogant and you will take a fancy to some other lover.'

It was said: 'Gold shines in a house like the sun in the world, and no one can do without it except for the austere, who hate this world and are grieved at the necessity of dwelling in it. But the true ascetic is he who leads an austere life in youth, whereas that virtue is false if one feigns to restrain the desires of a worn-out and decrepit soul but only abstains in the gloomiest period of life.'

It was said: 'He who attains luxury beyond his station no longer recognizes his former friends.'

It was said: 'Wealth ruins women because their passion dominates reason.'

It was said: 'Never give your children, wife or servants more than they require, for they will only obey you so long as they need you.'

'It would be better,' continued the neighbour, 'that all the money should remain in my hands, so that I might employ it more efficiently while you free yourself and marry me.'

'But', rejoined the woman, 'I feel the very same mistrust that you do of me, and have not the slightest intention of entrusting my part of the treasure. Why should you bear this grudge towards me? Was it not I who pointed out the existence of the treasure to you rather than to any other person?'

It was said: 'It is only in consequence of corruption that justice and equity merit gratitude; for it is, in fact, only he who does more than he is obliged to who is deserving of gratitude. He who gives those around him what he owes them, merits commendation, but not thanks.'

On hearing these words the neighbour, compelled by malice, indignation and fear lest the woman accuse him to her relations, killed her and flung her corpse into the place where they had dug the treasure. As day began to dawn, he did not stay to cover up the body but in all haste loaded the treasure on his shoulders and went his way.

Scarcely was he gone when the miller came to fasten the ass to the handle of the millstone within the circle, and gave a shout to urge him forward. The animal advanced a few steps and then, finding the pit and the corpse before him, stood still. The miller beat him vigorously, and the ass writhed and twisted about without moving forward a single step. His master, who could not possibly see the obstacle that prevented the advance of the poor beast, took a knife and began to prick him. Having done so a few times in vain, and becoming more enraged, the miller dealt him a violent blow in the side. As the whole knife cut the animal, the ass fell down dead. While this was going on, the morning had grown lighter so that, finally, the miller saw the hole and found in it his dead wife. He pulled her out, and discovered underneath her the vestiges of the treasure. In rage and despair at the simultaneous loss of his money, wife and ass, the miller committed suicide.

Continuation of the Fable of the Bear and the Monkey

When the monkey stopped his tale, the bear rejoined: 'I see clearly from your parable that the ass had a sufficient excuse for his conceit, but what excuse can you have?'

The monkey replied: 'This: that my sight is failing me, and that I am even fearful of losing it altogether. Now, if you choose to have me cured, that is your affair.'

'And who do I have,' responded the bear, 'who can restore your eyesight, upon which depends your selection of fruits and, consequently, my welfare?'

'There is no shortage of physicians,' answered the monkey, 'but those who are wise consult only those of their own species. The monkeys of this country have amongst them a very famous and skilled physician, and I have no doubt that, if I went to see him, my eyes would be healed. Perhaps even the very sight of him would do me good.'

The bear agreed to this idea and the monkey was taken to a physician celebrated for his cunning and craft. When the pair reached their destination the physician monkey escaped up a tree, but the bear, stationing himself at its foot, described his servant's illness, entreating for a cure. The cunning monkey replied: 'Let him come up here, that I may examine him with my own eyes.' Whereupon the bear, lengthening the cord that held the monkey, sent him up.

As the other physician began to examine the monkey's eyes and to ask him a number of questions, the prisoner was able to describe the life he led with the bear and implored his friend to teach him a stratagem so that he might obtain his deliverance. On hearing this, the shrewd monkey said, 'You can count on me persuading him to stay up all night, and then you must choose your opportunity to escape when he falls asleep. But take care that he does not feign sleep and watch you.'

Then, dismissing him and turning to the bear, he continued: 'Before I prescribe anything, I must inform you of the matter with your slave, for it is absurd to assume that he who is ignorant of the disease can prescribe a cure. You should therefore know that the reason why monkeys enjoy such good health, and are so sharp-sighted, slim and lively, is because it is their nature to be very wakeful, and to take several excursions at night.'

Accordingly, it was said: 'Too much sleep brings destruction and ravishes away life.'

It was said: 'He who is addicted to slumber can never attain his goal.'

It was said: 'The common definition of liberality, that it consists in giving away things of great value, is not correct. For, in that case the sluggard would be the most liberal of all men, since he gives away his own life without hope of compensation.'

'Doubtless',continued the cunning physician monkey, 'by withdrawing your servant from his mode of life, you have introduced the principle of dissolution into his frame, as was the case with the little bird that was caught for the king's daughter.'

Tell me about that,' said the bear, and the monkey continued:

The King's Daughter and the Little Bird

A king had a daughter who was the apple of his eye. She fell ill and became so weak that she could no longer eat or drink. The physician who attended her prescribed that she should be

moved to a country house with a delightful garden watered by
several streams. This was done accordingly.

The very day of her arrival, she saw a richly feathered bird
poised on a gazebo of vines, pecking at the grapes and singing
the sweetest of songs compounded with many tender
melodies. On seeing and hearing this, the maiden was so
cheered that she immediately asked for something to eat.

It was said: 'The melody that goes straight to the heart is
that which proceeds from the lips of beauty. Since it moves
both senses and feelings – as these two forces emulate each
other – the melody acts like compound medicines. At once
more salutary and more efficient than simple ones.'

The bird then flew away, and did not return for the
remainder of the day. Its absence caused the maiden much
anxiety. Still, when the bird reappeared at the same hour the
following day, she was greatly relieved and delighted, and
proceeded to eat and drink. When the bird flew away, as it
had done the first day, she relapsed into the same state of
uneasiness.

The king was informed of these developments. He gave
orders to catch the bird. The servants succeeded in doing so
and placed it in a cage, which the damsel watched constantly.
She took great delight in it, and now ate and drank with
abandon. When the physician – who knew nothing about the
bird – saw her thus regaining strength, he attended to her
with redoubled diligence, as he now hoped for a permanent
cure. The bird, meanwhile, spent several days without singing
or eating, and the beauty of its feathers began to fade. The
maiden, therefore, fell back into her former state or even a
worse one, as she was overwhelmed by a new anxiety. Her
father was again informed of what had transpired and he
began to regret that he had ordered the capture of the bird.

It was said: 'Do not be the student of one who answers every question before having considered all its aspects before reflecting on its corollaries and deduced either from the questions themselves or from his own answers and prepared himself to refute objections that an opponent might raise, or before obviating the possibility of the latter detecting contradiction in his own principles. This is the same reason you should not seek advice from an inexperienced youth, who would not be able to trace from the beginning to the end the consequences of the measures he would propose to you. Rather, choose to be a disciple of he who ponders the conclusion of a dispute before answering — in the same way that, if you desired advice, you would ask it from an experienced man, who would be able to scrutinize the matter from the surface to the core and would be able to see its beginning and its end.'

The perplexed physician was distraught with the princess's deteriorating health. He concluded that it must be the result of special circumstances and inquired into the matter. When the story of the bird was related to him, he immediately suggested that the whole garden should be enclosed in a great net and, once this was done, he set the bird at liberty within it. The animal, returning to its customary dwelling and habits, was as lively and beautiful as ever, and resumed its delightful singing. The princess improved in health, too, until she recovered from her illness.

Continuation of the Fable of the Bear and the Monkey

When the Monkey ended his parable, the bear said to him: 'I have heard your stories and understood your meaning. If you will now prescribe that which will restore my slave to health, I will do whatever you direct.'

'I prescribe', replied the cunning physician-monkey, 'that you remain a considerable part of the night where you go to feed in the daytime. There is no doubt that this will prolong your life, increase your appetite and enjoyment, enliven your spirits, soothe your sleep and, simultaneously, restore your slave's health.'

Thanking the physician for this advice, the bear proceeded to his pasture ground, where the monkey supplied him with bad fruit all day long. But at night, it exhibited more liveliness and alacrity. He began to throw down an occasional good fruit, as it had done in earlier times. The early part of the night having passed, the bear led him back to the cave and imprisoned him in it.

The next morning, they resumed their usual activities. Over the course of the next few days, the monkey pretended that his sight improved at night, enhancing his choices of fruit. The bear, however, did not trust the monkey. On the contrary, he held him to be a deceitful hypocrite. As the monkey multiplied his stratagems, the bear became more suspicious.

Finally, one night when the bear wanted to go to his lair, the monkey attempted to detain him, exclaiming every now and then: 'Here, here, are some juicy ones!' The bear, in compliance with his fierce and rugged nature but also to verify his suspicions – consented to stay, as there was a bright moonlight that would enable him to keep a better watch over the monkey while he pretended to be asleep. Feigning a profound slumber, he began to snore as the monkey attempted his escape. The bear drew on the cord with such force that he broke the monkey's back and killed it instantly.

Continuation of the History of Bahram Gour

Bahram listened to Jalis and praised him, persuaded by the advice, and addressed the sage: 'What a blessing it is for me to have you at my side, and how refreshing it is to my spirit to hear the precepts that you have taught me. The examples that you have set before me, and the wise sayings you have uttered, have resounded in my ears. Have faith, for if you live until I accede the throne you will be the first to enter my chambers and the last to leave them. You will regulate my conduct according to your advice, trust God for the rest.' Jalis, prostrating himself at these words, implored Heaven to fulfill Bahram's wishes.

On a spring day, Yezdejird was in one of his favourite haunts where the pavement had been strewn with flowers until it appeared covered with carpets of velvet and bouquets of gems. The king was in a good mood when Bahram entered the hall. Taking his place nearby in fulfilment of his office, and turning his eyes on the bystanders all about the hall, Bahram was entranced by the sight of the flowers. This reminded him of his stay at the court of Nu'man. He recalled banquets in beautiful gardens, where they drank amidst flowers bathed in dew; the delight of going forth into the country at the peep of dawn to rouse wild beasts from their lairs and take pleasure in chasing, overtaking and capturing them. While he was absorbed in such thoughts Bahram remained silent, his eyes fixed on the ground, breathing deeply, with a troubled disposition. Yezdejird, meanwhile, was stealthily observing his son. When the young man regained his composure he lifted his eyes and perceived that he had attracted his father's glances; he instantly regretted having done so. It was not long before Yezdejird, changing from his previous good humour, bent his head. Whereupon the guests and all the company rose to their feet, for it was the custom of the court of Persia that whenever the king appeared silent and displeased, all those present – without exception – should leave and remain motionless in awe and silence.

Present in the hall on this occasion was one of the king's jesters, a man of quick speech and wit, gifted with a lively imagination and a talent for uttering shrewd sayings on the spur of the moment. Guessing that the sight of his son sad and silent in the midst of a festive gathering had caused the king's displeasure, he endeavoured to serve Bahram and gain a favour. He began to think of a suitable ploy to shield the youth from the displeasure if the king. At that moment, Yezdejird raised his head and looked at him as if to call on him for a jest that might divert him. The jester prostrated himself. Then, rising on his knees and sitting on his heels, said: 'Your abject slave entreats the king's permission to relate a very curious adventure that happened to him.' Yezdejird signalled his acquiescence and the jester began his story.

The King of Persia's Jester

The humble slave claimed that he was, in his youth, a great admirer of women. When he saw a beautiful one he would desperately fall in love with her, but would soon grow tired of her, for constancy formed no part of his nature.

It was said: 'If you love at first sight, you may stumble and fall.'

It was said: 'Take care of your eyes, for a pernicious attachment often rises from their boldness. It is also related that a certain devotee, who was doing penance on pilgrimage and had with him as his fellow traveller a beautiful young woman, who veiled her eyes with his own *hijab*. When inquired for this reason, he replied: 'Because it is the glances of her eyes and not those of others, which awaken love.'

It was said: 'An inconstant man deserves that all his wishes be frustrated.'

It was said: 'Instability is the mark of a vulgar mind and not a lofty spirit.'

It was said: 'To give up one true love for another is as if a man changed his religion.'

Now it came to pass, continued the jester, that the king's slave was on a journey in Sind, passing through one of the cities of that province, when he fell in love with a woman who surpassed all others that were ever seen. He was moved by the beauty of her face; her height; the perfect symmetry of her limbs; her demeanour; the gracefulness of her movements; the fascination of her eyes; and the charm of her appearance. The king's slave at once followed her, so amazed that he scarcely knew where he was going, until she entered her house. He took up his post before her door and remained there day and night.

The woman sent for him to request that he leave, bidding him to take care lest her kinsfolk should harm him. But the king's slave only answered her messengers with his passionate lamentations. He concluded by saying that no human being could compel him to leave that doorway and, even if it were to cost him his life, he could not refrain from contemplating her beauty. The woman did not reply but sent another message to which he replied as before. Finally, she sent a third message, in these terms: 'I suspect you to be of a fickle nature, capable of taking advantage of me. Were it not for this, I would hasten to make you happy. Nevertheless, I will consent to marry you on condition that you wed no other wife. But I warn you, should you ever forsake me, not only will I put you to death without fail but before killing you, I will make such an example of you that you will become a legend. If, on these conditions, you still persist in your wish, then come. But if not, save yourself before it is too late.'

It was said: 'There are four kinds of fools who deserve no pity when some mishap befalls them. These are: he who accuses a physician of imposture because he is truthfully informed of his ailment; he who assumes a burden beyond his strength; he who wastes his substance in pleasure; and he who embarks upon an undertaking after he has been warned of its perils.'

It was said: 'He who opens your eyes, helps you; he who warns you, rouses you from sleep; he who speaks plainly is a sincere friend who honours you; and he who protests and warns you of that which he will do neither fails in his duty nor deceives you.'

The king's servant, continued the jester, accepted the bargain, pledging to observe its terms. He married the woman and lived with her for some time in peace. It so happened that a young female friend of hers came to visit. The ever-observant husband contemplated her and was captivated by her beauty. His whole soul turned towards her. He followed this young woman to her house, took up his post at her door and began to weary her with messages until she complained to his wife.

When the wife heard what had transpired, she complained, reproached him, reminded him of the conditions stipulated between them and asked him to desist from this pursuit. This, unfortunately, rendered him more obstinate. His wife perceived his wickedness, made an incantation that transformed him into a hideous slave and employed him in the meanest and most labourious tasks.

This punishment, however, did not change the man's nature. Nor did it produce any other effect than that of causing him to fall in love with another slave whom he courted with particular perseverance. Having exhausted her patience, the slave woman complained to her mistress as well.

It was said: 'Nature is more powerful in man than education. For our dispositions are original and strengthened by faculties that increase with our development. Supported by improving capabilities, our dispositions become citizens of the soul that is their dwelling. There, they luckily obtain a power beyond that of education, which is foreign and casual.'

It was said: 'The master who least likely attains his objective is the one who expects his pupil to assist him in subduing his own nature. For how can this occur when natural dispositions are stronger, more cherished, and have far more hold on the soul of the disciple than any master can boast of? The wisest instructor is he who requires his pupil to conceal the evil that is in one's nature.'

When the wife heard of her husband's latest adventure, she was filled with indignation and cast a fresh spell on him. She transformed him into an ass and set him to perform the hardest labour and bear the heaviest burdens, a condition in which he remained for a long time. Nevertheless, the hard labour did not quench his natural disposition, or prevent him from failing in love, this time with a jenny. Although the ass never saw the jenny, he began to bray and run after her with an eagerness that could only be restrained by blows. Naturally, the king's servant experienced a very hard life.

One day, the disconsolate wife paid a visit to the daughter of the king of that country, and was standing with her in an open gallery that commanded a view of the neighbourhood. On this same day a frail old man had hired the king's servant-ass and had laden him with earthenware goods in two sacks. The old man was driving to the palace of the princess when, near the palace, stood the jenny who was the animal's flame. He had so little control over himself that he immediately set off towards her, braying. People assembled to beat him and the goods he was carrying fell to the ground. The old man called for help as all the children gathered around to assault the poor animal. The jenny ran away, kicking with all her might, while the king's servant persisted in his pursuit. The king's daughter, on watching this absurd scene, could not contain her laughter. Yet, the distressed wife said to her, 'Oh, daughter of the king, I could tell you the story of this ass that will astonish you far more than what you have heard or seen.'

'I should be very glad to hear it,' replied the princess, and the woman, acknowledging that it was her husband, proceeded to relate the whole story from the beginning. The princess was greatly surprised and amused when, finally, she pleaded with her to let the husband go free. The woman consented and, having removed the spell, restored the king's servant to his former shape. His first thought was to escape from Sind.

End of the Story of Bahram Gour

At this joint, the jester stopped his tale and Yezdejird, who had been convulsed with laughter both by the story and by the manner of its narration, recovered his gravity and dignity. He then said angrily to the jester: 'Wretch, what was it that moved you to fabricate this evil falsehood? Do you not know that we have forbidden our subjects to lie, and that if they commit such a crime, we punish them?'

It was said: 'Falsehood is like poison. It may cause death if used alone but, when mixed in medicine by an apothecary, may be of service. A king may not permit falsehood except when used for the good of the state, for example to deceive an enemy or conciliate the disaffected. Likewise, kings must only allow such poisons to be kept in the hands of sound men, who would know how to withhold them from those with evil hands.'

'O most fortunate prince', replied the jester, 'this tale that I have related, contains precepts that may be beneficial to the person who accepts them correctly. But the motive that induced me to relate it is such that it may be revealed to none, save the king himself.' Yezdejird thereupon signalled those present to leave the hall. The king turned to the jester and said: 'Well, what is it?'

'The king's servant', replied the jester, 'desires to intimate that his illustrious son, Bahram, is desperately in love.'

'And with whom?' inquired Yezdejird.

'With the daughter of the *asbahbaz* (army commander),' answered the jester.

'Considering that which we have observed this evening in Bahram,' replied the king, 'it appears that you may have divined the truth. Nor can we blame the youth on that account, since he assuredly does not degrade himself by bestowing his love on the daughter of the guardian of our kingdom and leader of our faithful subjects. Bahram shall, therefore, obtain the fulfilment of his wish and you shall be rewarded for having apprised us of it. But do not say a word of it to anyone, until our purpose shall have been carried into execution.'

Then the king gave permission to Bahram, his guests, courtiers and the musicians to return to their seats in the hall.

They all resumed their occupation, and Yezdejird enjoyed the evening's festivities once again, listening to music until the company dispersed. The jester, having left with the others, followed Bahram and apprised him of the facts concerning his conversation with the king. Bahram thanked and rewarded him.

Yezdejird married his son to the daughter of the army commander. The youth, nevertheless, did not compel his soul to be content with his father's service because his soul accommodated that which understanding required from him. Thus Bahram remained at court, until a brother of Caesar arrived to negotiate a peace treaty and other matters with Yezdejird. The King of Persia received the Roman with sumptuous hospitality and accorded him great honour. Bahram, then seeing the lofty position in which Caesar's brother was held at court, pleaded with him to intercede with his father to send him back to Nu'man. At his recommendation, Yezdejird granted this desired permission, and Bahram returned to Arabia. He lived there happily until his father died which made him heir to the kingdom of Persia.

Elevation of Bahram Gour to the Throne of Persia

Although the chapter on contentment ends here, I will now complete the story of Yezdejird, the manner of his death, how his subjects reacted and by what means sovereignty passed to Bahram.

Yezdejird deviated widely from the right path and became tyrannical in his oppression and violation of the principles of justice and clemency — which his predecessors had observed — so that Persians grew impatient with his caprices. Distinguished elders assembled to look after their own interests by conspiring against him. Yet, it is more probable that the conspirators included those who had suffered from the injustice of the King. Several among them proceeded to pray to God to deliver them from Yezdejird, imploring for an end to his tyranny. The Lord, moved to compassion by their unhappy condition, granted their wish.

One day, when the King was in his *majlis*, the chamberlain informed him that an unbroken horse of unparalleled beauty, possessing all the qualifications most esteemed in a charger, flew in at full speed but stopped short before the palace gate. Everyone was struck with terror, and no one dared approach the animal, while even other horses fled in fright. Believing this to be a fable, Yezdejird rose to see for himself. He found that, indeed, the animal was of marvellous beauty. On approaching it, Yezdejird — increasingly bewitched by the animal's poise — began to stroke its forehead as it was standing perfectly quiet and gentle. Taking the horse by its forelock, Yezdejird intended to saddle and bridle the animal. As Yezdejird went round him and parted the animal's haunches, it apparently gave him a kick that threw him to the ground and killed him. Thereupon, according to several witnesses, the horse took to flight with a speed so tremendous that no one could tell which direction he had taken. Other witnesses maintained that Yezdejird mounted the animal, urging him to speed, when the horse — bearing him rapidly out of sight of all present — threw him into the sea. Only God knows which of these two versions may be true.

Believing that they were delivered from Yezdejird by heaven, the Persians decided to exclude his son from the throne as well. They feared he would follow in his father's footsteps and, therefore, bestowed the crown upon Chosroes, a scion of the dynasty of their ancient kings. Chosroes enjoyed universal popularity. He abrogated unjust laws decreed by Yezdejird and freed Persians from their odious system of government. Indeed, they had reason to bless their choice.

Meanwhile, news of these developments reached Nu'man, who informed Bahram and promised him support and assistance. He further volunteered his life and wealth to his service. Bahram thanked him and asked that Arab troops be prepared to invade Persian territories, but with orders not to shed blood. Nu'man, therefore, unleashed his troops on these forays, in which they grievously wasted and spoiled the country. Persian ambassadors approached Nu'man, demanding that he abstain from these acts of hostility, and to return to the allegiance due from a faithful vassal. Nu'man informed them that he was nothing more than a servant of King Bahram, and had done only that which he was commanded to do. He advised them to address King Bahram himself.

The Persian envoys presented themselves to Bahram and examined him carefully. They were greatly impressed with his beauty and majesty. Prostrating themselves before him, they implored his pardon for all their offences. Bahram spoke to them courteously, held out brilliant hopes and concluded by bidding them safe journey home. He further assured them of his good intentions since he wished nothing but public safety and welfare, and that he would immediately return to make them acquainted with his person and defend his own rights. He asked the envoys to prepare for his reception and dismissed them with many honours.

Meanwhile ten squadrons, each consisting of a thousand valiant Arab horsemen, were assembled under Nu'man's orders, for Bahram. The latter advanced at their head to attack the Persian territory. Nu'man preceded Bahram's troops with a force more powerful than any the Persians could muster. The Arabs reached Jundi-Shahpour, in those days the capital of Persia, and set up their camp at the foot of its walls. Then the lords of the country, headed by the Mobedan-mobed, went forth to meet Bahram. A throne was immediately erected in the midst of the camp and Bahram was seated upon it while Nu'man stood before him. All the Persian chiefs, one after another, prostrated themselves before Bahram and took up their designated posts.

When this ceremony was concluded, Bahram nodded to the Mobedan-mobed to speak; the latter praised God and thanked him for the mercy he had shown towards his creatures, then proceeded to recall Yezdejird's tyranny and how God had summoned him hence. He dwelt on the repugnance felt by Persians to bestow the crown on his son, fearing that he would tread in his father's footsteps. Moreover, he posited, Persians knew that Bahram had grown up amongst Badu Arabs, who enriched themselves on the spoils of other countries and disliked Persians. It might be reasonable to suppose, concluded the Mobedan-mobed, that Bahram may have acquired the same propensity, and entreated him to withdraw his claims to the throne. Persians would agree to pay him tribute for the sake of peace, the chief religious leader pressed, but, as far as the crown was concerned, the Mobedan-mobed insisted that they would never consent to bestow it on him. Moreover, he emphasized that they would leave no means to withhold it from him, by force if necessary.

When the Mobedan-mobed ended his speech, Bahram replied. After praising God and thanking Him for all His benefits, the young man acknowledged the truth in the charges of tyranny and iniquity raised against Yezdejird by the Persian speaker. He declared that he had always desired to obtain sovereign power in order to erase all traces of this past tyranny, to raise a new edifice on the basis of justice and allow his subjects to enjoy the fruits of a mild and beneficent rule — so that they may forget the harshness and cruelty of his father's. In conclusion, he said that although he had no intention of giving up his paternal inheritance, or of shunning any peril to regain it, he would propose a trial of courage. The crown and the other insignia of royalty would he placed in the midst between two untamed lions. He would himself come to the spot, together with Chosroes, the usurper of the throne. Of the two of them, whoever should have the courage to take the crown from between the claws of the lions would retain it, being the one most worthy of sovereignty.

Bahram added that, if he were willing to expose himself to this risk, it was only from tenderness towards his subjects whom he desired to save from the miseries of war, as well as from his firm confidence in the favour and assistance of God, because he was conscious of the uprightness of his purpose, and purity of his intentions. In short, he desired nothing else than the prosperity of the country and of its inhabitants.

The Persian chiefs accepted Bahram's proposal, hoping through this means to be rid of him without exposing themselves to the consequences of war. Nevertheless, they returned to the city full of admiration for the beauty, courtesy, eloquence, and regal dignity of Yezdejird's son. Locating two fierce lions, they kept them fasting for three days, and on the fourth carried them out of the city in two iron cages. Each lion had an iron chain around its neck to which a stake was also attached. The two stakes were fixed into the ground, leaving enough space between the two so that the lions might be able to touch each other. The crown and insignia of royalty were placed where both animals could reach to defend them. The cages were opened and the two lions came forth. An immense multitude of Persians had, meanwhile, assembled at the grounds. Arab troops from the camp, hastening to watch, were likewise present, on the opposite side.

Then Bahram stepped out from his pavilion, his loins protected with a belt into which he had tucked up the skirts of his garments. Advancing in front of the ranks, he called aloud on Chosroes: 'Make haste and come forth, O rebel. Come, O usurper of the inheritance of my forefathers! Come and take the royal crown which you have ravished from him to whom it belonged.'

'You', replied Chosroes, 'must first encounter the trial to which you have chosen to expose yourself, since you come as the challenger and have offered yourself voluntarily. Moreover, you lay claim to the kingdom by right of succession, whereas I never laid claim to it at all; it was offered to me and I accepted it.'

Bahram did not reply but advanced unarmed towards the lions when the Mobedan-mobed, seeing him resolved to encounter this peril, cried out: 'You are going to meet your death, O Bahram – but the guilt will not be ours.'

'It is well,' replied the young man, 'as I take full responsibility and act only from tenderness for you. No one shall deter or restrain me.'

'Since you are determined to have it so at all costs,' resumed the religious leader, 'confess your sins to Almighty God – entreat his forgiveness – and implore his help.' Bahram rehearsed his sins, expressed his penitence, and exclaimed: 'Oh, Lord God, help me,' and then drew close to one of the lions.

The savage animal sprang on him but the young man avoided it with great dexterity. Bahram threw some dint on the lion's face, and climbed on its back through an agile move. He gave the animal such a terrific squeeze with his knees that the brute extended his paws, hung out his tongue, and lay senseless and motionless on the ground. Meanwhile the other lion sprang forward to attack Bahram, but could not advance beyond the length of its chain. The young man shielded himself with the head of the lion that was under him and then, seizing the other by its ears, began striking their skulls together until both fell dead. He then rose on his feet, gave thanks to God for His protection and assistance, unwound the skirts of his garment from his girdle and, taking the crown, placed it on his head. 'Long live King Bahram, the son of a King,' cried Chosroes, 'and may the inheritance of his ancestors, that the Lord has now bestowed upon him, prosper in his hand: let us all be ready to obey him.'

And all the Persians thereupon hailed him King, shouting their approval. The Mobedan-mobed approached Bahram, took him by the hand and led him to the throne. He invested him in his own hands with the insignia of royalty and paid him homage. All the Lords of Persia followed his example. Bahram then mounted his horse, entered his capital and his father's palace, and distributed largesse with a liberal hand amongst the valiant and the needy. He, moreover, bestowed great largesse upon Nu'man, invested him with the garments of royalty, crowned him, and rewarded the Arabs who had assisted him in his undertaking according to their ranks. He faithfully observed all his promises, governed with mildness and justice and earned his people's praises until his death.

The Persians recorded many marvellous actions performed by Bahram. Two of these actions are, indeed, worthy of great attention. They have been inscribed in my work titled *Notices of Remarkable Children*. God be praised for the grace that He bestowed on this monarch.

5

Self-denial

Verses From the Holy Qur'an

The Lord our God, blessed be His name, addressed the wisest
of all His vicars, the most learned of those charged with the
execution of His divine pleasure – to fulfill His decrees and
observe His precepts, whether explicitly stated or understood
– thus:

> Do not regard with envy what we have given some among
> them to enjoy – the flower of the present life – for with
> this we seek only to try them. Better is your Lord's
> provision, and more lasting. (20:31)

This saying was revealed to the Prophet with a choice: to
be a Prophet-king or a Prophet-servant of God. He chose to
have nothing whatsoever, rather than to have power, and
nothing else.

Gabriel informed him of the Lord's commandment: The
choice is given to you, who guides men on the right path, to
reach your decision.

Choose the gift of prophecy together with a virtuous life
that will allow you to gather the seventh arrow tomorrow.

Or else sovereignty, before which the most distant nations will bow down in terror with their foreheads in the dust.

And he made his choice of giving himself to the Lord, to attain the highest virtue and happiness.

Traditions Concerning Muhammad

An example of self-denial attributed to the Prophet and extracted from the tradition of Ibn Mas'ud – may God be well pleased with him – reports that the Prophet said:

'A king who lived in the time of our forefathers was seized with fear – by which he meant, the fear of God, praised and magnified be His name. He gave up all power and travelled until he reached the shores of the Nile. Settling in a modest home, he began to make bricks, by which trade he earned a livelihood. News of this humble individual reached the ruler who sent him the following message: "Wait for me where you are; for I will come and seek you." Accordingly, he too abdicated his throne and joined the first king, and they lived together for the rest of their lives.'

To this, 'Abdallah ibn Mas'ud adds: 'If we were in Egypt, I could show you the tombs of these two kings, with the inscription recording that which God's apostle has told us.'

Prose and Verse on the Wisdom of Self-denial

It is related that Sulayman ibn 'Abd al-Malik, proud in his vainglory because of the power he had attained, said one day to 'Umar ibn 'Abd al-'Aziz, may God have mercy on him: 'Tell me, 'Umar, what do you think of our nation?'

'O Prince of the Faithful,' he replied, 'it would be a pleasure, were it not of so little worth; a blessing, if it had anything worthwhile; a power, if it were not to perish; a happy nation, if it did not end in sorrow; a delight, if it was not filled with suffering; and a glory, if it was accompanied by virtue.' At these words the Caliph broke down and cried. On the same subject, I have composed the following verses:

Oh, wretched man who are tormented and beguiled by that which you do not need;
If your conquests were as vast as Chosroes's; if you possessed so much treasure as he accumulated and enjoyed;
Yet would also be tormented by an impotent desire to obtain more;
For a life of peace is not granted on earth, except to the wise, who know how to abstain;
Seek, therefore, to practice abstinence, a virtue followed only by the chosen.

Be on your guard against an evil mansion, for within it breathes a poison; there inevitable torment endures. Although its appearance may be noble, what is visible from far only fills a seeker with hope.

Our world is a house filled with idle pastimes and borrowed goods.
A house filled with subtlety, with the eager pursuit of profit, with traffic and with booty.
You have a soul for your capital: Oh! Take heed that this treasure is not spoiled.
Do not exchange your soul for banquets, perfumes, and splendid garments.
And reflect that all which Solomon once possessed is no longer worth so much as a spark of fire.

In a *Qasid*a on the same subject, I have written:

We live in a country that favours its adversaries and breaks faith with its allies.

A country that is powerless to oppose those who conspire against it but which bars the path of its peaceable inhabitants.

He who seeks to make it his home wishes what is contrary to the customs of the place.

Oh, how ready are its people, when assembled in the great temple, to oppose the stranger that threatens it!

Leave this inhospitable land; lay aside your desire to go forth in it; do not be courteous to those who live there.

Desist from accepting its vanities; and if thou have acquired any, give them up to the first bidder.

I swear that I have done my utmost to warn those that hear me.

I have proclaimed that this country is hastening, alas towards its doom.

When God knows that only abstinence from the lusts that infect it can ensure the country's safety from threatening disasters.

Again, I have written the following verses on the same subject:

Let abstinence be your shield; abstinence that signifies disdain of what is superfluous and which attracts you, then tyrannizes over you, and lastly proves your ruin.

You cannot abstain from the things that are necessary for life but you can do so from every excess.

Whether revelling in luxury, and delicate living, or hardening you in griping avarice.

Much as one sees and hears, we know of no man who has ever accumulated treasure with glory.

The covetous man is afflicted by his sin with constant anxiety.

And, in the end, he cannot escape from destiny; that judge against whom we close our doors in vain.

The Daughter of the King of Najaf and the Muslim Commander Sa'ad ibn Abi Waqqas

Hurqa, Nu'man ibn Mundhir's daughter, asked for an audience with Sa'ad ibn Abi Waqqas, may God be well pleased with him, in Qadisiya. She presented herself before him, followed by all her maidens, clad in sackcloth and black vests, a horrible sight to witness. Hurqa could not be distinguished from her maidens, because they were all wearing long garments, covered with veils much like nuns. They all saluted Sa'ad, who inquired: 'Which of you is Hurqa?'

'I am,' replied Nu'man's daughter.

'You are Hurqa!?' exclaimed Sa'ad.

'Yes,' returned the woman. 'O Emir, why do you ask me the second time? Sadly, the world is but a temporary place, and the same conditions never continue for any length of time. Its guests are ever changing and hurled from one innovation to another. We were the sovereigns of this country, where tribute was gathered for us, and whose inhabitants obeyed us for a long period of time. But when our time was up, fate determined our destiny, our sceptre was broken and the crowds of mighty men who thronged around us ran away. Such is fortune, O Sa'ad, nor are there any upon whom it has bestowed a benefit without following it up with a disaster that wrings the heart. Such is fortune that grants joy and alternates it with sorrow.' Then Hurqa recited the following two verses:

We once ruled people and public injury was our injury; now we are reduced to poverty on the same level with the poorest of our subjects.

Curse be upon the world that does not grant good fortune but turns its back to you.

While Hurqa was addressing Sa'ad, 'Amr ibn Ma'adikarb al-Zubaydi entered and, seeing her, exclaimed: 'Are you Hurqa who travelled from the palace to the church on richly coloured carpets made of silk?

'The same,' she replied.

And he resumed: 'What has befallen you? Who has robbed you of your celebrated charms, dried up the sources of your wealth, and quenched the impulses of your revenge?'

'O 'Amr,' she replied, 'the trials of fortune are such that they place kings on the same level as abject slaves. They rob the mighty of his power and humble the proud. We, however, anticipated this calamity and therefore do not complain.'

Sa'ad then asked her where she was from. When she told him and requested shelter, the ruler granted Hurqa protection and support. Astonished at Sa'ad's generosity, she responded with the following verse:

He has fulfilled the duties of a protector and has displayed nothing but courtesy; for it is only from noble souls that a noble soul receives honour.

Abdication of the Caliph Mu'awiya ibn Yazid

Having discussed the abdication of kings, we shall now broach the form that refers to the traditions of the Prophet quoted at the beginning of this chapter: that is, self-denial in the realm of sovereignty, the act of abdicating the throne.

We will not discuss the self-denial of kings who abstained from the luxuries of sovereignty without abdicating the throne. Nor those who undertook the twofold charge of governing men according to the rules of eternal justice and of attending the worship of God while abstaining from earthly luxuries as David, peace be onto him, did among prophets, and as Abu Bakr did amongst the upright Caliphs. This virtue is not included in the subject matter of this book, and is of a different dimension than that which we have analysed and presented herein. Let us now implore God's assistance and resume our previous task.

As a young man, Mu'awiya ibn Yazid ibn Mu'awiya was diligent in his studies, learned, introverted and inclined to worship God, rejecting what was gaudy and glittering. Elevated to the throne of the Caliphate when he was barely seventeen years old, the idea of 'rule' quickly became an abomination so that, repenting of having to assume such a heavy burden on his own shoulders, he consulted his kinsfolk on his contemplated abdication. They opposed his decision and argued with him for twenty days, doing their utmost to prevent him from renouncing the throne. Finally, concluding that they could not deter him from his determination, they pleaded with him to designate a successor. Mu'awiya replied: 'How can you suppose that, having swallowed the bitter pill of abdicating, I could further burden myself by appointing my successor? If I had thought it desirable for any living man, I

would assuredly have retained the throne.' He then addressed
his people, informing them that he felt unable to sustain the
weight of government and concluded by exhorting them to
choose a successor as they saw fit. He released them from
their oath of allegiance and returned to his home, where he
refused to see any living soul. He lived for about twenty-five
days before he died.

'Ali ibn al-Jahm, in his poem in the *Rajiz*, alludes to the
history of this Caliph in the following verses:

> He was succeeded by his son, Mu'awiya the weak,
> A man filled with piety and wisdom,
> Who ruled for a month and a half,
> And was overtaken by a cruel death.
> He left his people without imposing on them a successor,
> Dreading the importance of his act, applying the virtue of
> denial.

Although 'Ali ibn al-Jahm's rendition implies that
Mu'awiya met his death without having resigned the
Caliphate, the historical facts are known to everyone as I have
related them. It thus became customary to call this Caliph by
the diminutive of his name, because he was not held in esteem
on account of his abdication. That is why he received the
surname of Abu Layla, which is customary to bestow upon
those who are underprivileged people.

Mu'awiya was prompted to self-denial and abdication by a
dialogue he overheard between two of his maidens. These two
girls, one of whom was of singular beauty, were arguing, when
the first one said: 'You see that by your beauty you have
captivated the greatest prince in the world.'

'And what sovereignty,' she replied, 'can be compared with beauty? Beauty is the judge above all kings where supreme power resides.'

'And what is the advantage of supreme power,' returned the first lady?

'A king either walks on a straight path, his duties bearing witness to his gratitude to God, and in this case, he is deprived of all rest and his whole life is poisoned. Or, he allows his passions to guide him and revels in luxury, neglecting his duties and becoming ungrateful towards God, and in this case he ensures for himself the flames of hell.' These words left a deep impression on the mind of the young Mu'awiya and led ultimately to his abdication.

Abdication of Nu'man

'Uday ibn Zayd al-'Abadi al-Tamimi, a man held in high favour by the king of Persia – whom he served as secretary and interpreter – was once sent to the Roman Empire as ambassador, where he learned wisdom and became acquainted with its traditions. Some add that he became a Christian and practised self-denial. 'Uday's father Zayd ruled the city of Najaf for Mundhir ibn Ma' al-Sama'. For all these reasons, 'Uday enjoyed a good reputation with the kings of Najaf, of the tribe of Lakhm.

One day 'Uday was with Nu'man ibn 'Umru' al-Qays, King of Najaf, in the castle of Khawarnak (to which we have alluded earlier), when the king turned his gaze on the surrounding country. It was spring, and the ground was blossoming with flowers. The king stood for a while, contemplating nature, and became absorbed in earnest thought. 'Uday did not venture to question him on the reasons for his sadness, until the king said, 'Must all that I see be destroyed?'

'The king knows that it is so,' replied 'Uday.

'Then', resumed Nu'man, 'what is the worth of possessing such perishable assets?' He then wandered about the world on pilgrimage, delaying his conversion to Christianity.

Nu'man had a great predilection for the flowers that were dubbed after him as 'Shaqa'iq al-Nu'man,' because he devoted special care to the species in a royal preserve. One beautiful spring day, the king visited a *shaqiqa* (sandy plain) covered with these anemones. He contemplated them with great attention, admiring the symmetry and brilliant colour of their petals, the greenness of their stalks and the way dew fell drop by drop on the ground when a breeze rocked the flowers. His soul delighted at this sight.

On the ground he spread a carpet of silk in various colours, resembling a garden with many species of flowers upon which a tent of scarlet *dibaj* was erected, furnished with seats, cushions, pillows, couches and other similar articles. The tent was covered in a robe of scarlet silk, dyed with *bahraman*, which allows the most brilliant dye to shine. The king was seated in his pavillion, the plain enamelled with flowers before his eyes, surrounded by his friends — amongst whom was 'Uday ibn Zayd. The ruler enjoyed his friends' conversation as they listened to music and consumed wine.

When this temporary moment of joy subsided, Nu'man reverted to sounder reflection. He discussed various issues with 'Uday in the manner described at the beginning of this section. 'Uday seized the opportunity to warn him as we have recorded, doing his utmost to rouse the king from thoughtlessness. Nu'man listened to him openly, and, no longer wishing to remain idle, mounted his horse and returned towards Najaf with 'Uday riding by his side. When they reached a burial ground a short distance from city walls, 'Uday said: 'O King, may every curse be far removed from you. Do you hear the voice that comes from these tombs?'

'What does it say?' asked Nu'man.

The poet answered, 'Listen: "You who ride in haste to pass over these grounds, remember that we were once like you, and you shall one day be like us."'

On hearing these words, Nu'man remembered certain things as his troubled soul was further awakened. When the two riders reached a cluster of trees shaken by the wind and overshadowing a little lake, 'Uday, said to the king: 'May every curse be far removed from you. Do you hear the language of these trees?'

'What does it says,' asked the king?

'Uday replied: 'Listen: "Turn your thoughts on yourself as you see us; reflect that you are about to overstep the fatal limit, beyond which the uncertainties of time are not felt, where calamity cannot reach.

"How many others have here dismounted from their mounts, and quenched their thirst with wine and clear waters? They poured liquor from precious flasks decorated with ribbons. Their horses were covered with rich garments, and they lived happily for a while, without hurry and trusting time.

"But they had not yet reached the climax of their lives, when they were cut off by Fate; Fate, that carries off the lowly as well as the mighty, and hurls him who follows after his own desires from one turnabout to another."'

'Uday recited these verses to Nu'man as he had done earlier ones, pointing to certain tombs near a cluster of habitations between the first burial ground and the little wood. When they reached the palace, Nu'man said to the poet: 'Come to me tomorrow at daybreak as I plan to share some news with you.'

Returning the following day as requested, 'Uday found the king dressed as a pilgrim, in unrefined canvas clothes. Nu'man then took leave and departed. He was never heard from again.

Nevertheless, the prince who became a hermit was none other than Nu'man ibn Mundhir, called the Elder, of whom 'Uday was not a contemporary; he only mentioned him in his poems. 'Uday lived during the reign of Nu'man ibn Mundhir the Younger, and undertook to admonish this prince in the manner related here. Consequently he converted to Christianity, but did not become a pilgrim. The latter, moreover, is the same Nu'man who ordered the poet 'Uday's execution, and ruled over the kingdom until he himself was put to death by Chosroes. As to the rest, God only knows the truth, as the following verses by 'Uday attest:

> You who speak evil of Fate, are you exempt from all blame, are you free from the weaknesses of human nature?
>
> Do you possess an agreement that specifies your days, or are you not a fool deceived by the vanities of the world?
>
> Awaken and remain forever in the world, you who have seen death, or tell me whether man has any power to defraud the sepulchre of its prey.
>
> Where is Chosroes Anushirvan, the greatest amongst monarchs, gone?
>
> Where did Sapor go before him, and those of the fair-skinned race, the gallant kings of the Romans?
>
> Why are there no memorials for anyone of them?
>
> And the monarch who built Tikrit, where flow the Tigris and Euphrates, filled his palace with marble and

raised its roofs so high that birds made their nests on its ridges.

Thoughts of death never entered his mind, and behold, when the kingdom was taken from him, his gates were deserted by all.

And remember the lord of Khawarnak, who was looking down from the towers of his castle, and was moved by thoughtful reflections.

At first he rejoiced, contemplating his possessions, the land that obeyed him, the majestic river and the palace that lay before his eyes.

But turning quickly to wisdom, he exclaimed: 'What happiness can there be in a life that ends in a grave?'

Favourites of fortune, kings, and lawgivers, are all buried within a tomb.

And their ashes are as the withered leaf that is whirled in the air by the wind.

Abdication of a Greek King

It is related that a Greek king, on rising one morning from bed, put on clothes brought to him by a maiden. When he was dressed, the maiden presented him a mirror, in which the ruler contemplated himself and, seeing that he had a white hair in his beard, said to her: 'Give me those scissors.' When she brought him the scissors, he cut out a white hair and gave it to her. The quick-witted and cultivated lady placed the hair in the palm of her hand, held it to her ear, and remained for some time listening to it. The king inquired what she was doing. 'I am listening to this white hair,' she replied, 'because its appearance disturbed the highest dignity that exists on earth; a king is enraged against it, and seeks to exterminate it.'

'And what do you gather from it' asked the king?

The lady replied: 'I hear it utter a language that my tongue does not dare repeat, for fear of angering the king.'

'Say what you will,' returned the monarch, 'and fear nothing as long as you tread the paths of wisdom.' The maiden thus continued:

'The white hair says, "oh powerful ruler on earth, I knew that you would seize me and scold me. Therefore, I did not show myself above your skin until I had laid my eggs and hatched them; seeing my little ones come forth, I have bequeathed onto them the charge of making you pay the penalty of my death. And they are already grown and have set to work to avenge me, so that they will either kill you all of a sudden, or they will trouble you and undermine your strength until death shall seem a relief."'

'Write down that discourse,' said the king. When the lady completed her task, the king read it again and then hastened with all speed to a temple of great renown, where he exchanged his regal robes for the tunic of priests in the sanctuary. Once this became known to his subjects, they hastened to the temple, vying with each other in their prayers asking him to return to the palace and rule his kingdom. But he would not hear of it. He insisted that they consent to his abdication and appoint another king in his place. His subjects would not yield and tried in vain to dissuade him from his intention. Finally the priests intervened, and it was stipulated that the king should stay and worship God in the sanctuary, that he would administer the affairs of state as he thought fit and delegate the rest to others. And this he did as long as he lived.

Conversion of an Ossetian King to Christianity

Ossetia was once ruled by a heathen king, proud and ruthless, who even in youth was so arrogant that whenever he appeared in public he allowed no one to raise his voice except to praise him and to give thanks for his goodness. One of the king's ministers was a Christian who believed in God (may his name be glorified) but, fearing his ruler, had concealed his faith. The counsellor aimed to convert his monarch and seized upon every opportunity to do so, although he had gained several converts throughout the country.

One day, as the king was riding along the road, an old man raised his voice to petition him on some business, whereupon the ruler commanded his guards to seize him. When they laid hands on him, the old man exclaimed, 'God is my Lord.' On hearing these words, the minister ordered that he should be released. Naturally, the king was somewhat displeased by this behaviour, although he did not reverse the order on the spot lest people conclude that someone had dared to contradict his command. Rather, he kept silent, making it appear as though the minister had acted according to the king's mind. The ruler remained silent until he returned to the palace when he summoned his counsellor and asked him: 'What moved you to contradict my order in the presence of slaves?'

'If the king will allow me,' replied the minister, 'I hope not to displease him, for I acted out of loyalty, affection and anxiety for his welfare.'

'Tell me what you have in mind,' replied the king, 'for I will not judge you harshly.'

The minister then appealed to him to hide in the hall, so that he might see and hear everything that occurred. The king consented. A magnificent bow, which had been made for the king's special use, was brought to the counsellor by the bow-maker. Noticeably, the craftsman had inscribed his own name on it. The minister gave the bow to a page to hold, saying to him: 'The bow-maker will enter shortly. When I start speaking to him, you will read his name – which is written here – aloud. When you are sure that the bow-maker has heard you, break the bow.'

The bow-maker arrived and the page followed the minister's instructions to the letter. Seeing his work thus destroyed, the bow-maker could not restrain himself from raising his hands against the page, who was fatally wounded.

'Brute', exclaimed the minister, 'how dare you slay my page?' 'My lord', replied the bow-maker, 'that bow was a masterpiece of beauty and perfection, a labour of love. Why then did your page destroy it?'

'Perhaps he did not know that you were its creator,' said the counsellor.

'But the bow informed him of my identity,' rejoined the bow-maker.

'How so?' inquired the minister.

'My name is written on it; your page read it, and I heard him,' replied the bow-maker.

As this was all that the counsellor hoped for, he dismissed the bow-maker and turned to the king: 'I have illustrated,' he said, 'that what I did was done from fidelity and affection to the king. The king decried an old man who proclaimed that God was his Lord. Now, was I not right to fear that this Lord, against whose power there are no defences, might turn against the king?'

'Has that old man, then, another Lord besides myself?' exclaimed the king.

'Let the king reflect,' replied the minister, 'that he is young, whereas that man is very old. The king assuredly could not have been the old man's master before your accession to the throne.'

'He belonged to my father,' replied the king.

And the minister returned, 'How can a man remain a servant when his master is no more? O king, the old man was speaking of the Master who gave him his being, of Him who made a man and who preserved him alive; He alone has a right to his service and gratitude; He is my Lord, the Lord of everything; He is God!'

'You have kindled a spark in my bosom that will not be quenched,' replied the king. 'I now perceive that both masters and slaves must necessarily have an immortal Lord above them; but if you know this Lord, aim to show him to me,' asserted the king.

'Assuredly, I know him,' rejoined the counsellor.

The king continued: 'Teach me then to know Him, and I promise to be your disciple as long as I live.'

'To lead you to know Him is my first duty,' answered the minister, 'and, as to making yourself my disciple, you should know that He, in whose footsteps you will tread, will never be your slave, but would willingly shed his life's blood to save you from the torture of doubt in matters of faith.'

The minister then sought to instruct him in the revelation of God – whose name is praised – who enlightened the believer-prince. Turning to his counsellor, he inquired: 'Are there not any particular ways of serving our Lord so that by putting them into practice, His favour may be obtained?'

'Assuredly there are,' replied the minister. 'God himself,' he continued, 'has commanded the observance of certain acts of piety. He who performs them is accepted of Him and obtains the promise of divine grace and favour.' The counsellor then described to the believer-prince how to pray and fast. He further enlightened the king of several other religious teachings of Jesus, on whom be the peace and blessings of God. The king applied himself to these acts of piety until they had become second nature.

Finally, one day the king said to his counsellor: 'Why do you not proclaim faith in God to the people as you have done to me?' To which the minister replied:

'Most noble prince, Ossetians are a tough nation, intellectually slow and spiritually intractable, and I would not feel safe were such words to pass my lips.'

'Well, then, if you will not, I will do so myself,' replied the king.

'You should know,' replied the counsellor, 'that if respect for his name does not suffice to defend him from the rage of the people, he will not even be able to defend himself. No, rather, I will give my life for that of the king. When they put me to death, as they assuredly will, the king should be cautious not to repeat the attempt.'

Determined to satisfy his king, the counsellor convened a meeting of the civil magistrates, judges, priests, sages and chief men of the country, and called on them to worship God, whose name be praised. They immediately rushed on him and killed him. Then, carrying the minister's corpse into the king's presence, they informed him of the crime and of its punishment, declaring that they suspected the king of believing in the same faith and asked him to speak his mind. The king, concealing his real sentiments, told them that they had done well in slaying the counsellor, and sent them away. But it was not long before he abdicated the throne and shut himself up in a monastery, where he lived until God called him to Himself. In the meantime, the Lord avenged the minister by exterminating his murderers.

Self-denial of Babak, Son of Ardashir, the First Sassanid

It is related that Ardashir ibn Babak ibn Sassan, in his youth and at the commencement of his power, had a son who was called Babak after his grandfather. This child grew up into a handsome man, promising in intellect. Ardashir was extremely attached to him, and entrusted his education to a philosopher, a man of comprehensive views with sound principles of wisdom and inclined to a life of great austerity. The philosopher was to look after the youth as his own son. By mutual consent, the philosopher moved his pupil from Ardashir's house and instilled such a course of instruction that the young man was quickly enabled to bear the weight of philosophical learning and the burden of self-denial.

When Ardashir aspired to supreme power in Persia, he frequently consulted his son and found in Babak all that he could wish, as he successfully attained his objectives — with one exception: the young man always sought, both through his words and actions, to inspire his father with a great dislike for the things of this world. Babak represented worldly vices as unworthy, set forth their uselessness and constantly repeated that all must look to the fearful end of their delusion. Naturally, this troubled Ardashir, even if he was otherwise overjoyed with his son's virtues.

It was said: 'He who offers princes that which does not please them must not complain if they fail to react.'

It rarely occurs that a prince is able to fix his mind so steadfastly on one idea as to devote his whole attention to it, without dragging others to share his indecision. The reason for this is that a prince finds himself immersed in many different matters, each of which may require attention, so that scarcely may he be inclined towards one before he is diverted by another. Therefore, when you see a prince absorbed in one idea, never seek to force upon him another, because that will prevent him from addressing the first.

Ardashir tolerated his son's peculiarity because of the love he bore him and also out of pity, in the hope of curing him. One day, the ruler asked his son: 'Babak, do you know who your father is?'

'Most fortunate prince,' he replied, 'I have two fathers. One is the author of my being and the other that of my salvation – and I acknowledge and revere both of them.'

'Explain which is the father who is the author of your being,' replied Ardashir.

The young man answered him in nearly these words: 'It is he who fills the eyes of his people with glory, their ears with the sound of his praise, who inspires their understandings with reverence and their hearts with affection. The monarch whose clemency embraces all things, whose justice never errs, whose government is upright and the vigour of his arm so strong that the heart of the guilty tremble as their swords fall to the ground. It is he who preserves the just from injustice, the monarch whose valour enables men and whose moderation and generosity captivate their affections.'

'And who,' resumed Ardashir, 'is the father you look upon as the author of your salvation?'

'A sage,' replied Babak, 'who knows the dignity of his own soul, honours and serves it.'

'Tell me in what way he serves his soul?' asked Ardashir.

The young man replied: 'When he contemplates his soul, the sage perceives in it a fertile soil, rejoicing in every good gift of God. He sees in it springs of water, lofty trees, mature fruit, cool shelters and undying breezes. But there lurk the lions of anger, the panthers of ignorance, the wolves of perfidy, the wild boars of violence, the dogs of avarice, the hyenas of folly, the serpents of injustice, the scorpions of envy. He, therefore, expels all these dangerous animals, and watches over and defends his property, so that they may not return and render it a habitation of unqualified prosperity, without any fusion of evil.'

Ardashir, more than ever convinced that these words indicated his son's aversion to rule, was deeply grieved. He said to him: 'Wisdom, Babak, will never be sufficient to those who possess it, especially if one is capable of governing others, or if one envisages to be governed and subjugated.'

'Most fortunate prince,' replied his son, 'you have undoubtedly hit the mark. But the man who is governed and subjugated is he who is driven by his own passions that torment him at the expense of others.'

'Nevertheless,' replied Ardashir, 'the greatest monarchs have exerted themselves for the good of their subjects, being moved thereto not by their own passions, but by the desire to find grace in the eyes of the Lord, who gives understanding and loves the benefactors of the human race.'

'But,' answered Babak, 'it is not every monarch upon whom such grace is bestowed, but only on those who, irrespective of their personal interests, place themselves on a level with the poorest of their subjects and so illustrate their selflessness. It is those who devote their power and all the time required to the affairs of state, thus escaping the charge of indolence. It is those who deny every breath of passion when it behooves them to take with one hand and give with the other, to raise one person to a post of confidence and dismiss another, to grant or refuse and to punish or pardon. It is by these means that they avoid every shadow of injustice. Therefore, to possess these qualities is more singular than the sphinx, more marvellous than alchemy, and rarer than red gold. Meanwhile, if the king will grant me permission, I will relate to him a parable that will indicate who is the lord and the conqueror, and who is the subjugated and the slave.'

'Tell me,' replied Ardashir, and Babak continued:

The Tame and Wild Elephants

It is related that a king owned a tame and trained elephant that he valued highly. One day, the king's huntsmen caught a wild elephant, which the trainers could not tame. They thought of introducing it to the trained elephant in the hope that it might do the same things. Accordingly, this was attempted, but without success. The new elephant became intractable. In order to force it into submission the trainers resorted to discipline, kept the animal in solitary confinement and deprived it of food. While the wild elephant was undergoing these hardships, the tame animal said to it: 'You are damaging your own interests, acting very unwisely, and must be ignorant, for if you knew all the good that the trainers wished for you, you would assuredly not behave in this manner.'

It was said: 'Stupidity is a veil that prevents understanding from enlightening the right path.'

It was said: 'The ignorant is no better than a walking corpse among the living, who stumbles, and who is rotten.'

It was said: 'As you would not give your honourable kinswoman to one who did not ask her in marriage, abstain from compromising your dignity.'

The wild elephant then asked its tame companion what it really was that the trainers wanted to do with him. The latter replied: 'To better feed you, provide you with abundant drink, clean your stall, give you servants to wait on you, guard you, take care of you and lead you forth at appointed hours so that the people will assemble in crowds to admire you.

'Moreover, you will be covered with beautiful draperies, preceded by percussion and other musical instruments that move the affections and excite the imagination. You will be publicly honoured, so that no animal shall venture to cross your path nor even blow a breath of air in your direction.'

'I must try it,' replied the wild elephant. Placing aside his wildness and stubbornness, he lent himself to everything that was required of him. Thereupon it was caressed, served and held in honour, and everything supplied to him in great abundance. Then, on the day of the festival, every attention was paid to it. The elephant was rubbed down with utmost care and covered with fine clothes; a richly adorned carriage was placed on its back into which mounted several soldiers armed with weapon sashes, helmets and iron clubs. A guard armed with a spear seated himself astride on his neck. A covering of armour was drawn over its trunk and a sword was fastened to it. Attendants armed with shields and iron clubs posted themselves on either side of the elephant, holding on to its tusks. Then the drums and castanets sounded, and the procession went into motion, led by the elephant.

When the wild elephant returned to its stable, however, it said to its tame counterpart: 'I tried what you suggested and assessed all the advantages you spoke of. Yet, there are certain questions about which I would like additional explanation.'

'Ask whatever you like,' replied the tame elephant.

'What were the heavy burdens that were placed on my back? The carriage with the soldiers and implements of war? What did they put around my trunk and at the end of it, and why did the attendants hold on to my tusks? Why did a man ride on my neck?'

'They covered your trunk with a coat of arms to protect it from wounds,' answered the tame elephant. 'They fastened onto the end a sword with which you might fight an enemy. As for those who held your tusks, their business was to ward off the foe if they should attack you, and to aid you in the assault. Lastly, the man who rode on your neck was there to guide you wherever it was necessary to go.'

'It is for this, then,' replied the wild elephant, 'that they feed me so well, supply me with clear water, keep me and the litter on which I lie so delicately clean, utter my name with applause and cover me with fancy clothes. I now clearly understand that the advantage is not equal to the annoyance, nor the benefit to the injury. Henceforth I shall assuredly be the most eager of those who have ever eagerly desired their freedom.'

It was said: 'He who worries about others, takes their burdens on his own shoulders.'

It was said: 'As desire places you in submission to others and enslaves you the more it presses, it is clear that men are slaves of worldly goods, and those who need more have the heaviest weight to bear.'

It was said: 'If the meaning of slavery is to serve others then there are three kinds of slaves: kings, lovers and those who receive benefits. For all three are in captivity, both outwardly and inwardly. And of these, the most enslaved is the king, because he is bound to serve his subjects both with body and mind. This is so because the ruler must govern them; instruct them; defend them; provide for their prosperity; restrain the disobedient; assist the oppressed; ensure free movement; strengthen frontiers; devise and apply laws; collect excessive wealth and expend it for the public good; prevent revolution; and eliminate civil discord and sedition. Besides all this, the king stands in need of his subjects; endures various difficulties; must protect himself; carry on the duties of state; seek out those who are able to give him good and honest counsel; and be prepared to repulse enemies.'

The tame elephant listened to the discourse of its wild colleague and understood that it was the one that was foolish, thoughtless, and lacking depth. It, therefore, replied to the wild elephant: 'The wise have well said that ignorance covers the eyes with a bandage, and alters the substance of things, and that he who is in error is deserving of forgiveness unless he is smitten with admiration for his own errors; for if it reaches that pitch, he becomes totally blind.'

Then, turning to the wild elephant, it said: 'In return for the wise counsel that you have given me, and for the manner in which you have opened my eyes to the truth, I will show you a cunning device through which you may recover your freedom. I am better acquainted than you are with the manners and customs of men and therefore can more easily find a way to escape from their hands — after which I will follow you and be your servant for the rest of my life.'

The two elephants then agreed to pretend to be afflicted with an illness that attacks camels and elephants in their hinds, making them tremble with such force that, whenever they endeavour to stand on their legs, it causes them to fall. Bleeding the animal and making it walk slowly cures this illness. Thus, no sooner did the two elephants appear to be suffering from this illness that the keepers hastened to apply the prescribed remedy, and took them to an open plain where they could walk freely. Once they reached a certain distance from any habitation, the two elephants seized the opportunity and fled, thus recovering their freedom.

Continuation of Babak's Story

When Ardashir heard his son's story to the end, he was troubled by it, and fixed his eyes onto the ground without speaking. He despaired even of bringing his son to consent to his wishes. Ardashir then rose, making a sign to Babak to follow him; he took him to the treasury where the crown jewels were kept. He showed Babak these treasures and called his attention to their immense value. When he finished showing his son this display, Ardashir said to him: 'To whom, Babak, would you leave all this wealth? To someone, perhaps, whom you love better than yourself, and who is more worthy of it?'

'Most fortunate prince', replied his son, 'if you will permit me, I will relate to you a parable which will serve as an answer to your question.'

'Tell me the parable,' answered Ardashir, and Babak continued.

The Herdsman and the Hermit

It is related that a herdsman kept oxen belonging to inhabitants in a village who was diligent in leading them to pasture and who performed this task with complete satisfaction. The proprietors appreciated the herdsman's value for his care as well as the increase in the number of cattle, and always praised him. They were so pleased with him and had such implicit confidence in his integrity that they never required of him an account of the herd.

It was said: 'You love the one you have confidence in, who is faithful, and deserving of affection.'

It was said: 'Kindness and fidelity are praised by everyone and favoured by all.'

The herdsman regularly spent the hours of noon in the neighbourhood of a monastery, where he would stretch out in the shade, lamenting his hard life. A hermit, who lived at the monastery and who was moved to compassion by the poor man's complaints, one day asked him: 'Herdsman, what ails you so that I never hear you do anything but complain?'

'I complain', replied the herdsman, 'of the great trouble that I must endure in keeping the cattle, preserving it from all danger and driving it in search of the richest pastures. For I do this because no one else does, and it costs me incredible exertion.'

'And what motive', continued the hermit, 'induces you to give yourself so much trouble for the comfort of others? Surely, you and your next of kin have the most right to your care and attention.' 'But', answered the herdsman, 'if I did not perform this task, the herd would not be nearly so numerous or flourishing as you see. The day when it was first entrusted to my care, its numbers were scanty, and the cows were lean and dry. They neither adorned the meadows nor filled the pails with milk.'

'You are evading my question,' replied the monk, 'even as one who refuses to answer an inquiry and will not attend to it. I merely ask you the reason why you exert yourself for the benefit of others, and prefer the convenience of your neighbour to your own happiness. You tell me of the troubles you endure and the great care and anxiety that you display. Now try to explain your motives for all this zeal and diligence.'

'For the pains I take with the cattle,' replied the herdsman, 'I gain this: that I can eat what I please and give to whomever I please the flesh of any of the animals that may perish by falling over precipices. Then I make use of the milk and other produce of the herd much like their owners themselves. Lastly, I lead them to graze wherever I think fit. They are, in fact, like my own property managed by myself.'

The hermit listened carefully and answered: 'This is exactly the way a simple monk deceived himself before, at last, he became aware of the folly of his belief.'

'Tell me how this came about,' responded the herdsman. The hermit then told him the following story.

The Restoration of a Deserted Monastery

A monk was on pilgrimage when he reached a monastery that had been in its heyday a splendid edifice, but whose walls were now crumbling because of neglect. The location was enchanting, with a vast and fertile territory extending in front of it, watered by clear streams. Yet very few monks, who were destitute, inhabited the monastery.

The beauty of the spot captivated the pilgrim-monk. He stopped there and, as a vigorous, active and industrious man, restored the ruined walls, cultivated the farm and cleaned out the canals that had been dredged for irrigation. Waters flowed once again through the canals as this monk planted various trees throughout the land. Consequently, monastery revenues greatly increased. Several monks were attracted to the facility as the community grew in size and wealth. The pilgrim-monk appointed himself headmaster. He then bought slaves and burdened them with farming duties and, little by little, added the neighbouring territory to the domain of the convent. Extensive vine, olive and almond tree farms were planted, and both productions and revenues augmented. The monk, eager to accumulate wealth, began to reject applications from the needy and, within a short period of time, amassed a considerable treasure.

It was said: 'Wealth is like water. He who does not open a gate to carry off its overflow drowns in it.'

It was said: 'The assistance we provide others through our wealth and influence is the amulet that preserves them both.'

Perceiving that the pilgrim-monk defrauded and left them empty-handed while he took everything, the monks complained. They spoke against him, and all those who had formerly shown him respect now turned against him until, finally, they openly clashed. The monks publicly admonished the pilgrim-monk to divide the monastery's wealth and devote a portion to charity.

To this the pilgrim-monk replied: 'Why should I give you that which is mine, and which I have gained with difficulty by the labour of my own hands?'

'That has nothing to do with it,' retorted the monks; 'these riches belong to God, and each one of us has a right to his share, although you have a claim to a larger portion as a reward for the manner in which you have administered and augmented the revenue.'

'Well', replied the pilgrim-monk, 'you shall see whose wealth this is.'

During the night he ordered his slaves to cut down a thousand vines and as many olive and almond trees. It was a sad sight to contemplate. Not knowing who was responsible for this destruction, the monks immediately notified the pilgrim-monk of the calamity. He, in turn, scolded them sharply, saying: 'The trees are my property, what does it matter to you whether they are preserved or destroyed?' All rushed on him with blows and abuse once they understood that he was the author of the mischief. Finally, they expelled the monk from the monastery, and he left a poor man – just as he had come.

But as he departed, he looked around at the land he had brought into cultivation and the plantations he had created. Appreciating this impressive but sombre sight, he sighed deeply and reflected with grief on how he had wasted his youth, his strength and the best years of his life in an undertaking that accrued no benefits. Then he went on his way in loneliness and obscurity, poverty and weakness, muttering these words:

'The wise were right when they said: The world is a road that we travel on but do not inhabit. It is a temporary shelter but not a lasting home. It is a narrow bridge that, if crossed with caution, leads the traveller to a happy home. But he who lingers on it to amuse himself, falls from it, and is lost.

'If you enjoy the goods of this world in peace, tomorrow they may corrupt you. They are yours one moment but are torn from your grasp the next. Therefore, among all the favourites of fortune, he is wise he who provides against her treachery: for which all he has to do is prepare his mind for the uncertainties that may deprive him of his possessions before a fatal summons compels him to leave. Who sets his affections on this world's goods cannot be well prepared for eternity.

'No one assuredly can leave his possessions with ease. But one can prepare one's mind through abstinence during the course of this uncertain and transitory life. Instead, one can accumulate a treasure of good deeds, as reward for the afterlife.

'He who is accustomed to luxury will miss its loss more bitterly than who is does not cherish it. If luxury is suddenly yanked away from such an individual he will be filled with sorrow.

'Let him who longs to obtain power know how to abdicate. Let him who seeks to accumulate wealth cultivate such virtues as may serve him for an escort as he prepares to meet his maker.

'Vulgarity destroys peace and ushers in sorrows.'

The monk then resumed his pilgrimage and, a short while later, died.

Conclusion of the Story of the Herdsman and the Hermit

The herdsman reflected on the parable thus presented to him, and perceived the wisdom of the maxim contained in it. 'May God reward you,' he said, 'for the admonition you have given me. Still, now that your allusions have conveyed a lesson that I have taken home, now that you have opened my understanding to good counsel and cleansed my mind from the rust of folly, tell me what you think I ought to do in the circumstances in which I am placed.'

The hermit answered: 'I have given you proof of the error into which you have fallen, regarding that which was committed to your charge — to watch over and guard — as belonging to you. I removed from your eyes the bandage of ignorance that benefited others but to your detriment, all for the sake of scanty gains and vain as well as false innovations. Therefore, restore the cattle to their owners, and think of yourself. Deliver yourself from beasts of prey, poisonous vipers, howling mastiffs, rapacious eagles, muttering devils, hideous snares and deadly poisons. You will thus be able to escape from damnation and ascend into the world of light.'

Disappearance of Babak

Having concluded these parables, Babak was silent, and Ardashir remained absorbed in reflection on the reasoning put forth by his son. Troubled and agitated, he then rose to his feet, burning with indignation. Babak immediately left the palace and wondered off no one knew where.

Conclusion

Abu Hashim ibn Muhammad ibn Zafar, the poor and lowly servant of God, content to abide His holy will, whose sins may God forgive, says: 'With God's assistance, I have brought the task I set out to undertake to its end. I now commend myself to God, so that He may spare me the suffering of being deprived of the light of His countenance and excluded from His favour. I likewise implore Him that He may support me under the trial of interrogation, that He may spare me the necessity of answering by groans, that He would deliver me from sin and save me from an evil end. To Him only do I turn, for He is the God of mercy and of blessings.'

Bibliography

'Abd al-Hafiz, 'Adil Fathi Thabit. *Shar'iyyat al-Sulta fil-Islam* [Legitimation of Authority in Islam], Alexandria: Dar al-Jama'at al-Jadida lil-Nashr, 1996.

'Abd al-Majid, Abu Nahla Ahmad bin. *Kitab al-Sulwanat fi Musamarat al-Khulafa' wal-Sadat* [Book of Consolations in Conversations with Caliphs and Noblemen], Cairo: Dar al-Thaqafa, 1978.

Abdesselem, A. Ben. 'Al-Turtushi,' *The Encyclopedia of Islam*, New Edition, Leiden & London: E. J. Brill and Luzac & Co., 1965, pp. 739–740.

Akhtar, Shabbir. *A Faith for All Seasons: Islam and the Challenge of the Modern World*, Chicago: Ivan R. Dee, 1990.

Amari, Michele. *Biblioteca Arabo-Sicula*, Volume I, Torino-Roma: Ermanno Loescher, 1880.

—— *Solwan; or Waters of Comfort by Ibn Zafer*, Volumes I and II, London: Richard Bentley, 1852.

Arkoun, Mohammed. *Rethinking Islam*, translated and edited by Robert D. Lee, Boulder, Colorado: Westview Press, 1994.

Arié, Rachel. *Miniatures Hispano–Musulmanes*, Leiden: E. J. Brill, 1969.

Avernel (ed.). *Lettres, instructions diplomatiques et papiers d'état du cardinal de Richelieu*, 8 volumes, Paris, 1853–1877.

Bagley, Frank Ronald Charles. *Ghazali's Book of Counsel for Kings*, London: Oxford University Press, 1964.

Beaucaire, Horric de (ed.). *Mémoires du cardinal de Richelieu*, Paris, 1908.

Bell, Daniel. *The End of Ideology*, New York: Free Press, 1962.

Bosworth, C. E. 'Kay Ka'us,' *The Encyclopedia of Islam*, New Edition, Leiden & London: E. J. Brill and Luzac & Co., 1965, p. 815.

Bowen, H. and C. E. Bosworth. 'Nizam al-Mulk,' *The Encyclopedia of Islam*, New Edition, Leiden & London: E. J. Brill and Luzac & Co., 1965, pp. 69–73.

Brockelmann, C. 'Ibn 'Abd Rabbih,' *The Encyclopedia of Islam*, New Edition, Leiden & London: E. J. Brill and Luzac & Co., 1965, pp. 676–677.

―― 'Al-Mawardi', *The Encyclopedia of Islam*, New Edition, Leiden & London: E. J. Brill and Luzac & Co., 1965, p. 869.

Carlyle, Thomas. 'The Leader as Hero,' in Barbara Kellerman, (ed.), *Political Leadership*, Pittsburgh, Pennsylvania: University of Pittsburgh Press, 1986, pp. 5–9.

Chauvin, Victor. *Bibliographie des Ouvrages Arabes*, Liège: Imprimerie H. Vaillant-Carmanne, 1892.

Chiarelli, Leonard C. *Sicily During the Fatimid Age*, Doctoral Dissertation, Department of History, University of Utah, June 1986.

Clausewitz, Karl von. *On War*, translated by O.J. Matthijs Jolles, Washington D.C.: Infantry Journal Press, 1950.

Collins, John M. *Grand Strategy*, Annapolis, MD: Naval Institute Press, 1973.

Damaj, Muhammad Ahmad (ed.). *Sulwan al-Muta' fi 'Udwan al-Atba'* [Consolation for the Ruler During the Hostility of Subjects], Beirut: Mu'assasat 'Izz al-Din lil-Tiba'a wal-Nashr, 1995.

Al-Dawani, Muhammad ibn As'ad Jalal al-Din. *Akhlaq-i Jalili* [Practical Philosophy of the Muhammadan People], translated by W. T. Thompson, London: Luzac, 1839.

Dekmejian, R. Hrair. 'Charismatic Leadership in Messianic and Revolutionary Movements,' in *Religious Resurgence*, edited by Richard T. Antoun and Mary Elaine Hegland, Syracuse, New York: Syracuse University Press, 1987, pp. 82–93.

―― *Egypt Under Nasir*, London: University of London Press, 1972.

―― *Islam in Revolution*, Syracuse, New York: Syracuse University Press, 1995.

―― 'Marx, Weber and the Egyptian Revolution,' *The Middle East Journal* 30:2, Spring 1976, pp. 161–162.

Al-Dhahabi, al-Imam Shams al-Din Muhammad ibn Ahmad ibn 'Uthman. *Sirat A'lam al-Nubala'* [Biography of Most Learned Nobles], Volume 20, Beirut: Mu'assasat al-Risala, 1985.

Djait, Hichem. *Europe and Islam: Cultures and Modernity*, Berkeley and Los Angeles: University of California Press, 1985.

Donohue, John J. and John L. Esposito (eds.). *Islam in Transition: Muslim Perspectives*, New York: Oxford University Press, 1982.

Elcock, Howard. *Political Leadership*, Cheltenham, UK: Edward Elgar, 2001.

Enayat, Hamid. *Modern Islamic Political Thought*, Austin: University of Texas Press, 1982.

Erasmus. *The Education of a Christian Prince*, edited by Lisa Jardine, Cambridge: Cambridge University Press, 1997.

Esposito, John L.. *Political Islam: The Challenges of Change*, Annandale, Virginia: United Association for Studies and Research, 1995.

—— (ed.). *Voices of Resurgent Islam*, New York: Oxford University Press, 1983.

Etzioni-Halevy, Eva. *The Elite Connection: Problems and Potential of Western Democracy*, Cambridge, United Kingdom: Polity Press, 1993.

Hourani, Albert. *Islam in European Thought*, New York: Cambridge University Press, 1991.

Foster, Michael B. *Masters of Political Thought*, Volume I, Cambridge, Missouri: Houghton Mifflin Co., 1941.

Friedrich, Carl J. and Zbigniew K. Brzezinski, *Totalitarian Dictatorship and Autocracy*, New York: Fredrick A. Prager, 1963.

Gabrieli, Francesco. *The Arabs: A Compact History*, translated by Salvator Attanasio, Westport, Connecticut: Greenwood Press, 1981.

—— 'Ibn al-Mukaffa',' *The Encyclopedia of Islam*, New Edition, Leiden & London: E. J. Brill and Luzac & Co., 1965, pp. 883–885.

Graham, A. C. *Disputers of the Tao*, La Salle, Illinois: Open Court Co., 1988.

Greene, Thomas H. *Comparative Revolutionary Movements*, 3rd edn, Englewood Cliffs, New Jersey: Prentice Hall, 1990.

Halliday, Fred. *Islam and the Myth of Confrontation: Religion and Politics in the Middle East*, London: I.B. Tauris, 1995.

Hantaux (ed.). *Maximes d'état et fragments politiques du cardinal de Richelieu*, Paris, 1880.

Hitti, Philip K. *History of the Arabs*, 10th edn, London: Macmillan, 1970.

Islam: Opposing Viewpoints, n. p., n. c., USA: Greenhaven Press, 1995.

Al-Jabiri, Muhammad 'Abid. *Al-'Aql al-Akhlaqi al-'Arabi* [Arab Ethical Reason]. Beirut: Markaz Dirasat al-Wahda al-'Arabiyya, 2001.

Jones, Charles O. (ed.). *Preparing to be President: The Memos of Richard E. Neustadt*, Washington DC: The American Enterprise Institute Press, 2000.

Ibn Jubayr, Abu al-Husayn Muhammad ibn Ahmad. *Rihla* [Travels], Leiden: E. J. Brill, 1907.

Kellerman, Barbara (ed.). *Political Leadership*, Pittsburgh, Pennsylvania: University of Pittsburgh Press, 1986

Kelsay, John. *Islam and War: A Study in Comparative Ethics*, Louisville, Kentucky: Westminster/John Knox Press, 1993.

Keshk, Muhammad Jalal. *Al-Sa'udiyyun wal-hal al-Islami* [The Saudis and the Islamic Solution], Washington, D.C.: n.p. 1982.

Khadduri, Majid. *Arab Contemporaries: The Role of Personalities in Politics*, Baltimore and London: The Johns Hopkins University Press, 1973.

—— *Arab Personalities in Politics*, Washington, DC: The Middle East Institute, 1981.

Ibn Khaldun. *The Muqaddima* [Introduction (to the Science of History)], translated by F. Rosenthal, abridged and edited by N. J. Dawood, New Jersey: Princeton University Press, 1967.

Ibn Khallikan, Abu al-'Abbas Shams al-Din Ahmad ibn Muhammad Abu Bakr. *Wafayat al-A'yan wa Anba' Abna' al-Zaman* [Obituaries of Eminent Men and Histories of Leading Contemporaries], Volume 4, Cairo: Maktabat al-Nahda al-Misriyya, 1948.

Lambton, Ann K. S. 'Al-Dawani,' *The Encyclopedia of Islam*, New Edition, Leiden & London: E. J. Brill and Luzac & Co., 1965, p. 174.

Laoust, Henri. 'Ibn Taymiyya,' *The Encyclopedia of Islam*, New Edition, Leiden & London: E. J. Brill and Luzac & Co., 1965, pp. 951–955.

Lecomte, G. 'Ibn Kutayba,' *The Encyclopedia of Islam*, New Edition, Leiden & London: E. J. Brill and Luzac & Co., 1965, pp. 844–847.

Machiavelli, Niccolò. *The Discourses*, edited with an introduction by Bernard Crick, using the translation of Leslie J. Walker, S. J., with revisions by Brian Richardson, London and New York: Penguin Books, 1970.

—— *The Prince*, translated with notes by George Bull, with an introduction by Anthony Grafton, London and New York: Penguin Books, 1999.

—— *Selected Political Writings*, Edited and translated by David Wootton, Indianapolis, Indiana: Hackett Publishing Co., 1994.

Madani, Ahmad T. *Al-Muslimun fi Siqilliya wa Janub Italiya* [The Muslims in Sicily and South Italy], Cairo: n. p., 1948.

Makdisi, George. 'Ibn Taimiya: A Sufi of the Qadiriya Order,' *American Journal of Arabic Studies* I (1974), pp. 118–129.

Modelski, George. 'Kautilya: Foreign Policy and International System in the Ancient Hindu World,' *American Political Science Review* 58:3, September 1964, pp. 549–551.

Molesworth, William (ed.). *The English Works of Thomas Hobbes*, 11 volumes, London, 1839–1845.

Mosca, Gaetano. *The Ruling Class*, edited and revised by Arthur Livingston, New York: McGraw-Hill, 1939.

—— *Histoire des Doctrines Politiques*, Paris: Payot, 1936.

Montesquieu, Charles L. *Oeuvres Complètes de Montesquieu*, Paris: Gallimard, 1951.

Al-Munajjid, Salah al-Din (ed.). *Shaykh al-Islam Ibn Taymiyya: Siratuhu wa Akhbaruhu 'inda al-Mu'arrikhin* [Shaykh Ibn Taymiyya: Biography and Views According to Historians], Beirut: Dar al-Kitab al-'Arabi, 1976.

Neustadt, Richard E. *Presidential Power*, New York: John Wiley & Sons, 1960.

—— *Presidential Power and Modern Presidents: The Politics of Leadership from Roosevelt to Reagan*, New York: The Free Press, 1990.

Oakeshott, Michael (ed.). *Leviathan: Or the Matter, Form, and Power of a Commonwealth Ecclesiastical and Civil*, Oxford: Blackwell, 1946.

Pellat, Ch. 'Al-Djahiz,' *The Encyclopedia of Islam*, New Edition, Leiden & London: E. J. Brill and Luzac & Co., 1965, p. 385.

Plutarch. 'Timoleon and Aemilius Paulus', in Barbara Kellerman, (ed.), *Political Leadership*, Pittsburgh, Pennsylvania: University of Pittsburgh Press, 1986, pp. 350–51.

Przeworski, Adam and Henry Teune. *The Logic of Comparative Social Inquiry*, New York, New York: John Wiley, 1970.

Ibn Qutaiba, Abu Muhammad 'Abdallah. *Adab ul-Kātib* [Training of the Advisor], edited by Max Grunert, Leiden: E. J. Brill, 1900.

—— *Kitab al-Ma'arif* [The Book of Knowledge], edited by F. Wtisten-feld, Gottingen, 1850.

—— *Kitab al-Sh'ir wal Shu'ara'* [Book of Poetry and Poets], edited by M. J. de Goeje, Leiden: E. J. Brill, 1904.

—— *'Uyun al-Akhbar* [Sources of Information], edited by C. Brockel-mann, Leiden: E. J. Brill, 1900.

Richelieu, Cardinal. *Political Testament*, in J. H. Robinson, (ed.), *Readings in European History*, 2 volumes, Boston: Ginn, 1906.

Rizzitano, Umberto. 'Ibn Zafar 'Abd Allah,' *The Encyclopedia of Islam*, New Edition, Volume III, Leiden: E. J. Brill, 1971, p. 970.

—— *Storia e Cultura nella Sicilia Saracena*, Palermo: S. F. Flaccovio, 1975.

Rodinson, Maxime. *Europe and the Mystique of Islam*, translated by Roger Veinus, London: I.B. Tauris, 1987.

Rosenthal, F. 'Ibn al-Tiktaka,' *The Encyclopedia of Islam*, New Edition, Leiden & London: E. J. Brill and Luzac & Co., 1965, p. 956.

—— 'Ibn Abi Tahir Tayfur', *The Encyclopedia of Islam*, New Edition, Leiden & London: E. J. Brill and Luzac & Co., 1965, pp. 692–693.

Rosenthal, Erwin I. J. *Political Thought in Medieval Islam*, Greenwood Press: Westport, Connecticut, 1985.

Al-Rumi, Yaqut. *Kitab Irshad al-'Arib ila Ma'rifat al-Adib* [Book of Intelligent Guidance and Refined Learning], Volume VII, Cairo: Matba'al Hindiyya, 1925.

Sabine, Geoge H. *A History of Political Thought*, 3rd edn, New York, New York: Holt, Rinehart and Winston, Inc., 1961.

Salibi, Kamal S. 'Ibn Djama'a,' *The Encyclopedia of Islam*, New Edition, Leiden & London: E. J. Brill and Luzac & Co., 1965, pp. 748–749.

Al-Sayyid, Rudwan (ed.). *Al-Harakat al-Islamiyya wa-Athariha fi al-Istiqrar al-Siyasi fi al-'Alam al-'Arabi* [Islamic Movements and Political Stability in the Arab World]. Abu Dhabi: The Emirates Centre for Strategic Studies and Research, 2002.

The Sea of Precious Virtues [Bahr al-Fava'id]. Translated, edited, and annotated by Julie Scott Meisami. Salt Lake City, Utah: University of Utah Press, 1991.

Al-Siqilli, Muhammad Ibn Zafar. *Sulwan al-Muta' fi 'Udwan al-Atba'* [Consolation for the Ruler During the Hostility of Subjects], various manuscripts at the Bibliothèque Nationale, Paris, France.

Skinner, Quentin. *The Foundations of Modern Political Thought*, Vol. II, Cambridge: Cambridge University Press, 1978.

—— 'Political Philosophy' in *The Cambridge History of Renaissance Philosophy*, ed. by Charles B. Schmitt, et al., Cambridge: Cambridge University Press, 1988, pp. 389–90.

Spencer, Herbert. 'The Great Man Theory Breaks Down,' in Barbara Kellerman, (ed.), *Political Leadership*, Pittsburgh, Pennsylvania: University of Pittsburgh Press, 1986, pp. 10–15.

Stowasser, Barbara Freyet (ed.). *The Islamic Impulse*, Washington, DC: Center for Contemporary Arab Studies, Georgetown University, 1987.

Ibn al-Tiqtaqa, Muhammad ibn 'Ali. *Al-Fakhri* [On the systems of government and Muslim dynasties], translated by C. E. J. Whitting, London: Luzac, 1947.

Tzu, Sun. *The Art of War*, translated by Thomas Cleary, Boston & Shaftesbury: Shambhala Publications, Inc., 1988.

Watt, W. Montgomery. 'Al-Ghazali,' *The Encyclopedia of Islam*, 2nd edn, Leiden & London: E. J. Brill and Luzac & Co., 1965, Encyclopedia of Islam II, pp. 1038–1041.

Weber, Max. *Economy and Society*, translated and edited by Guenther Roth and Claus Wittich, New York: Bedminster Press, 1968.

Who's Who in America, Volume 2, 53rd edn, 1999.

Wilson, Woodrow. 'Leaders of Men,' in Barbara Kellerman, (ed.), *Political Leadership*, Pittsburgh, Pennsylvania: University of Pittsburgh Press, 1986, pp. 428–437.

Bin Yousef, Ahmad and Ahmad Abul Jobain. *The Politics of Islamic Resurgence: Through Western Eyes*, North Springfield, Virginia: The United Association for Studies and Research, 1992.

Index